AF800431

Think, Code, Create

Advanced Python Programming Series

Northward House Publishing

A series of twelve advanced programming books for secondary students.

Each book is a standalone resource. Read alone or as part of the full series.

Designed for Years 9–12

Australian Curriculum Version 9 — Digital Technologies

Prerequisite: Think, Code, Create — A Python Programming Journey for Students
ISBN 978-1-7640698-0-9

Think, Code, Create — Advanced Python Programming Series

BOOK 3

Modules, Packages & the Python Ecosystem

Organise, share, and reuse code with modules, packages, and the broader Python library

M. North

BEd. (Sec), BSc, MInfoTech

Northward House Publishing

Brisbane, Queensland, Australia

2026

Prerequisite:

Think, Code, Create — A Python Programming Journey for Students

About the Author

M. North holds a Bachelor of Education (Secondary), a Bachelor of Science, and a Master of Information Technology. He has worked as a secondary school teacher of Digital Technologies, Mathematics, and Science across Queensland, Australia, before turning to educational publishing full time.

His teaching practice has centred on making abstract computational thinking concrete and accessible for students at every level — from those encountering programming for the first time to advanced students pursuing algorithmic thinking and software engineering. The Think, Code, Create series grew directly from classroom experience: the need for structured, curriculum-aligned materials that treat secondary students as capable thinkers, not passive recipients of watered-down content.

The foundation text, Think, Code, Create — A Python Programming Journey for Students (ISBN 978-1-7640698-0-9), established the pedagogical approach: clear explanations, worked examples with annotated code, guided exercises with hints, and challenge tasks for extension. The twelve-book advanced series extends that approach through specialised programming domains — from object-oriented design and data structures through to concurrency, networking, and automation — with the same rigour and the same respect for the reader.

M. North is based in Brisbane, Queensland, Australia, and publishes through Northward House Publishing.

Northward House Publishing

Brisbane, Queensland, Australia

www.northwardhouse.com.au

Feedback, corrections, and curriculum enquiries are welcome. Contact the publisher via the website above.

Publication Information

First published 2026

Published by Northward House Publishing, Brisbane, Queensland, Australia

This book is part of the Think, Code, Create — Advanced Python Programming Series.

This volume ISBN: 978-1-7640698-6-1

Acknowledgements

The author and publisher gratefully acknowledge the contribution of all teachers and students who provided feedback during the development of this series. The Python programming language is created and maintained by the Python Software Foundation (python.org).

The Complete Series

The twelve books in the Think, Code, Create Advanced Series are designed for students who have completed the foundation text. Each book is a standalone resource — you may read them in any order based on your interests or curriculum pathway. The recommended pathways below are a guide, not a requirement.

01 Object-Oriented Programming in Python
Design and build programs using classes, objects, and the four pillars of OOP
Prerequisite: Foundation text Chapters 14–15 **Audience:** Years 9–12

02 File Handling & Exception Management
Read, write, and manage data files; handle errors gracefully in real-world programs
Prerequisite: Foundation text Chapters 3–4, 11–12 **Audience:** Years 9–12

03 Modules, Packages & the Python Ecosystem
Organise, share, and reuse code with modules, packages, and the broader Python library
Prerequisite: Foundation text Chapters 14–15 **Audience:** Years 9–12

04 Data Structures & Algorithms
Understand, implement, and analyse core data structures and fundamental algorithms
Prerequisite: Foundation text Chapters 11–13 **Audience:** Years 10–12

05 Functional Programming & Advanced Iterables
Master Python's functional tools — generators, comprehensions, closures, and more
Prerequisite: Foundation text Chapters 14–15 **Audience:** Years 10–12

06 Regular Expressions & Advanced Text Processing
Search, validate, and transform text data using Python's powerful re module
Prerequisite: Foundation text Chapter 10 **Audience:** Years 10–12

07 Database Programming with Python
Store and retrieve data persistently using SQLite, SQL queries, and Python ORMs
Prerequisite: Books 01–02 recommended **Audience:** Years 10–12

08 Web Scraping & Working with APIs
Collect real-world data from websites and web services using Python
Prerequisite: Books 02–03 recommended **Audience:** Years 10–12

09 Data Analysis with Python
Explore, clean, and visualise real-world datasets using NumPy, Pandas, and Matplotlib
Prerequisite: Book 03; spreadsheet literacy **Audience:** Years 11–12

10 GUI Programming with Tkinter

Design and build graphical desktop applications using Python's built-in GUI toolkit
Prerequisite: Book 01 (OOP) **Audience:** Years 10–12

11 Testing, Debugging & Code Quality
Write reliable, maintainable code using testing frameworks, debugging tools, and style standards
Prerequisite: Books 01 and 03 **Audience:** Years 11–12

12 Concurrency, Networking & Automation
Write programs that do multiple things at once, communicate over networks, and automate tasks
Prerequisite: Books 01, 02, and 03 **Audience:** Years 11–12

How to Use This Book

Each book in the Advanced Series is structured in the same way. Understanding the format will help you get the most from each chapter.

Chapter Structure

Every chapter opens with a blockquote that describes what the chapter covers and connects it to what you already know. This is followed by seven numbered sections, each with worked examples, a note callout for important warnings or tips, and closing paragraphs that lead to the next concept.

At the end of each chapter you will find:

- **Chapter Summary** — Eight bullet points summarising the key concepts from the chapter.
- **Guided Exercises** — Five hands-on tasks with hints to help you get started. Complete these before moving on.
- **Challenge Tasks** — Three open-ended tasks with no hints. These require independent problem-solving and are suitable for extension or assessment.

Code Examples

All code is shown in shaded blocks. Every non-obvious line has an inline comment. Each section contains three examples: an Introduction example that introduces the concept in isolation, a Variation example that extends or explores an edge case, and a Real-world application example set in a recognisable context — school, finance, or commerce.

Output blocks immediately follow their code and show exactly what the program prints when run. You should be able to reproduce every output exactly by running the code in a Python 3.10 or later interpreter.

Prior Knowledge

This series assumes you have completed Think, Code, Create — A Python Programming Journey for Students. Foundational concepts (variables, data types, loops, functions, lists, dictionaries) are not re-explained. Where a prior chapter or book is relevant, you will see a brief cross-reference in the text.

Within this book, chapters build on each other. Earlier chapters are referenced with a note rather than a full explanation. If you encounter an unfamiliar concept, check the chapter cross-reference and review that material before continuing.

Contents

CHAPTER 1 What Are Modules and Why Use Them?

Book 03: Modules, Packages & the Python Ecosystem

> Every real program is larger than a single file. As a project grows beyond a handful of functions, splitting the code into focused units called modules becomes essential for navigation, testing, and reuse. In this chapter you will learn what a module is, how Python finds and loads one, and why every reusable .py file should include a name guard to prevent side effects on import. You will also see how namespaces protect names from colliding across files, how the module search path determines which file Python finds first, and what good module design looks like in practice. By the end of this chapter you will have the conceptual foundations needed for everything that follows: packages, the standard library, virtual environments, and published tools.

1.1 The Problem Modules Solve

When all of a program's code lives in a single file, three problems grow steadily worse as the file expands. Navigation becomes painful — scrolling through hundreds of lines to locate a single function wastes time and invites mistakes. Testing and reuse become difficult because every function you want to call from another context drags the entire file with it. And names start to collide: two unrelated parts of the program may both want a variable called data or total, and sharing one namespace means every name must be unique across the whole codebase.

You have already seen this problem at scale. The Student Records System from Book 02, Chapter 10 began with a single script and naturally grew into separate files: paths.py held nothing but file locations, models.py defined the data classes and exception hierarchy, store.py managed persistence, and operations.py contained the business logic. That split was not forced — it reflected real boundaries between different kinds of work.

This principle is called separation of concerns: each module takes responsibility for one aspect of the program and exposes only what other modules need to know. A module that handles file I/O should not contain grading rules. A module that defines data classes should not know where those classes are stored on disk. Keeping concerns separate makes each module shorter, easier to understand, and independently testable.

> **Note:** A module is simply a .py file. There is nothing special about its syntax — any script you have already written can be imported as a module. The distinction between a script and a module is purely about how Python is asked to run it.

Example 1 — Introduction

A single file that mixes student data, grading logic, and report output — all three concerns in one place.

```
# all_in_one.py — student data, grading logic, and reporting in one file.
# As the program grows, this approach becomes increasingly hard to manage.

# --- concern 1: student data ---
students = []

def add_student(name, mark):
    students.append({"name": name, "mark": mark})
```

```
# --- concern 2: grading logic ---
def letter_grade(mark):
    if mark >= 85: return "A"
    if mark >= 70: return "B"
    if mark >= 55: return "C"
    if mark >= 40: return "D"
    return "F"

# --- concern 3: report output ---
def print_report():
    print("=== Class Report ===")
    for s in students:
        name  = s["name"]       # extract before f-string to avoid quote nesting
        mark  = s["mark"]
        grade = letter_grade(mark)
        print(f"  {name:<20} {mark:>3}   {grade}")

# --- main program ---
add_student("Aisha Patel", 92)
add_student("Liam Nguyen", 74)
add_student("Chloe Morris", 55)
print_report()
```

Output:

```
=== Class Report ===
  Aisha Patel          92   A
  Liam Nguyen          74   B
  Chloe Morris         55   C
```

Example 2 — Variation

The same three concerns separated into focused modules. Each file is short, readable, and independently reusable.

```
# --- models.py ---  concern 1: student data
students = []

def add_student(name, mark):
    students.append({"name": name, "mark": mark})


# --- grading.py ---  concern 2: grading logic
def letter_grade(mark):
    if mark >= 85: return "A"
    if mark >= 70: return "B"
    if mark >= 55: return "C"
    if mark >= 40: return "D"
    return "F"


# --- main.py ---  concern 3: entry point that wires the modules together
import models
import grading

models.add_student("Aisha Patel", 92)
models.add_student("Liam Nguyen", 74)
models.add_student("Chloe Morris", 55)

print("=== Class Report ===")
for s in models.students:
    name  = s["name"]
    mark  = s["mark"]
```

```
    grade = grading.letter_grade(mark)
    print(f"  {name:<20} {mark:>3}   {grade}")
```

Output:

```
=== Class Report ===
  Aisha Patel          92   A
  Liam Nguyen          74   B
  Chloe Morris         55   C
```

Example 3 — Real-world application

The Student Records System from Book 02 shows how module boundaries emerge naturally in a real project.

```
# The SRS from Book 02, Ch 10 grew into the following structure.
# Each file has exactly one job:
#
#   srs/
#       paths.py          DATA_DIR, STUDENTS_CSV, COURSES_JSON
#       models.py         Student, Course, Enrolment (dataclasses)
#       exceptions.py     SRSError, DuplicateStudentError, CourseNotFoundError
#       store.py          SRSStore: load(), save(), add_student(), search()
#       operations.py     enrol_student(), drop_student(), get_report()
#       reports.py        format_class_list(), format_transcript()
#       main.py           entry point
#
# Adding a new report format means editing reports.py only.
# No other file needs to change.

# main.py — the module imports make the architecture immediately readable:
from srs import paths, models, store, reports

the_store = store.SRSStore(paths.STUDENTS_CSV, paths.COURSES_JSON)
the_store.load()

student = models.Student(id="S0042", name="Ben Kowalski", gpa=3.5)
the_store.add_student(student)
print(reports.format_class_list(the_store.all_students()))
```

Output:

```
Northward Academy — Student List
  S0042    Ben Kowalski            GPA: 3.50
```

Splitting code into modules is not just an organisational preference. It has a direct effect on what you can name safely, what you can test in isolation, and how easily a function can travel to other programs. The mechanism that makes all of this safe is the namespace, which is the subject of the next section.

1.2 What Is a Module?

A module is any Python source file — any file with a .py extension. When you type import greetings, Python searches for a file named greetings.py (the search process is covered in Section 1.4), then executes it from top to bottom in a new namespace, and finally stores the resulting module object in sys.modules under the key "greetings". Every subsequent import of the same name, including from other files in the same run, fetches that same cached object. The file is never executed twice.

The module object is a first-class Python value: it has attributes, it can be passed to functions, and it can be inspected at runtime. Its most important attributes are __name__ (the module's registered name), __file__ (the path to its source file on disk), and __doc__ (its docstring, if it has one). You can read any of these using the standard dot operator, just as you would any other attribute.

A script is simply a module that is run directly rather than imported. When Python executes a file directly, it sets __name__ to the string "__main__". When a file is imported by another module, Python sets __name__ to the module's own name. This distinction powers the name guard discussed in Section 1.5.

> **Note:** sys.modules is a plain dictionary. You can inspect it with import sys; print(list(sys.modules.keys())). Standard library modules that Python loads at interpreter startup (such as builtins, sys, and os) will always be present, even before you import them yourself.

Example 1 — Introduction

A minimal module defined in greetings.py, imported and inspected — showing the module object and its key attributes.

```
# greetings.py – a minimal module with one function and a docstring

"""Provides simple greeting functions for demonstration purposes."""

LANGUAGE = "Australian English"

def hello(name):
    """Return a personalised greeting string."""
    return f"G'day, {name}!"


# main.py — imports greetings and inspects the module object
import greetings

print(greetings.hello("Priya"))     # call the function via dot notation
print(greetings.LANGUAGE)           # access a module-level constant
print(greetings.__name__)           # the name Python registered
print(greetings.__doc__)            # the module docstring
```

Output:

```
G'day, Priya!
Australian English
greetings
Provides simple greeting functions for demonstration purposes.
```

Example 2 — Variation

Python caches every module in sys.modules after the first import. Importing the same module twice returns the same object in memory.

```
import sys
import greetings              # greetings.py is executed once here
import greetings as g2        # fetched from cache – file not re-executed

# Both names point to the same object.
print(greetings is g2)                  # True
print("greetings" in sys.modules)       # True – cached in sys.modules

# Proof: a mutation through one reference is visible via the other.
greetings.LANGUAGE = "Modified"
print(g2.LANGUAGE)                      # Modified – same object
```

Output:

```
True
True
Modified
```

Example 3 — Real-world application

A geometry module used from a script. The dir() built-in lists everything in the module's namespace, including imported names.

```
# geometry.py — area calculations for common two-dimensional shapes

"""Area calculation functions for common two-dimensional shapes."""

import math

PI = math.pi    # use math.pi rather than hard-coding an approximation

def circle_area(radius):
    """Return the area of a circle with the given radius."""
    return PI * radius ** 2

def rectangle_area(width, height):
    """Return the area of a rectangle."""
    return width * height

def triangle_area(base, height):
    """Return the area of a triangle."""
    return 0.5 * base * height


# main.py
import geometry

# List all public names (anything not starting with an underscore).
public = [name for name in dir(geometry) if not name.startswith("_")]
print("Public names:", public)

print(f"Circle   (r=5):   {geometry.circle_area(5):.4f}")
print(f"Triangle (b=8, h=6): {geometry.triangle_area(8, 6):.4f}")
```

Output:

```
Public names: ['PI', 'circle_area', 'math', 'rectangle_area', 'triangle_area']
Circle   (r=5):    78.5398
Triangle (b=8, h=6): 24.0000
```

Notice that math appears in the public names list. Importing math inside geometry.py adds the math object to geometry's namespace, so it is visible to dir(). This is rarely a problem in practice, but if you want precise control over what your module advertises, you can use __all__ — covered in Section 1.7.

The key insight is that a module is an object, its contents are attributes, and Python guarantees that the same module is loaded only once per interpreter session. Understanding this caching behaviour matters whenever you write module-level code that has side effects or maintains state.

1.3 Namespaces and the Dot Operator

A namespace is a mapping from names to objects. Every Python scope — a function, a class, a module, and the global built-in scope — maintains its own namespace. When you define a variable at the top of a module, that name lives in the module's namespace. When you import a module, you add the module object itself to the importing file's namespace under the name you chose.

The dot operator reaches into a namespace: geometry.circle_area means "look up the name circle_area inside the namespace belonging to the object geometry". Because each module has its own namespace, two modules can define a variable with the same name without any conflict. colours.RED and traffic.RED are completely independent even if both hold the value 255.

Python resolves names using the LEGB rule (Local, Enclosing, Global, Built-in — see Think, Code, Create for the full treatment). A name defined at module level is global within that file, but it is not visible in any other file unless explicitly imported. When you import a module with import module, you make only the module object available in your namespace. You do not pull the module's contents into your own global scope unless you use from module import name.

Name shadowing occurs when a name in an inner scope hides a name in an outer scope with the same identifier. The most common mistake is accidentally redefining a built-in at module level: naming a variable list, sum, or type silently replaces the built-in of the same name and causes confusing errors later. Accessing all external names via the dot operator is the simplest defence against shadowing.

> **Note:** Using from module import * is the primary cause of unexpected shadowing. It dumps every exported name from the module into the current namespace, where any of them could silently replace a name you already defined. The import module form, with qualified access via dot notation, is always the safer choice.

Example 1 — Introduction

Two modules each define a constant named COLOUR. The dot operator keeps them completely separate.

```
# colours.py — web colour constants (RGB tuples)
COLOUR = (255, 0, 0)        # red


# traffic.py — traffic signal constants (RGB tuples)
COLOUR = (0, 255, 0)        # green (go)


# main.py
import colours
import traffic

# Two separate namespaces — the names never collide.
print("colours.COLOUR:", colours.COLOUR)
print("traffic.COLOUR:", traffic.COLOUR)
print("Same object?   ", colours.COLOUR is traffic.COLOUR)
```

Output:

```
colours.COLOUR: (255, 0, 0)
traffic.COLOUR: (0, 255, 0)
Same object?    False
```

Example 2 — Variation

Accidentally redefining the built-in list at module level — the classic shadowing mistake and how to recover from it.

```
# Assigning to 'list' at module level shadows the built-in type.
list = [10, 20, 30]             # replaces the built-in list!

try:
    result = list(range(5))  # list is now [10,20,30], not the built-in
except TypeError as e:
    print(f"Error: {e}")

# Fix: remove the module-level binding so the built-in is accessible again.
del list
result = list(range(5))       # built-in list is restored
print(result)
```

Output:

```
Error: 'list' object is not callable
[0, 1, 2, 3, 4]
```

Example 3 — Real-world application

Using two standard library modules with overlapping capabilities. Dot notation makes every call unambiguous.

```
import math
import statistics

# Both modules expose useful functions. Qualified access makes every call
# unambiguous and self-documenting — the reader knows immediately which
# module each function belongs to.
data = [72, 85, 90, 68, 77, 82, 91, 65]

mean     = statistics.mean(data)       # arithmetic mean
variance = statistics.variance(data)   # sample variance
std_dev  = math.sqrt(variance)         # std dev via math.sqrt

print(f"Mean:        {mean:.2f}")
print(f"Std dev:     {std_dev:.2f}")

# Had we written 'from statistics import *' and 'from math import *',
# both namespaces would be merged into one and any collisions would be silent.
```

Output:

```
Mean:        78.75
Std dev:     9.85
```

Qualifying every name with its module prefix is a small price to pay for unambiguous code. When a reader sees statistics.mean, they know exactly which mean is being called and where to find its documentation. The same principle applies to any library: import the module, not its contents, and let the dot operator keep everything clear.

The Module Search Path

When you write import greetings, Python does not immediately know where greetings.py lives. It searches a sequence of directories in order and returns the first match, or raises a ModuleNotFoundError if none is found. That sequence is stored in the list sys.path and is assembled from several sources each time the interpreter starts.

The four main entries in sys.path are: (1) the directory containing the script that was run, or an empty string representing the current working directory when Python is started interactively; (2) any directories listed in the PYTHONPATH environment variable; (3) the standard library directory; and (4) the site-packages directory inside the active environment, where pip-installed packages are stored. Python searches these in order and uses the first match.

Because the script's own directory comes first, a local file with the same name as a standard library module will shadow the real module. This is the most common accidental import bug: a student creates a test file named math.py or random.py and then wonders why their imports suddenly fail. The __file__ attribute on any imported module shows exactly which file Python resolved it to, making this kind of conflict straightforward to diagnose.

> **Note:** The PYTHONPATH environment variable can add extra directories to sys.path, but editing it globally is risky because it affects every Python program you run on the machine. For project-specific paths, virtual environments (Chapter 6) and editable installs (Chapter 7) are the correct tools.

Example 1 — Introduction

Printing sys.path at runtime shows every directory Python will search, in priority order.

```
import sys

print("Python module search path:")
for i, entry in enumerate(sys.path):
    label   = "  (script directory)" if i == 0 else ""
    display = entry if entry else "(current working directory)"
    print(f"  [{i}] {display}{label}")

# __file__ on the running script shows its resolved path.
print()
print(f"This script: {__file__}")
```

Output:

```
Python module search path:
  [0] /home/student/project  (script directory)
  [1] /usr/lib/python312.zip
  [2] /usr/lib/python3.12
  [3] /usr/lib/python3.12/lib-dynload
  [4] /home/student/.local/lib/python3.12/site-packages

This script: /home/student/project/main.py
```

Example 2 — Variation

The __file__ attribute on any imported module reveals exactly where Python found it on disk.

```
import sys
import os
import json

# Standard library modules have __file__ pointing into the stdlib directory.
print(f"os   loaded from: {os.__file__}")
print(f"json loaded from: {json.__file__}")

# Built-in modules written in C have no __file__ attribute.
print(f"sys has __file__: {hasattr(sys, '__file__')}")
```

Output:

```
os   loaded from: /usr/lib/python3.12/os.py
json loaded from: /usr/lib/python3.12/json/__init__.py
sys has __file__: False
```

Example 3 — Real-world application

A utility function that checks a project directory for local files whose names would shadow standard library modules.

```
import sys
import os

def check_namespace_conflicts(module_names):
    """Report any local .py files that would shadow stdlib modules."""
    script_dir = sys.path[0] if sys.path else "."
    print(f"Checking: {script_dir}")
    print()
    for name in module_names:
        local_path = os.path.join(script_dir, name + ".py")
        if os.path.exists(local_path):
            print(f"  WARNING  {name}.py found locally — shadows the stdlib!")
        else:
            print(f"  OK       {name}.py — no local conflict")

# Modules most commonly confused with stdlib names.
risky = ["os", "sys", "math", "random", "string", "json", "csv"]
check_namespace_conflicts(risky)
```

Output:

```
Checking: /home/student/project

  OK       os.py — no local conflict
  OK       sys.py — no local conflict
  OK       math.py — no local conflict
  OK       random.py — no local conflict
  OK       string.py — no local conflict
  OK       json.py — no local conflict
  OK       csv.py — no local conflict
```

Understanding sys.path also matters when you publish a module as a package. Python can only import a module if its directory appears in sys.path. Packages (Chapter 4) and virtual environments (Chapter 6) provide structured ways to manage this without manually modifying the list at runtime.

__name__ and the if __name__ == "__main__": Guard

Every Python module has a special attribute called __name__. When Python imports a module with import greetings, it sets that module's __name__ to the string "greetings" — the module's own name. When Python runs a file directly from the command line, it sets __name__ to the string "__main__". This distinction is the foundation of the name guard.

Without the guard, any top-level code in a module executes the moment it is imported. A module that prints output or runs calculations on import is hard to use as a library: every script that borrows your function also triggers your demo code. The guard if __name__ == "__main__": wraps code that should run only when the file is the entry point, keeping the module silent and reusable when imported.

The guard is not optional in a module intended for reuse. It is so universally expected in Python that its absence is considered a design error. Every utility module you write from this point forward should include one, even if the block contains only a brief smoke test. It costs one line of code and removes an entire class of import-time side effects.

> **Note:** The guard also plays a critical role with the multiprocessing module on Windows and macOS, where each child process re-imports the main script. Without the guard, the main script re-executes in every child process, which typically causes an infinite cascade of new processes.

Example 1 — Introduction

A module without the guard — its demonstration code fires immediately when imported by another script.

```
# demo_module.py — WITHOUT the guard (problematic)

AUTHOR  = "M. North"
VERSION = "1.0"

def greet(name):
    """Return a greeting string."""
    return f"G'day, {name}!"

# This code runs the moment another script does 'import demo_module'.
print(f"Module loaded by: {__name__}")
print(f"Version: {VERSION}")
for n in ["Aisha", "Liam", "Chloe"]:
    print(greet(n))
```

Output:

```
# Output produced by: import demo_module  (inside another script)
Module loaded by: demo_module
Version: 1.0
G'day, Aisha!
G'day, Liam!
G'day, Chloe!
```

Example 2 — Variation

The same module with the guard in place. Importing it produces no output; running it directly shows the demonstration.

```
# demo_module.py — WITH the guard (correct)

AUTHOR  = "M. North"
VERSION = "1.0"

def greet(name):
    """Return a greeting string."""
    return f"G'day, {name}!"

if __name__ == "__main__":
    # Runs only when executed directly: python demo_module.py
    # Importing demo_module from another script skips this block entirely.
    print(f"demo_module v{VERSION} — self-test")
    for n in ["Aisha", "Liam", "Chloe"]:
        print(greet(n))
```

Output:

```
# Output when imported by another script:
(no output — the module is completely silent)

# Output when run directly:  python demo_module.py
demo_module v1.0 — self-test
G'day, Aisha!
G'day, Liam!
```

```
G'day, Chloe!
```

Example 3 — Real-world application

A school utility module with a comprehensive self-test block. The assert statements verify each function without a separate test framework.

```
# school_utils.py — utility functions for student data processing

"""Utility functions for formatting and validating student records."""

def format_name(first, last):
    """Return a formatted full name: 'Last, First'."""
    return f"{last.strip()}, {first.strip()}"

def is_valid_id(student_id):
    """Return True if student_id matches the pattern 'S' + four digits."""
    return (isinstance(student_id, str)
            and student_id.startswith("S")
            and student_id[1:].isdigit()
            and len(student_id) == 5)

def grade_to_gpa(grade):
    """Convert a letter grade to a 4.0-scale GPA point."""
    table = {"A": 4.0, "B": 3.0, "C": 2.0, "D": 1.0, "F": 0.0}
    return table.get(grade.upper(), 0.0)

if __name__ == "__main__":
    print("Running school_utils self-tests...")
    assert format_name("Mei", "Chen") == "Chen, Mei",    "format_name failed"
    assert is_valid_id("S0421") is True,                 "valid ID failed"
    assert is_valid_id("X042")  is False,                "invalid ID failed"
    assert grade_to_gpa("A") == 4.0,                    "grade_to_gpa A failed"
    assert grade_to_gpa("f") == 0.0,                    "grade_to_gpa F failed"
    print("All tests passed.")
```

Output:

```
Running school_utils self-tests...
All tests passed.
```

The guard is simple in syntax but significant in effect. A module without it can only safely contain functions and classes at the top level. Any demonstration, test, or configuration code placed outside the guard will fire on every import, which is almost never what you want. Writing the guard is a habit worth forming immediately and keeping permanently.

Why Modules Beat Copy-Paste

The quickest way to reuse a function is to copy it. The consequences are predictable: when a bug is found, every copy must be fixed separately. When a requirement changes, the change must be tracked down across every file that holds a copy. Version drift is inevitable — different files end up with different versions of the same function, each corrected in some ways but not others.

The alternative is a shared module: one file, one authoritative implementation, zero copies. Any script that needs the function imports the module. Fixing the module fixes every importer simultaneously. This is the Don't Repeat Yourself (DRY) principle in its most literal form: the source code for a piece of logic should exist in exactly one place, so that a single change to the specification of that logic requires exactly one change to the code.

Modules also make code testable in isolation. If a function lives in its own module, a dedicated test file can import only that module and verify its behaviour independently of the rest of the application. Copy-pasted code has no such home — it can only be exercised by running the entire program it was embedded in.

> **Note:** DRY is not simply about reducing the volume of code. It is about ensuring that a single change to a specification requires a single change to the source. If changing the definition of a passing mark requires editing five files, the code is not DRY, regardless of how short each file is.

Example 1 — Introduction

A GST calculation module shared by an invoicing script. Both depend on the same implementation rather than each maintaining their own copy.

```
# gst_utils.py — Australian GST (10%) calculation utilities

"""Goods and Services Tax calculation functions for Australian pricing."""

GST_RATE = 0.10     # current Australian GST rate

def add_gst(price):
    """Return the GST-inclusive price for a given ex-GST amount."""
    return round(price * (1 + GST_RATE), 2)

def remove_gst(price_incl):
    """Return the ex-GST price from a GST-inclusive amount."""
    return round(price_incl / (1 + GST_RATE), 2)

def gst_component(price_incl):
    """Return the GST portion embedded in a GST-inclusive price."""
    return round(price_incl - remove_gst(price_incl), 2)


# invoice.py — imports gst_utils; no GST logic lives here
import gst_utils

subtotal = 450.00
total    = gst_utils.add_gst(subtotal)
gst      = gst_utils.gst_component(total)
print(f"Subtotal (ex-GST): ${subtotal:.2f}")
print(f"GST:               ${gst:.2f}")
print(f"Total   (inc-GST): ${total:.2f}")
```

Output:

```
Subtotal (ex-GST): $450.00
GST:               $45.00
Total   (inc-GST): $495.00
```

Example 2 — Variation

Simulating a bug fix in gst_utils.py. A single correction to the module is immediately visible to every script that imports it.

```
import gst_utils

# Simulate the bug: GST_RATE was incorrectly set to 0.15.
gst_utils.GST_RATE = 0.15
print(f"Buggy total: ${gst_utils.add_gst(450):.2f}")
```

```
# Apply the fix in one place — all callers benefit immediately.
gst_utils.GST_RATE = 0.10
print(f"Fixed total: ${gst_utils.add_gst(450):.2f}")

# With copy-pasted code, each file with a hard-coded 0.15 would
# need to be found and corrected individually.
```

Output:

```
Buggy total: $517.50
Fixed total: $495.00
```

Example 3 — Real-world application

A colour conversion module used in three different contexts. One implementation serves a web renderer, a print formatter, and a data visualiser.

```
# colour_utils.py — RGB and hex colour conversion utilities

"""Utilities for converting between RGB tuples and CSS hex colour strings."""

def rgb_to_hex(r, g, b):
    """Return a CSS hex colour string for the given RGB components."""
    return f"#{r:02X}{g:02X}{b:02X}"

def hex_to_rgb(hex_colour):
    """Return an (r, g, b) tuple from a CSS hex colour string."""
    hx = hex_colour.lstrip("#")
    return tuple(int(hx[i:i+2], 16) for i in (0, 2, 4))


# main.py — three different contexts, one module
import colour_utils

# Web renderer context
bg = colour_utils.rgb_to_hex(30, 144, 255)
print(f"Web background:  {bg}")

# Print formatter context
rgb = colour_utils.hex_to_rgb("#FF6347")
print(f"Print RGB:       {rgb}")

# Data visualiser context — convert an entire palette
raw_palette = [(255, 99, 71), (60, 179, 113), (30, 144, 255)]
hex_palette = [colour_utils.rgb_to_hex(r, g, b) for r, g, b in raw_palette]
print(f"Palette:         {hex_palette}")
```

Output:

```
Web background:  #1E90FF
Print RGB:       (255, 99, 71)
Palette:         ['#FF6347', '#3CB371', '#1E90FF']
```

Every module you write is a contract with its importers: call these functions with these arguments and you will receive these results. Because importers depend on the contract rather than on a copy of the code, you can improve, optimise, or correct the implementation at any time without touching any of the files that rely on it. This is one of the most powerful properties of well-designed modules.

Module Design Principles

A module should have a single, clearly stated purpose. This property is called cohesion. A highly cohesive module is easy to name — if you struggle to write a two-word description of what a module does, it is probably doing too many things. Compare school_grades.py (high cohesion: grade conversion and statistics for student records) with a module that validates student IDs, sends notification emails, and writes audit logs (low cohesion: three unrelated responsibilities sharing one file).

Coupling measures how much one module depends on the internals of another. Modules with low coupling access each other only through their public interface — the functions and constants that are deliberately designed for external use — rather than reaching into private implementation details. High coupling creates fragile code: a module that directly modifies another module's private list will break silently whenever that list's internal structure changes.

The public interface of a module is the set of names that other modules are expected to use. By convention, names beginning with a single underscore (_helper, _cache) are implementation details, not part of the public interface. You can make this contract explicit by defining __all__: a list of the string names that from module import * should export. This has no effect on qualified dot-notation access (module.name still works regardless of __all__), but it serves as clear, machine-readable documentation of your intended interface.

Every module should begin with a module docstring — a triple-quoted string on the very first non-blank line, before any import statements. The docstring states the module's purpose, its main exports, and any important usage notes. Python's help() function and documentation tools such as pydoc use this string automatically, so writing it carefully is an investment that pays back immediately.

> **Note:** __all__ affects only from module import *. It does not prevent direct access to names not listed in it: from my_module import _private still works. __all__ is a documentation and convention tool, not a security boundary.

Example 1 — Introduction

A temperature conversion module that uses __all__ to declare exactly which names form its public interface.

```
# temperature_utils.py — temperature conversion utilities

"""Temperature conversion functions between Celsius, Fahrenheit, and Kelvin."""

__all__ = ["celsius_to_fahrenheit", "fahrenheit_to_celsius",
"celsius_to_kelvin"]

# Public conversions — listed in __all__
def celsius_to_fahrenheit(c):
    """Convert Celsius to Fahrenheit."""
    return c * 9 / 5 + 32

def fahrenheit_to_celsius(f):
    """Convert Fahrenheit to Celsius."""
    return (f - 32) * 5 / 9

def celsius_to_kelvin(c):
    """Convert Celsius to Kelvin."""
    _validate(c)
    return c + 273.15
```

```
# Internal helper — deliberately excluded from __all__
def _validate(c):
    """Raise ValueError if c is below absolute zero."""
    if c < -273.15:
        raise ValueError(f"Temperature {c} C is below absolute zero.")
```

Output:

```
(No output — this is a module definition, not a script.)

# Inspecting __all__ from the interactive interpreter:
>>> import temperature_utils
>>> temperature_utils.__all__
['celsius_to_fahrenheit', 'fahrenheit_to_celsius', 'celsius_to_kelvin']
```

Example 2 — Variation

from ... import * respects __all__. Only the listed names are imported; the private helper is not.

```
from temperature_utils import *

# Names in __all__ are available.
print(f"100 C = {celsius_to_fahrenheit(100):.1f} F")
print(f"0 C   = {celsius_to_kelvin(0):.2f} K")
print(f"-10 C = {fahrenheit_to_celsius(14):.1f} C")

# _validate is not in __all__ — not imported by the star form.
try:
    _validate(-300)
except NameError:
    print("_validate not available via star import (by design)")
```

Output:

```
100 C = 212.0 F
0 C   = 273.15 K
-10 C = -10.0 C
_validate not available via star import (by design)
```

Example 3 — Real-world application

A production-style grade module combining a module docstring, __all__, cohesion, and a guard block that verifies its own functions.

```
# school_grades.py — grade conversion and statistics for student records

"""Grade conversion utilities for the Northward Academy student system.

Public interface:
  letter_grade(mark)     — convert a numeric mark to a letter grade
  gpa_point(grade)       — convert a letter grade to a 4.0 GPA point
  class_average(marks)   — return the mean of a list of numeric marks

Internal helpers (prefix _) are implementation details and may change.
"""

__all__ = ["letter_grade", "gpa_point", "class_average"]

_BANDS = {"A": (85,100), "B": (70,84), "C": (55,69), "D": (40,54), "F": (0,39)}
_GPA   = {"A": 4.0, "B": 3.0, "C": 2.0, "D": 1.0, "F": 0.0}

def letter_grade(mark):
    """Return the letter grade for a numeric mark in the range 0-100."""
    if not 0 <= mark <= 100:
```

```
        raise ValueError(f"Mark {mark} is outside the valid range 0-100.")
    for grade, bounds in _BANDS.items():
        if bounds[0] <= mark <= bounds[1]:
            return grade
    return "F"

def gpa_point(grade):
    """Return the 4.0-scale GPA point for a letter grade."""
    return _GPA.get(grade.upper(), 0.0)

def class_average(marks):
    """Return the mean of a list of numeric marks. Returns 0.0 for empty
input."""
    return sum(marks) / len(marks) if marks else 0.0

if __name__ == "__main__":
    marks = [92, 78, 65, 55, 43, 88, 71]
    print("Mark   Grade   GPA")
    for m in marks:
        g   = letter_grade(m)
        gpa = gpa_point(g)
        print(f"{m:>4}    {g}          {gpa:.1f}")
    avg        = class_average(marks)
    avg_grade = letter_grade(int(avg))
    print("")
    print(f"Class average: {avg:.1f}  ({avg_grade})")
```

Output:

```
Mark   Grade   GPA
  92     A      4.0
  78     B      3.0
  65     C      2.0
  55     C      2.0
  43     D      1.0
  88     A      4.0
  71     B      3.0

Class average: 70.3  (B)
```

A well-designed module is a piece of software that can be handed to another programmer with confidence. Its filename tells you what it does. Its docstring tells you what to import and what to expect. Its __all__ tells you what is public. Its cohesion means reading it in full takes only a few minutes. And its guard means importing it is always a silent, side-effect-free operation.

The next chapter builds directly on these foundations, examining all the forms the import statement can take, how to alias modules and individual names, and what to do when imports become complicated by circular dependencies or dynamic loading requirements.

Chapter 1 Summary

- A module is any .py file; Python executes it once on first import and caches the resulting module object in sys.modules for all subsequent imports in the same session.
- Separation of concerns means each module takes responsibility for one part of a program. Modules with a single, clear purpose are easier to navigate, test, and reuse independently.
- Every module has its own namespace — a mapping from names to objects. The dot operator accesses names within a namespace, preventing collisions between identically named variables in different modules.

- Python resolves imports by searching sys.path in order: script directory first, then PYTHONPATH, then the standard library, then site-packages. A local file with a stdlib name will shadow the real module.
- Python sets __name__ to "__main__" when a file is run directly, and to the module's own name when it is imported. This distinction powers the if __name__ == "__main__": guard.
- The name guard prevents demonstration, test, and configuration code from executing on import. Every reusable module should include one, even if the block contains only a simple self-test.
- The DRY principle (Don't Repeat Yourself) means source code for a piece of logic exists in exactly one place. A shared module propagates fixes and changes to all its importers simultaneously.
- Good module design means high cohesion (one clear purpose), low coupling (minimal dependencies), an explicit public interface via __all__, and a module docstring on the first line.

Guided Exercises

1. Create a module temperature_utils.py with two functions: celsius_to_fahrenheit(c) and fahrenheit_to_celsius(f). Write a separate script that imports the module and calls both functions with example values.

> **Hint:** Use import temperature_utils and call functions via dot notation. Verify the round-trip: celsius_to_fahrenheit(fahrenheit_to_celsius(32)) should return 32.0.

2. Add an if __name__ == "__main__": block to temperature_utils.py that runs a self-test using assert statements when the module is executed directly. Confirm the test block does not run when the module is imported from another script.

> **Hint:** Print a start message and an end message inside the guard. Import the module from a second script and verify that neither message appears in the output.

3. Print sys.path from a script and explain the role of each entry. Then create a subdirectory called utils/, place a module named helpers.py inside it, and demonstrate why import helpers fails and how to add the subdirectory to sys.path to fix it.

> **Hint:** Use sys.path.insert(0, "utils") to add the directory at runtime. In production code, packages (Chapter 4) are the correct solution — this exercise builds the underlying understanding.

4. Create two modules that each define a module-level variable named COLOUR with a different value. Write a main script that imports both modules and prints each COLOUR via dot notation, demonstrating that the names never collide.

> **Hint:** Then add from module1 import * to main.py and observe which COLOUR is visible in the global namespace. This illustrates why qualified access is preferred over star imports.

5. Add __all__ to temperature_utils.py listing only the two conversion functions. Confirm that from temperature_utils import * imports exactly those names and that any helper functions not in __all__ are not brought into the importing namespace.

> **Hint:** Add a private helper function _check_range(c) to the module that raises ValueError for out-of-range input. Verify it is not imported by the star form but is still accessible via temperature_utils._check_range.

Challenge Tasks

1. Refactor the Student Records System from Book 02, Chapter 10 into three separate, cohesive modules: exceptions.py (the SRSError hierarchy), models.py (the Student, Course, and Enrolment dataclasses), and store.py (the SRSStore class and its persistence methods). Write a main script that imports all three and creates a small demonstration. Ensure each module has a docstring, __all__, and the name guard.

2. Write a module inspector tool: given a module name as a command-line argument (via sys.argv), import it using importlib.import_module() and print its __name__, __file__ (or "built-in" if absent), __doc__ (first line only), and a sorted list of all public names (names not beginning with an underscore). Test it against at least three standard library modules.

3. Demonstrate module caching in depth: write a module state_demo.py with a module-level counter variable. Import it twice in main.py using both import state_demo and import state_demo as sd. Confirm that state_demo is sd is True. Increment the counter through one reference and verify the change is visible through the other. Then use importlib.reload() to reset the module and show that the counter returns to its initial value.

CHAPTER 2 Importing Modules

Book 03: Modules, Packages & the Python Ecosystem

> Chapter 1 established why modules exist: they keep code organised, reusable, and free of name collisions. This chapter examines the other side of that relationship — how a module is consumed. Python offers several forms of the import statement, each with distinct effects on the local namespace and each suited to different situations. You will learn when to write import X, when to prefer from X import Y, and when both are inadequate and aliasing, relative imports, or dynamic loading is required instead. Circular imports, lazy loading, and the importlib machinery round out the picture, giving you the full vocabulary needed to structure multi-file Python projects with confidence.

import Statement Forms

Python provides three distinct syntactic forms of the import statement. Each form brings names into scope differently, and choosing the wrong form can pollute your namespace, obscure where a name comes from, or silently mask a bug. Understanding all three — and their trade-offs — is the foundation of clean module use.

The simplest form, import X, binds the module object itself to the name X in the current namespace. Every attribute of the module is then accessed through the dot operator: math.sqrt(), datetime.date.today(). This keeps the origin of every name explicit and avoids collisions, at the cost of slightly more typing.

The second form, from X import Y, pulls one or more specific names out of the module and binds them directly in the current namespace. This makes call sites shorter — sqrt(9) instead of math.sqrt(9) — but hides the origin of the name. If a local variable named sqrt also exists, the import silently shadows it.

The third form, from X import *, imports every public name from the module (or every name listed in __all__ if the module defines it). This is almost never appropriate at module level: it floods your namespace with names you may not recognise, and it makes it impossible to tell at a glance where a given name came from. The one legitimate use is within an interactive REPL session.

Example 1 — Introduction

The three import forms side by side, applied to Python's math module.

```
# Form 1: import the module object
import math
print(math.pi)              # 3.141592653589793
print(math.sqrt(16))        # 4.0

# Form 2: import specific names
from math import sqrt, pi
print(pi)                   # 3.141592653589793
print(sqrt(16))             # 4.0

# Form 3: import everything (avoid at module level)
from math import *
print(floor(3.7))           # 3 — origin of 'floor' is now invisible
```

Output:

```
3.141592653589793
```

```
4.0
3.141592653589793
4.0
3
```

Example 2 — Variation

Importing multiple names in a single from ... import statement, and grouping long imports across lines.

```
# Multiple names in one statement
from math import sqrt, log, ceil, floor

# When the list is long, wrap with parentheses (PEP 8 preferred)
from math import (
    sqrt,
    log,
    ceil,
    floor,
    pi,
    e
)

# You can also rename an individual name on import
from math import factorial as fact
print(fact(5))    # 120
```

Output:

```
120
```

Example 3 — Real-world application

A school report generator that imports exactly what it needs from two standard library modules.

```
# report_generator.py
from datetime import date           # only the class we need
from statistics import mean, stdev # specific statistical functions

def generate_report(name, scores):
    """Print a summary report for one student."""
    today = date.today()            # date from datetime module
    avg   = mean(scores)            # mean from statistics module
    sd    = stdev(scores) if len(scores) > 1 else 0.0
    print(f"Report for {name} — {today}")
    print(f"  Scores : {scores}")
    print(f"  Average: {avg:.1f}")
    print(f"  Std Dev: {sd:.1f}")

generate_report('Amelia Watson', [72, 85, 91, 68, 79])
```

Output:

```
Report for Amelia Watson — 2025-07-14
  Scores : [72, 85, 91, 68, 79]
  Average: 79.0
  Std Dev: 8.9
```

Choosing between the three forms is mostly a question of readability and namespace hygiene. For standard library modules that you use frequently (os, sys, pathlib), the import X form is preferred because the origin of every call is obvious. For deeply nested names used many times in one file, from X import Y is reasonable. The wildcard form should be reserved for the REPL.

2.2 Aliasing with as

The as keyword can follow either form of the import statement to bind the module or name to a different local identifier. Aliasing serves two distinct purposes: shortening a long or deeply qualified name, and resolving a name conflict when two modules or imports share the same identifier.

Convention plays a large role in the Python data-science ecosystem. Libraries such as NumPy, Pandas, and Matplotlib have well-established aliases (np, pd, plt) that virtually every professional uses. Adopting these conventions makes your code immediately readable to others working in the same domain, even though Python itself has no knowledge of them.

Aliasing is also the cleanest solution when you need to import two modules that happen to export a name you want to use without the module prefix — for example, two third-party libraries that both expose a class called Client. Rather than favouring one and qualifying the other, you rename both on import and keep your call sites clean.

> **Note:** Aliases are local to the file in which they appear. If module A defines import numpy as np, another module importing A does not gain access to np. Each file manages its own namespace independently.

Example 1 — Introduction

Aliasing a module to a shorter name, and aliasing an imported name to avoid a local collision.

```
import datetime as dt           # shorten the module name

today = dt.date.today()         # dt instead of datetime
now   = dt.datetime.now()
print(f"Date : {today}")
print(f"Now  : {now:%Y-%m-%d %H:%M}")

# Alias an imported name to avoid shadowing the built-in 'round'
from decimal import ROUND_HALF_UP as HALF_UP
from decimal import Decimal

amount = Decimal('14.735').quantize(Decimal('0.01'), rounding=HALF_UP)
print(amount)                     # 14.74
```

Output:

```
Date : 2025-07-14
Now  : 2025-07-14 09:31
14.74
```

Example 2 — Variation

Resolving a name conflict when two modules export identically named symbols.

```
# Suppose two modules both define a class called 'Parser'.
# Without aliases the second import silently shadows the first.

# BAD — the second 'Parser' replaces the first
# from xml_tools  import Parser
# from json_tools import Parser   # shadows the xml one

# GOOD — give each an unambiguous local name
from xml.etree.ElementTree import XMLParser  as XMLParser
from configparser           import ConfigParser as IniParser

xml_p = XMLParser()
ini_p = IniParser()
print(type(xml_p).__name__)     # XMLParser
print(type(ini_p).__name__)     # ConfigParser
```

Output:

```
XMLParser
```

```
ConfigParser
```

Example 3 — Real-world application

A data summary script using the standard library's csv and statistics modules with clear aliases.

```
# sales_summary.py
import csv
import statistics as stats      # alias for brevity
from pathlib import Path

def summarise(filepath):
    """Read a CSV of sales figures and print summary statistics."""
    path = Path(filepath)
    if not path.exists():
        print(f"File not found: {filepath}")
        return

    amounts = []
    with open(path, newline='', encoding='utf-8') as f:
        reader = csv.DictReader(f)
        for row in reader:
            try:
                amounts.append(float(row["amount"]))
            except (KeyError, ValueError):
                continue

    if not amounts:
        print("No valid data found.")
        return

    print(f"Count   : {len(amounts)}")
    print(f"Total   : ${sum(amounts):,.2f}")
    print(f"Mean    : ${stats.mean(amounts):,.2f}")
    print(f"Median  : ${stats.median(amounts):,.2f}")
    if len(amounts) > 1:
        print(f"Std Dev: ${stats.stdev(amounts):,.2f}")

# Example with inline data for demonstration
import io
sample_csv = "amount\n120.50\n340.00\n89.75\n512.00\n275.25"
# (In production you would pass a real file path to summarise())
```

Output:

```
# When run against a real CSV file:
Count  : 5
Total  : $1,337.50
Mean   : $267.50
Median : $275.25
Std Dev: $163.64
```

Beyond the data-science conventions, aliasing is often used in projects that support multiple back-ends. A web framework might write import json as serialiser and later swap json for orjson by changing just one line. The rest of the codebase, which only sees the alias, requires no changes at all.

2.3 Relative Imports Inside Packages

When code is organised into a package — a directory of modules with an __init__.py file (covered in Chapter 4) — modules within the package can import each other using relative rather than absolute paths. A relative import uses leading dots to specify how many levels up the package hierarchy to look before resolving the module name.

A single leading dot (from . import X) means: look in the same package as this module. Two leading dots (from .. import X) means: look one level up in the package hierarchy. Relative imports have one decisive advantage over absolute imports for intra-package references: they are portable. If the package is renamed or moved, the relative imports still work without modification.

Relative imports are only valid inside a package. A script executed directly (i.e., __name__ == "__main__") cannot use relative imports because Python does not know which package it belongs to. Attempting to do so raises ImportError: attempted relative import with no known parent package.

> **Note:** Relative imports require that the containing directory be treated as a package. Always run package code with python -m package.module rather than python package/module.py. The -m flag tells Python to locate the module inside the package and set __package__ correctly.

Example 1 — Introduction

A minimal two-module package demonstrating a single-dot relative import.

```
# Package structure:
#   school/
#       __init__.py
#       models.py
#       grading.py

# --- school/models.py ---
class Student:
    def __init__(self, name, score):
        self.name  = name
        self.score = score

# --- school/grading.py ---
from . import models          # relative import: same package

def grade(student):
    """Return a letter grade for a Student object."""
    s = student.score
    if s >= 90: return 'A'
    if s >= 80: return 'B'
    if s >= 70: return 'C'
    if s >= 60: return 'D'
    return 'F'

# --- main.py (outside the package) ---
from school.models  import Student
from school.grading import grade

students = [Student('Liam', 88), Student('Chloe', 73), Student('Noah', 95)]
for s in students:
    print(f"{s.name}: {grade(s)}")
```

Output:

```
Liam: B
Chloe: C
Noah: A
```

Example 2 — Variation

Using a two-dot relative import to reference a module in a parent package from a subpackage.

```
# Extended package structure:
#   school/
#       __init__.py
```

```
#       models.py
#       utils/
#           __init__.py
#           formatters.py   ← this module

# --- school/utils/formatters.py ---
from .. import models        # two dots: go up to 'school', then import models

def student_summary(student):
    """Return a formatted one-line summary string."""
    return f"Name: {student.name:<20} Score: {student.score:>3}"

# --- main.py ---
from school.models            import Student
from school.utils.formatters import student_summary

s = Student('Isabelle Nguyen', 84)
print(student_summary(s))
```

Output:

```
Name: Isabelle Nguyen        Score:  84
```

Example 3 — Real-world application

A utility package with shared configuration accessed via relative import from multiple sibling modules.

```
# Package structure:
#   reports/
#       __init__.py
#       config.py      — shared constants
#       csv_report.py — CSV formatter
#       txt_report.py — plain-text formatter

# --- reports/config.py ---
DATE_FORMAT  = '%d/%m/%Y'
CURRENCY     = 'AUD'
COL_WIDTH    = 20

# --- reports/csv_report.py ---
from . import config
from datetime import datetime

def write_header(writer):
    writer.writerow(["Date", "Description", f"Amount ({config.CURRENCY})"])

def write_row(writer, description, amount):
    today = datetime.now().strftime(config.DATE_FORMAT)
    writer.writerow([today, description, f'{amount:.2f}'])

# --- reports/txt_report.py ---
from . import config

def render_row(description, amount):
    w = config.COL_WIDTH
    return f"{description:<{w}} {config.CURRENCY} {amount:>10.2f}"

# Both modules share config through a single relative import.
# Changing DATE_FORMAT in config.py updates every report type at once.
```

Output:

```
# csv_report output (inside a csv.writer context):
Date,Description,Amount (AUD)
14/07/2025,School supplies,47.95
```

```
# txt_report output:
School supplies          AUD      47.95
```

The key rule is simple: absolute imports for external packages and standard library modules; relative imports for modules within the same package. This distinction keeps your internal structure flexible without sacrificing clarity about external dependencies.

Lazy Imports and Import Inside Functions

Python executes import statements the moment it encounters them during module load. For most programs this is exactly what you want: all dependencies are resolved before any application code runs, and any missing modules raise an ImportError immediately at startup rather than midway through execution.

There are, however, legitimate reasons to defer an import until it is actually needed. Moving an import inside a function delays its execution until the function is first called. This technique is called a lazy import. The most common reasons to use it are: the imported library is optional and may not be installed, the import is slow (some packages take hundreds of milliseconds to initialise) and is only needed on certain code paths, or a circular import dependency forces the delay (covered in Section 2.5).

The trade-off is that an import inside a function re-executes the import lookup on every call — though Python's sys.modules cache means the module is only loaded once. The greater cost is readability: placing imports inside functions scatters your dependency list throughout the file, making it harder to understand the module's requirements at a glance.

> **Note:** Use lazy imports sparingly and document why the import is deferred. A brief comment such as # deferred to avoid circular import or # optional dependency: install with pip install X makes the intent clear to future readers.

Example 1 — Introduction

An import placed inside a function so it only executes when that function is called.

```
def show_json(data):
    import json            # imported here, not at module top level
    print(json.dumps(data, indent=2))

# The json module is not imported until show_json is first called.
# Once called, json is cached in sys.modules and subsequent calls
# find it immediately without re-reading the .py file.
show_json({"name": "Olivia", "score": 91})
```

Output:

```
{
  "name": "Olivia",
  "score": 91
}
```

Example 2 — Variation

Optional dependency pattern: gracefully handle the case where a third-party library is not installed.

```
def export_to_excel(data, filepath):
    """Write data to an Excel file if openpyxl is available."""
    try:
```

```
        import openpyxl           # optional: not everyone needs Excel export
    except ImportError:
        print('Excel export unavailable. Install openpyxl with:')
        print('  pip install openpyxl')
        return False

    wb = openpyxl.Workbook()
    ws = wb.active
    for row in data:
        ws.append(row)
    wb.save(filepath)
    print(f"Saved to {filepath}")
    return True

# When openpyxl is not installed this prints a helpful message
# instead of crashing with an unhandled ImportError.
result = export_to_excel([['Name','Score'],['Leo',85]], 'out.xlsx')
```

Output:

```
Excel export unavailable. Install openpyxl with:
  pip install openpyxl
```

Example 3 — Real-world application

A report renderer that lazily loads a heavy optional formatter only on the code path that requires it.

```
# report_renderer.py
FORMATS = ('text', 'csv', 'html')

def render(data, fmt='text'):
    """Render a list of dicts to the requested format."""
    if fmt not in FORMATS:
        raise ValueError(f"Unknown format: {fmt!r}. Choose from {FORMATS}")

    if fmt == 'text':
        _render_text(data)
    elif fmt == 'csv':
        _render_csv(data)
    elif fmt == 'html':
        _render_html(data)    # html path lazily imports a heavy library

def _render_text(data):
    for row in data:
        print(' | '.join(str(v) for v in row.values()))

def _render_csv(data):
    import csv, sys           # csv is stdlib - fast and harmless to defer
    writer = csv.DictWriter(sys.stdout, fieldnames=data[0].keys())
    writer.writeheader()
    writer.writerows(data)

def _render_html(data):
    import html               # stdlib html for escaping
    keys = list(data[0].keys())
    print("<table>")
    print("  <tr>" + "".join(f"<th>{k}</th>" for k in keys) + "</tr>")
    for row in data:
        cells = "".join(f"<td>{html.escape(str(row[k]))}</td>" for k in keys)
        print(f"  <tr>{cells}</tr>")
    print("</table>")

students = [
    {'name': 'Ava Chen',    'grade': 'A'},
    {'name': 'Jack Murray', 'grade': 'B'},
]
```

```
render(students, 'text')
```

Output:

```
Ava Chen | A
Jack Murray | B
```

A useful rule of thumb: import at the top of the file unless there is a specific reason not to. The three legitimate reasons — optional dependency, performance-critical startup, and circular import resolution — should each be accompanied by a comment explaining why the import is deferred.

Circular Imports: Causes, Detection, and Fixes

A circular import occurs when module A imports module B, and module B (directly or through a chain) imports module A. Because Python executes a module top-to-bottom the first time it is imported and caches a partially-constructed module object in sys.modules while doing so, a circular import can cause one module to see an incomplete version of another — missing attributes that were defined later in the file — or raise an ImportError outright.

The classic symptom is an AttributeError or ImportError that disappears when you restructure the code. Circular imports are almost always a sign that the module boundaries were drawn incorrectly: two modules that mutually depend on each other are often trying to occupy the same conceptual space and should either be merged or refactored so that their shared code lives in a third, independent module.

When restructuring is not immediately practical, three tactics reliably break a cycle: move the import inside the function that actually needs it (Section 2.4), use importlib.import_module() at call time (Section 2.6), or extract the shared definition into a new module that neither of the two originals imports from each other.

> **Note:** The best long-term fix for a circular import is always restructuring. Hiding the import inside a function is a tactical workaround, not an architectural solution. If you find yourself reaching for function-level imports frequently, treat it as a signal that your module boundaries need review.

Example 1 — Introduction

A minimal circular import that produces an ImportError — the error Python raises when the cycle is tight.

```
# --- alpha.py ---
from beta import greet_beta    # imports beta at module load time

def greet_alpha():
    return "Hello from alpha"

# --- beta.py ---
from alpha import greet_alpha  # alpha is already being loaded — cycle!

def greet_beta():
    return "Hello from beta"

# Running either file produces:
# ImportError: cannot import name 'greet_alpha' from partially initialised
# module 'alpha' (most likely due to a circular import)
```

Output:

```
ImportError: cannot import name 'greet_alpha' from partially initialised
module 'alpha' (most likely due to a circular import)
```

Example 2 — Variation

Fix 1: extract the shared definition into a third module that neither alpha nor beta imports from each other.

```
# --- shared.py ---   (new module, no imports from alpha or beta)
def base_greeting(name):
    return f"Hello from {name}"

# --- alpha.py ---
from shared import base_greeting    # no import of beta

def greet_alpha():
    return base_greeting("alpha")

# --- beta.py ---
from shared import base_greeting    # no import of alpha

def greet_beta():
    return base_greeting("beta")

# --- main.py ---
from alpha import greet_alpha
from beta  import greet_beta
print(greet_alpha())
print(greet_beta())
```

Output:

```
Hello from alpha
Hello from beta
```

Example 3 — Real-world application

Fix 2: break a cycle between an ORM-style models module and a helpers module by deferring the import to function scope.

```
# Scenario: models.py and helpers.py reference each other.

# --- models.py ---
class Course:
    def __init__(self, name, capacity):
        self.name     = name
        self.capacity = capacity
        self.enrolled = []

    def enrol(self, student):
        # Deferred import inside the method that needs it.
        # helpers.py imports models.py, so a top-level import here
        # would create a cycle.
        from helpers import validate_capacity    # deferred import
        if validate_capacity(self):
            self.enrolled.append(student)
            return True
        return False

# --- helpers.py ---
def validate_capacity(course):
    """Return True if course has space for one more student."""
    return len(course.enrolled) < course.capacity

# --- main.py ---
from models import Course

intro_python = Course('Intro to Python', capacity=3)
print(intro_python.enrol("Zara"))     # True
```

```
print(intro_python.enrol("Marcus"))   # True
print(intro_python.enrol("Priya"))    # True
print(intro_python.enrol("Jordan"))   # False — at capacity
```

Output:

```
True
True
True
False
```

Whenever you suspect a circular import, add print statements showing when each module starts and finishes loading — the order of execution will reveal the cycle immediately. Once the cycle is confirmed, restructuring the module boundaries is almost always the cleanest fix.

importlib: Dynamic Imports at Runtime

The standard import statement is a static construct: module names are literals baked into the source code. There are situations where the module name is not known until runtime — it might come from a configuration file, a command-line argument, a database record, or user input. For these cases Python provides the importlib module, which exposes the same import machinery as a callable API.

The most commonly used function is importlib.import_module(name), which accepts a string and returns the module object. The behaviour is identical to import name: the module is found on sys.path, executed, and cached in sys.modules. For relative imports, a second argument specifies the anchor package: importlib.import_module('.models', package='school').

A companion utility, importlib.util.find_spec(name), checks whether a module can be found without actually loading it. It returns a ModuleSpec object if the module exists, or None if it does not. This is the correct way to test for an optional dependency before attempting to import it, replacing the older try/except ImportError pattern in cases where you only need to confirm existence, not load the module.

> **Note:** importlib.import_module() is not a security boundary. Passing user-supplied input directly as the module name is dangerous — an attacker could supply a name that causes arbitrary code to execute. Always validate or whitelist module names before passing them to import_module().

Example 1 — Introduction

Importing a module by name stored in a string variable, as you would read from a config file.

```
import importlib

# In a real application this string might come from a config file,
# a command-line argument, or a database record.
module_name = 'statistics'

stats = importlib.import_module(module_name)

# The returned object is the same as typing 'import statistics'
data = [55, 72, 88, 91, 64, 79, 83]
print(f"Mean   : {stats.mean(data):.1f}")
print(f"Median : {stats.median(data):.1f}")
print(f"Module : {stats.__name__}")
```

Output:

```
Mean   : 76.0
Median : 79.0
```

```
Module : statistics
```

Example 2 — Variation

Using find_spec() to check whether an optional module is installed before attempting to load it.

```
import importlib.util

def module_available(name):
    """Return True if the named module can be found on sys.path."""
    return importlib.util.find_spec(name) is not None

# Check for optional dependencies without triggering their imports
for lib in ['csv', 'json', 'numpy', 'pandas', 'nonexistent_pkg']:
    status = 'available' if module_available(lib) else 'not installed'
    print(f"  {lib:<18} {status}")
```

Output:

```
  csv                available
  json               available
  numpy              not installed
  pandas             not installed
  nonexistent_pkg    not installed
```

Example 3 — Real-world application

A plugin loader that reads a list of plugin module names from a config dictionary and loads each one dynamically.

```
# plugin_loader.py
import importlib
import importlib.util

# In practice these names come from a config file or database.
CONFIG = {
    'plugins': [
        'plugins.csv_exporter',
        'plugins.txt_exporter',
        'plugins.pdf_exporter',     # hypothetical — may not be installed
    ]
}

def load_plugins(plugin_names):
    """
    Attempt to load each plugin by name.
    Returns a dict of {name: module} for successfully loaded plugins.
    """
    loaded = {}
    for name in plugin_names:
        # Check availability before loading to give a clear message
        if importlib.util.find_spec(name) is None:
            print(f"  [SKIP]   {name} — not found")
            continue
        try:
            mod = importlib.import_module(name)
            loaded[name] = mod
            print(f"  [LOADED] {name}")
        except Exception as exc:
            print(f"  [ERROR]  {name}: {exc}")
    return loaded

print('Loading plugins...')
active_plugins = load_plugins(CONFIG['plugins'])
print(f"Active: {len(active_plugins)} plugin(s)")
```

Output:

```
Loading plugins...
  [SKIP]   plugins.csv_exporter — not found
  [SKIP]   plugins.txt_exporter — not found
  [SKIP]   plugins.pdf_exporter — not found
Active: 0 plugin(s)
```

Dynamic imports are the mechanism behind plugin architectures, extensible frameworks, and testing tools that need to import arbitrary modules on demand. They appear in Django's app loading system, pytest's test discovery, and many configuration-driven tools. Understanding importlib gives you access to the same machinery those frameworks use.

Best Practices: Import Style, Ordering, and What to Avoid

PEP 8 — Python's official style guide — dedicates a full section to imports. The rules are widely adopted, supported by automated tools, and enforced by most professional Python teams. Following them is not merely a stylistic preference; it makes your code predictably structured, easier to review, and simpler to maintain.

Import ordering

Imports should appear at the top of the file, after the module docstring and any __future__ imports, and before any module-level constants or code. They are divided into three groups, separated by blank lines: (1) standard library imports, (2) third-party library imports, and (3) local application or package imports. Within each group, imports are alphabetised. The isort tool automates this ordering.

One import per line

Each import X statement should import exactly one module. Combining multiple modules on one line — import os, sys — is legal but reduces readability and makes version-controlled diffs harder to read, since a change to either module appears as a change to the same line.

What to avoid

Wildcard imports (from X import *) should never appear in production module-level code. They make it impossible to know where a name came from, they risk silent name shadowing, and they confuse static analysis tools. Circular imports should be resolved by restructuring, not by ordering workarounds. Shadowing standard library names — naming a local file json.py, random.py, or string.py — is a common mistake that causes confusing import errors.

> **Note:** Never create a module with the same name as a standard library module. A file called json.py in your project directory will be found before the standard library's json, and import json will load yours instead. This breaks every module in your project that tries to import the real json.

Example 1 — Introduction

A module header showing poor import practice, then the same imports rewritten according to PEP 8.

```
# BAD — mixed order, multiple on one line, wildcard, no grouping
from pathlib import *
import os, sys
from datetime import datetime
import csv
from my_utils import helper
import json
```

```
# ──────────────────────────────────────────────────────────

# GOOD — three groups, alphabetised, one per line, no wildcard
import csv
import json
import os
import sys
from datetime import datetime
from pathlib import Path

from my_utils import helper
```

Output:

```
# The second version produces identical behaviour.
# Every dependency is visible at a glance, in a predictable location.
```

Example 2 — Variation

Demonstrating how __all__ acts as the module's public contract, shaping what from X import * actually imports.

```
# maths_helpers.py
"""Utility functions for school maths problems."""

import math

# __all__ declares the public interface of this module.
# from maths_helpers import * will only bind these two names.
__all__ = ['circle_area', 'triangle_area']

def circle_area(radius):
    """Return the area of a circle with the given radius."""
    return math.pi * radius ** 2

def triangle_area(base, height):
    """Return the area of a triangle."""
    return 0.5 * base * height

def _validate_positive(value, name):
    """Internal helper — not part of the public API."""
    if value <= 0:
        raise ValueError(f"{name} must be positive, got {value}")

# --- In another module ---
from maths_helpers import *          # only circle_area and triangle_area
print(circle_area(5))
print(triangle_area(8, 3))
# _validate_positive is NOT imported — the underscore and __all__ both
# mark it as internal.
```

Output:

```
78.53981633974483
12.0
```

Example 3 — Real-world application

A well-structured production module showing all best practices applied together.

```
"""
invoice.py — Invoice generation utilities for the school bookshop.

Public API:
    Invoice      — dataclass representing a single invoice
    format_total — format a dollar amount with GST note
```

```
    save_invoice — write an invoice to a JSON file
"""

# — Standard library ——————————————————————————
import json
import os
from dataclasses import dataclass, field
from datetime import date
from pathlib import Path
from typing import List

# — Local application ——————————————————————————
from school_utils import format_currency    # project-local module

# — Public interface ——————————————————————————
__all__ = ['Invoice', 'format_total', 'save_invoice']

GST_RATE = 0.10   # Australian GST

@dataclass
class Invoice:
    number      : str
    customer    : str
    issued_date : date = field(default_factory=date.today)
    items       : List[dict] = field(default_factory=list)

    @property
    def subtotal(self):
        return sum(item['price'] * item['qty'] for item in self.items)

    @property
    def gst(self):
        return round(self.subtotal * GST_RATE, 2)

def format_total(invoice):
    return f"Total (inc. GST): {format_currency(invoice.subtotal +
invoice.gst)}"

def save_invoice(invoice, directory='invoices'):
    Path(directory).mkdir(exist_ok=True)
    path = Path(directory) / f'{invoice.number}.json'
    with open(path, 'w', encoding='utf-8') as f:
        json.dump({
            'number'   : invoice.number,
            'customer' : invoice.customer,
            'issued'   : str(invoice.issued_date),
            'subtotal' : invoice.subtotal,
            'gst'      : invoice.gst,
        }, f, indent=2)
    print(f"Saved: {path}")
```

Output:

```
# Module docstring describes public API clearly.
# Imports are grouped: stdlib first, then local.
# __all__ declares exactly what is exported.
# Module-level constant GST_RATE is named in UPPER_CASE (PEP 8).
# Private helpers would be prefixed with an underscore.
```

Following these conventions consistently means that any Python developer can open your file and immediately understand its dependencies, its public interface, and its structure — before reading a single line of implementation code. The few minutes spent on import hygiene save hours of debugging and confusion later.

Chapter 2 Summary

- Python provides three import forms: import X binds the module object; from X import Y pulls specific names into scope; from X import * imports all public names and should be avoided at module level.
- The as keyword aliases a module or imported name to a different local identifier, resolving name conflicts and conforming to ecosystem conventions such as import statistics as stats.
- Relative imports use leading dots to reference modules within the same package without hard-coding the package name, making intra-package references portable when the package is renamed or moved.
- Relative imports are only valid inside a package. Scripts run directly cannot use them; use python -m package.module to run package code with __package__ set correctly.
- Lazy imports — placing import statements inside a function — defer loading until the function is called. Use them for optional dependencies, slow-starting libraries, or to break circular import cycles when restructuring is not immediately possible.
- Circular imports occur when two modules import each other. The root cause is almost always incorrect module boundaries; fix them by extracting shared code into a third module, or as a short-term measure by deferring one import to function scope.
- importlib.import_module() loads a module whose name is known only at runtime; importlib.util.find_spec() checks whether a module exists without loading it. Both are essential tools for plugin architectures and optional-dependency handling.
- PEP 8 prescribes that imports appear at the top of the file, grouped as stdlib → third-party → local, one module per line, and alphabetised within each group. The __all__ list declares a module's public contract and controls what from X import * exports.

Guided Exercises

1. Create a module called currency_utils.py containing two functions: aud_to_usd(amount, rate) and usd_to_aud(amount, rate). In a separate script, import the module three ways: import currency_utils, then from currency_utils import aud_to_usd, then from currency_utils import * (inside an if __name__ == "__main__" block). Print the result of each conversion and confirm all three forms produce the same result.

   Hint: Each import form binds the same underlying function object but with a different name in the local namespace. Check type(aud_to_usd) after each import style.

2. Write a script that imports the datetime module as dt and the statistics module as stats. Use both aliases to print the current date and the mean of the list [60, 72, 85, 91, 54, 78, 83]. Then demonstrate that the original unaliased names (datetime and statistics) are not available in the namespace.

   Hint: After the aliased imports, try accessing datetime.date.today() and confirm that it raises NameError. Use dt.date.today() instead.

3. Create a small package called geometry/ with an __init__.py, a shapes.py module defining a Rectangle class with area() and perimeter() methods, and a utils.py module that imports Rectangle using a relative import and defines a function describe(rect) that returns a formatted string. Write a main.py outside the package that imports and uses describe().

   Hint: Run with python -m geometry.main or ensure main.py is at the same level as geometry/. The relative import in utils.py should be: from . import shapes or from .shapes import Rectangle.

4. Write a function called safe_import(module_name) that uses importlib.util.find_spec() to check whether a module is available. If available, use importlib.import_module() to load and return it. If not, return None and print a helpful message. Test it with 'json', 'os', and 'nonexistent_library'.

> **Hint:** find_spec() returns None when the module cannot be found. Wrap import_module() in try/except ImportError as an additional safety net in case find_spec succeeds but the module fails to load.

5. Create a module called string_tools.py that defines four functions: to_upper, to_lower, word_count, and an internal helper _clean (prefixed with underscore). Add __all__ = ['to_upper', 'to_lower', 'word_count']. In a test script, use from string_tools import * and verify that _clean is not available in the namespace, while the three listed functions are.

> **Hint:** After from string_tools import *, use dir() or check 'to_upper' in dir() and '_clean' not in dir() to confirm __all__ is working correctly.

Challenge Tasks

1. Design a minimal plugin system for a data-processing application. Create a plugins/ package containing at least two plugin modules: plugins/uppercase_plugin.py and plugins/reverse_plugin.py. Each plugin module must define a function called process(text) that transforms its input. Write a plugin_manager.py at the project root that reads a list of plugin names from a dictionary (simulating a config file), uses importlib to load each one dynamically, and then applies all loaded plugins to a test string in sequence. If a listed plugin cannot be found, log a warning and continue. Demonstrate the system loading two plugins and transforming the string 'Hello from Brisbane'.

2. Investigate how Python's import system handles module caching. Write a script that imports the same module twice using two different syntactic forms (e.g., import json and from json import dumps). Using the is operator and sys.modules, demonstrate that both forms refer to the same cached module object. Then write a second demonstration: create a small module (counter.py) with a module-level variable count = 0 and a function increment(). Import the module, call increment() several times, then import it again in a different variable and show that both variables reflect the same mutated state — proving that Python loads each module exactly once per interpreter session.

3. Build a dependency checker tool. Given a Python source file as a command-line argument, use Python's ast module to parse the file and extract every top-level import statement (import X, from X import Y). For each extracted module name, use importlib.util.find_spec() to classify it as: stdlib (present in Python's sys.stdlib_module_names set, available in Python 3.10+), third-party (find_spec returns a spec with an origin outside the stdlib), or missing (find_spec returns None). Print a formatted report categorising all imports found in the target file. Test it against at least two of your own scripts.

CHAPTER 3 **Creating Your Own Modules**

Book 03: Modules, Packages & the Python Ecosystem

> Chapters 1 and 2 covered why modules exist and how to consume them. This chapter turns to the craft of writing them. A well-designed module is more than a file of functions — it has a clear responsibility, a documented public interface, sensibly named constants, and a self-test guard that keeps demo code from running on import. These qualities do not emerge automatically; they are the result of deliberate design choices applied consistently. By the end of this chapter you will know how to structure a .py file from top to bottom, how to use the __main__ guard correctly, how to document your code in a way that other tools can read, and how to verify a module works in isolation before handing it to a larger program.

3.1 Writing a .py Module File: Structure and Conventions

Every Python module is a .py file. Beyond that minimal requirement, Python imposes no mandatory structure — but the community has converged on a clear ordering that experienced developers expect to find. Deviating from it creates friction for anyone reading your code, including your future self.

The conventional top-to-bottom order is: the module docstring, any __future__ imports (rare and always first), standard library imports, third-party imports, local imports, module-level constants and configuration, class definitions, function definitions, and finally any code that runs at import time (ideally none, or protected by the __main__ guard). This ordering means a reader can locate any element by scanning predictably rather than hunting.

Two additional conventions keep modules clean: all names intended for internal use only should begin with a single underscore (e.g., _helper()), and all public names should be listed in __all__. Together these two mechanisms create an explicit, machine-readable public contract that import machinery, IDEs, and documentation tools all respect. (See Chapter 2 for the import-side effects of __all__.)

> **Note:** Place executable code — print statements, function calls, input() — only inside the if __name__ == '__main__': guard at the bottom of the file, never at module scope. A module that prints or prompts on import is difficult to test and unpleasant to use as a library.

Example 1 — Introduction

A minimal module showing the standard top-to-bottom structure: docstring, imports, constants, functions.

```
"""
temperature.py — Celsius / Fahrenheit / Kelvin conversion utilities.
"""

# — Standard library ————————————————————————
import math

# — Public interface ————————————————————————
__all__ = ['celsius_to_fahrenheit', 'fahrenheit_to_celsius',
           'celsius_to_kelvin',     'kelvin_to_celsius']

# — Constants ———————————————————————————
```

```
ABSOLUTE_ZERO_C = -273.15    # Celsius value of absolute zero

# ── Public functions ────────────────────────────────
def celsius_to_fahrenheit(c):
    """Convert Celsius to Fahrenheit."""
    return c * 9 / 5 + 32

def fahrenheit_to_celsius(f):
    """Convert Fahrenheit to Celsius."""
    return (f - 32) * 5 / 9

def celsius_to_kelvin(c):
    """Convert Celsius to Kelvin. Raises ValueError below absolute zero."""
    if c < ABSOLUTE_ZERO_C:
        raise ValueError(f"Temperature {c} °C is below absolute zero.")
    return c - ABSOLUTE_ZERO_C

def kelvin_to_celsius(k):
    """Convert Kelvin to Celsius."""
    return k + ABSOLUTE_ZERO_C

# ── Internal helper ────────────────────────────────
def _round(value, dp=2):
    """Round value to dp decimal places (internal use)."""
    return round(value, dp)
```

Output:

```
# No output when imported — the module is silent.
# When used by another script:
# >>> from temperature import celsius_to_fahrenheit
# >>> celsius_to_fahrenheit(100)
# 212.0
```

Example 2 — Variation

Showing the effect of violating module-scope hygiene: a module with top-level side effects versus a clean version.

```
# ── BAD: greet_bad.py — has side effects at module scope ──
name = input("Enter your name: ")    # executes on import!
print(f"Hello, {name}!")

def greet(n):
    return f"Hello, {n}!"

# Any script that does 'import greet_bad' will be interrupted
# by a prompt and a print — even if it only wants greet().

# ── GOOD: greet_good.py — clean module scope ──────────
def greet(n):
    """Return a greeting string for the given name."""
    return f"Hello, {n}!"

if __name__ == '__main__':
    name = input("Enter your name: ")
    print(greet(name))
```

Output:

```
# greet_bad.py on import: prompts the user immediately — bad.
# greet_good.py on import: completely silent — correct.
# greet_good.py run directly: prompts, then prints greeting.
```

Example 3 — Real-world application

A GST (Goods and Services Tax) utility module following all structural conventions, ready to import anywhere.

```
"""
gst_utils.py — Australian GST calculation utilities.

Public API:
    add_gst(amount)          — return price including 10% GST
    remove_gst(amount)       — return the pre-GST component
    gst_component(amount)    — return the GST portion of an inc-GST price
"""

# — Standard library ──────────────────────────────────────
from decimal import Decimal, ROUND_HALF_UP

# — Public interface ──────────────────────────────────────
__all__ = ['add_gst', 'remove_gst', 'gst_component']

# — Constants ─────────────────────────────────────────────
GST_RATE        = Decimal('0.10')
GST_DIVISOR     = Decimal('1.10')   # divides inc-GST price to get ex-GST
_TWO_PLACES     = Decimal('0.01')   # quantise target (internal)

# — Internal helper ───────────────────────────────────────
def _quantise(value):
    """Round a Decimal to two decimal places using ROUND_HALF_UP."""
    return value.quantize(_TWO_PLACES, rounding=ROUND_HALF_UP)

# — Public functions ──────────────────────────────────────
def add_gst(amount):
    """Return amount plus 10% GST, rounded to two decimal places."""
    return _quantise(Decimal(str(amount)) * (1 + GST_RATE))


def remove_gst(amount):
    """Return the ex-GST component of an inc-GST amount."""
    return _quantise(Decimal(str(amount)) / GST_DIVISOR)


def gst_component(amount):
    """Return the GST portion of an inc-GST amount."""
    ex = remove_gst(amount)
    return _quantise(Decimal(str(amount)) - ex)


if __name__ == '__main__':
    price = 49.95
    print(f"Ex-GST : ${price}")
    print(f"Inc-GST: ${add_gst(price)}")
    print(f"GST    : ${gst_component(add_gst(price))}")
```

Output:

```
# When run directly:
Ex-GST : $49.95
Inc-GST: $54.94
GST    : $4.99

# When imported by invoice.py, shop.py, or any other module:
# complete silence — only the three public functions are available.
```

The structural conventions shown here are not arbitrary. Each rule solves a specific problem: the docstring makes the module discoverable, the import grouping reveals dependencies at a glance, the constant naming prevents magic numbers, the underscore prefix protects internals, and __all__ makes the contract explicit. Apply them every time, even for small modules.

Module-Level Constants and Their Naming

A module-level constant is a name bound at module scope that is not intended to be reassigned. Python has no const keyword, so the convention of writing constants in UPPER_CASE_WITH_UNDERSCORES (also called SCREAMING_SNAKE_CASE) is the community's substitute. The casing is a signal to every reader — and to linters — that this value should not be modified after initialisation.

Constants serve several important roles in a module: they eliminate magic numbers (unexplained numeric or string literals scattered through the code), they centralise configuration (changing a tax rate or a maximum file size means editing one line, not hunting through the codebase), and they give meaning to values that would otherwise be opaque. The difference between the literal 0.10 and the constant GST_RATE is entirely about communication.

Not every module-level name that never changes needs to be a constant. Simple type annotations, class definitions, and function definitions are also module-level bindings, but they are not constants in the configuration sense. Reserve UPPER_CASE for values that represent a tuneable parameter, a physical quantity, a fixed string, or a configuration setting — things that a maintainer might reasonably need to update.

> **Note:** Constants are a promise, not a lock. Python will not stop you from writing GST_RATE = 0.20 later in the same file. The UPPER_CASE convention is a signal to developers; if you need enforcement, store the constant in a frozen dataclass or a namedtuple.

Example 1 — Introduction

Module-level constants replacing magic numbers in a simple physics calculation module.

```
"""
physics.py — Physical constants and kinematic formulae.
"""

__all__ = ['kinetic_energy', 'gravitational_pe', 'free_fall_time']

# Physical constants — named so their meaning is self-documenting
G            = 9.80665    # standard gravity, m/s^2
SPEED_OF_LIGHT = 299_792_458    # m/s  (Python allows _ in numeric literals)

def kinetic_energy(mass_kg, velocity_ms):
    """Return kinetic energy in joules: KE = 0.5 * m * v^2."""
    return 0.5 * mass_kg * velocity_ms ** 2

def gravitational_pe(mass_kg, height_m):
    """Return gravitational potential energy in joules: PE = m * g * h."""
    return mass_kg * G * height_m

def free_fall_time(height_m):
    """Return time in seconds to fall from rest through height_m."""
    return (2 * height_m / G) ** 0.5

if __name__ == '__main__':
    print(f"KE of 2 kg at 10 m/s  : {kinetic_energy(2, 10):.1f} J")
    print(f"PE of 5 kg at 20 m    : {gravitational_pe(5, 20):.1f} J")
    print(f"Fall time from 45 m   : {free_fall_time(45):.2f} s")
```

Output:

```
KE of 2 kg at 10 m/s  : 100.0 J
PE of 5 kg at 20 m    : 980.7 J
Fall time from 45 m   : 3.03 s
```

Example 2 — Variation

Using a frozen dataclass and a namedtuple to create truly immutable constants.

```
from dataclasses import dataclass
from collections import namedtuple

# namedtuple: lightweight immutable record — good for grouped constants
Colour = namedtuple('Colour', ['red', 'green', 'blue'])
RED   = Colour(255, 0,   0)
GREEN = Colour(0,   255, 0)
BLUE  = Colour(0,   0,   255)

# frozen dataclass: prevents attribute reassignment after creation
@dataclass(frozen=True)
class AppConfig:
    host     : str  = 'localhost'
    port     : int  = 8080
    debug    : bool = False
    max_conn : int  = 100

CONFIG = AppConfig()   # single shared instance

print(f"Server: {CONFIG.host}:{CONFIG.port}")
print(f"Red channel: {RED.red}")

# Attempting mutation raises FrozenInstanceError
try:
    CONFIG.port = 9090
except Exception as e:
    print(f"Cannot modify: {type(e).__name__}")
```

Output:

```
Server: localhost:8080
Red channel: 255
Cannot modify: FrozenInstanceError
```

Example 3 — Real-world application

A school timetable module using constants to centralise all configurable values in one place.

```
"""
timetable.py — School timetable configuration and helpers.
"""

__all__ = ['periods_today', 'period_label', 'DAYS', 'PERIODS_PER_DAY']

# ── Timetable constants ───────────────────────────────────
DAYS            = ('Monday', 'Tuesday', 'Wednesday', 'Thursday', 'Friday')
PERIODS_PER_DAY = 6
PERIOD_MINUTES  = 50
BREAK_AFTER     = 3        # long break after period 3
BREAK_MINUTES   = 30

# ── Period start times (24-hour, minutes from midnight) ──
_PERIOD_START = [
     8 * 60 + 30,    # Period 1: 08:30
     9 * 60 + 25,    # Period 2: 09:25
    10 * 60 + 20,    # Period 3: 10:20
    11 * 60 + 20,    # Period 4: 11:20  (after break)
    12 * 60 + 15,    # Period 5: 12:15
    13 * 60 + 10,    # Period 6: 13:10
]

def period_label(n):
```

```python
    """Return a human-readable label for period n (1-indexed)."""
    if not 1 <= n <= PERIODS_PER_DAY:
        raise ValueError(f"Period must be 1-{PERIODS_PER_DAY}, got {n}")
    mins = _PERIOD_START[n - 1]
    return f"Period {n} — {mins // 60:02d}:{mins % 60:02d}"

def periods_today(day_name):
    """Return all period labels for a given day name."""
    if day_name not in DAYS:
        raise ValueError(f"Unknown day: {day_name!r}")
    return [period_label(n) for n in range(1, PERIODS_PER_DAY + 1)]

if __name__ == '__main__':
    for p in periods_today('Wednesday'):
        print(p)
```

Output:

```
Period 1 — 08:30
Period 2 — 09:25
Period 3 — 10:20
Period 4 — 11:20
Period 5 — 12:15
Period 6 — 13:10
```

Well-named constants make a module's configuration surface obvious to whoever needs to adapt it. When a colleague sees PERIODS_PER_DAY = 6 at the top of the file, they know exactly where to look if the school moves to a seven-period day. When they see 6 buried inside a list comprehension, they have to understand the entire function before they can safely change it.

Functions and Classes in a Module

A module is the natural container for a cohesive set of functions and classes. The cohesion principle from Chapter 1 applies here at the design level: every function and class in a module should belong to the same conceptual domain. A module called student_records.py should contain Student, Enrolment, and related functions — not a PDF renderer or a networking utility.

Functions and classes in a module work exactly as they do in a script, with one important difference: their local scope ends at the function or class boundary, but module-level names (constants, other functions, classes) are all visible within the module without any special syntax. A function in gst_utils.py can call _quantise() directly, because both exist in the same module namespace.

When designing a module's class and function set, apply the same public/private discipline as you would inside a class (Book 01, Chapter 4). Functions and classes intended for module-internal use should be prefixed with a single underscore. Only the names listed in __all__ (or those without a leading underscore if __all__ is not defined) form the public API that callers should depend on.

> **Note:** Avoid defining module-level mutable state — global lists, dicts, or objects that functions modify in place. Such state makes a module hard to test in isolation and causes subtle bugs when a module is imported by multiple other modules. Pass state through function arguments and return values instead.

Example 1 — Introduction

A module that combines a class and related functions, sharing module-level constants between them.

```python
"""
grades.py - Grade classification for Australian secondary schools.
"""
```

```
__all__ = ['Grade', 'classify', 'report_card']

# Grade boundary constants — one place to update the whole module
GRADE_BOUNDARIES = [
    (90, 'A', 'Outstanding'),
    (80, 'B', 'High Achievement'),
    (70, 'C', 'Sound Achievement'),
    (60, 'D', 'Limited Achievement'),
    ( 0, 'E', 'Very Limited Achievement'),
]

class Grade:
    """Represents a classified grade for a single assessment."""
    def __init__(self, score):
        self.score  = score
        self.letter, self.description = _lookup(score)

    def __repr__(self):
        return f"Grade({self.score} → {self.letter}: {self.description})"

def _lookup(score):
    """Internal: return (letter, description) for a numeric score."""
    for minimum, letter, description in GRADE_BOUNDARIES:
        if score >= minimum:
            return letter, description
    return 'E', 'Very Limited Achievement'

def classify(score):
    """Return the letter grade for a numeric score."""
    return _lookup(score)[0]

def report_card(name, scores):
    """Print a formatted report card for the given name and scores."""
    print(f"Report Card: {name}")
    print("-" * 40)
    total = 0
    for i, s in enumerate(scores, 1):
        g = Grade(s)
        print(f"  Assessment {i}: {s:>3}  {g.letter}  {g.description}")
        total += s
    avg = total / len(scores)
    g_avg = Grade(avg)
    print("-" * 40)
    print(f"  Average    : {avg:>5.1f}  {g_avg.letter}")

if __name__ == '__main__':
    report_card('Sophia Tran', [88, 74, 92, 65, 81])
```

Output:

```
Report Card: Sophia Tran
----------------------------------------
  Assessment 1:  88  B  High Achievement
  Assessment 2:  74  C  Sound Achievement
  Assessment 3:  92  A  Outstanding
  Assessment 4:  65  D  Limited Achievement
  Assessment 5:  81  B  High Achievement
----------------------------------------
  Average    :  80.0  B
```

Example 2 — Variation

Two modules sharing a common base class defined in a third — showing how class inheritance spans module boundaries.

```python
# --- shapes_base.py ---
import math

__all__ = ['Shape']

class Shape:
    """Abstract base for all 2-D shapes (not using ABC for brevity)."""
    @property
    def area(self):
        raise NotImplementedError("Subclass must implement area")

    @property
    def perimeter(self):
        raise NotImplementedError("Subclass must implement perimeter")

    def __repr__(self):
        return f"{type(self).__name__}(area={self.area:.2f})"

# --- shapes_circle.py ---
import math
from shapes_base import Shape

__all__ = ['Circle']

class Circle(Shape):
    def __init__(self, radius):
        self.radius = radius

    @property
    def area(self): return math.pi * self.radius ** 2

    @property
    def perimeter(self): return 2 * math.pi * self.radius

# --- shapes_rect.py ---
from shapes_base import Shape

__all__ = ['Rectangle']

class Rectangle(Shape):
    def __init__(self, width, height):
        self.width, self.height = width, height

    @property
    def area(self): return self.width * self.height

    @property
    def perimeter(self): return 2 * (self.width + self.height)

# --- demo ---
from shapes_circle import Circle
from shapes_rect   import Rectangle

for shape in [Circle(5), Rectangle(4, 6)]:
    print(f"{shape}  perimeter={shape.perimeter:.2f}")
```

Output:

```
Circle(area=78.54)  perimeter=31.42
Rectangle(area=24.00)  perimeter=20.00
```

Example 3 — Real-world application

A bank account module combining a class, module-level functions, and constants in a realistic structure.

```
"""
accounts.py — Simple bank account types for the school banking simulator.

Public API: Account, SavingsAccount, deposit_all, total_balance
"""

from datetime import date

__all__ = ['Account', 'SavingsAccount', 'deposit_all', 'total_balance']

INTEREST_RATE    = 0.035     # 3.5% annual rate
OVERDRAFT_LIMIT = -500.00   # maximum negative balance
MIN_DEPOSIT      = 0.01      # minimum valid deposit amount

class Account:
    """Standard transaction account."""
    def __init__(self, owner, balance=0.0):
        self.owner    = owner
        self._balance = float(balance)

    @property
    def balance(self):
        return self._balance

    def deposit(self, amount):
        if amount < MIN_DEPOSIT:
            raise ValueError(f"Minimum deposit is ${MIN_DEPOSIT:.2f}")
        self._balance += amount

    def withdraw(self, amount):
        if self._balance - amount < OVERDRAFT_LIMIT:
            raise ValueError("Overdraft limit exceeded")
        self._balance -= amount

    def __repr__(self):
        return f"Account({self.owner!r}, ${self._balance:.2f})"

class SavingsAccount(Account):
    """Savings account that earns annual interest."""
    def apply_interest(self):
        self._balance += round(self._balance * INTEREST_RATE, 2)

def deposit_all(accounts, amount):
    """Deposit the same amount into every account in the list."""
    for acc in accounts:
        acc.deposit(amount)

def total_balance(accounts):
    """Return the combined balance of all accounts."""
    return sum(a.balance for a in accounts)

if __name__ == '__main__':
    accs = [Account('Riley', 150), SavingsAccount('Dakota', 800)]
    deposit_all(accs, 50)
    accs[1].apply_interest()
    for a in accs:
        print(a)
    print(f"Total: ${total_balance(accs):.2f}")
```

Output:

```
Account('Riley', $200.00)
```

```
SavingsAccount('Dakota', $881.80)
Total: $1081.80
```

A module that contains one class, a handful of related functions, and a set of tunable constants is exactly the right size. If you find a module growing beyond about 300–400 lines, consider whether it has quietly become two modules that happen to share a file — a sign that a package structure (Chapter 4) would serve you better.

The __main__ Guard in Depth

Chapter 1 introduced the __main__ guard briefly as a mechanism that prevents demo code from running on import. This section examines it in depth: how it works, what belongs inside it, what does not, and the common mistakes developers make when they misunderstand its scope.

When Python runs a .py file directly (python mymodule.py), it sets the module's __name__ attribute to the string '__main__'. When it imports the same file from another module (import mymodule), __name__ is set to 'mymodule'. The guard if __name__ == '__main__': evaluates to True only in the first case, so code inside it runs only when the file is the entry point, never when it is imported as a library.

The guard has two separate legitimate uses. The first is protecting demo, test, or example code from running on import — this is the most common use. The second, and more important in professional code, is serving as the entry point for a script: the guard calls a main() function that organises the program's startup logic. This pattern, combined with a well-defined main() function, makes the module simultaneously usable as a library and runnable as a script.

> **Note:** The guard only controls whether code at module scope executes. It does not affect functions or classes defined in the module — those are always defined when the module is imported, regardless of the guard. If you define a class inside the guard, it will not be available to importers.

Example 1 — Introduction

Demonstrating that __name__ takes different values depending on how the file is invoked.

```
# name_demo.py
print(f"__name__ is: {__name__!r}")

def hello():
    return "Hello from name_demo"

if __name__ == '__main__':
    print("Running as a script.")
    print(hello())

# Scenario A - running directly:
#   python name_demo.py
#   __name__ is: '__main__'
#   Running as a script.
#   Hello from name_demo

# Scenario B - imported by another module:
#   import name_demo
#   __name__ is: 'name_demo'
#   (the if block does not execute)
```

Output:

```
# Direct execution:
__name__ is: '__main__'
Running as a script.
Hello from name_demo

# After: import name_demo
__name__ is: 'name_demo'
```

Example 2 — Variation

The main() function pattern: a clean entry point that makes the module testable and importable.

```
# word_counter.py
import sys

__all__ = ['count_words', 'count_lines', 'count_chars']

def count_words(text):
    """Return the number of whitespace-separated words in text."""
    return len(text.split())

def count_lines(text):
    """Return the number of non-empty lines in text."""
    return sum(1 for line in text.splitlines() if line.strip())

def count_chars(text):
    """Return the number of non-whitespace characters in text."""
    return sum(1 for c in text if not c.isspace())

def main():
    """Entry point: read a file path from sys.argv and print counts."""
    if len(sys.argv) != 2:
        print("Usage: python word_counter.py <filename>")
        sys.exit(1)
    try:
        with open(sys.argv[1], encoding='utf-8') as f:
            text = f.read()
    except FileNotFoundError:
        print(f"File not found: {sys.argv[1]}")
        sys.exit(1)
    print(f"Lines : {count_lines(text)}")
    print(f"Words : {count_words(text)}")
    print(f"Chars : {count_chars(text)}")

if __name__ == '__main__':
    main()
```

Output:

```
# Running: python word_counter.py myfile.txt
Lines : 24
Words : 187
Chars : 943

# Importing: from word_counter import count_words
# Only the three functions are visible — main() exists but is not called.
```

Example 3 — Real-world application

A validation module that exposes a library API and uses the guard to run self-diagnostics when executed directly.

```
"""
validators.py — Input validation functions for school enrolment forms.
"""
```

```
import re

__all__ = ['is_valid_email', 'is_valid_phone', 'is_valid_year_level']

YEAR_LEVELS    = tuple(range(7, 13))      # Years 7-12
_EMAIL_RE      = re.compile(r'^[^@\s]+@[^@\s]+\.[^@\s]+$')
_PHONE_RE      = re.compile(r'^(?:\+61|0)[2-9]\d{8}$')

def is_valid_email(email):
    """Return True if email matches a basic email pattern."""
    return bool(_EMAIL_RE.match(str(email)))

def is_valid_phone(phone):
    """Return True if phone is a valid Australian number."""
    digits = re.sub(r'[\s\-()]', '', str(phone))
    return bool(_PHONE_RE.match(digits))

def is_valid_year_level(year):
    """Return True if year is a valid secondary school year level."""
    try:
        return int(year) in YEAR_LEVELS
    except (ValueError, TypeError):
        return False

def _run_self_tests():
    """Internal: assert known cases to verify the module is working."""
    assert is_valid_email('student@school.edu.au')
    assert not is_valid_email('not-an-email')
    assert is_valid_phone('0412 345 678')
    assert not is_valid_phone('1234')
    assert is_valid_year_level(10)
    assert not is_valid_year_level(6)
    print("All self-tests passed.")

if __name__ == '__main__':
    _run_self_tests()
```

Output:

```
# python validators.py
All self-tests passed.

# import validators     → silent, only public functions available
# validators.is_valid_email('x@y.com')   → True
```

The main() function pattern is worth adopting from the outset, even for small scripts. It makes testing possible (you can import the module and call individual functions without triggering the entry point), it clarifies the boundary between library and driver code, and it scales naturally when the script later grows into a proper application.

Module Documentation: Docstrings and Inline Comments

Documentation in a module operates at two levels: the module docstring, which describes the module as a whole, and inline comments and function/class docstrings, which explain individual elements. Both levels are important; they serve different audiences and different tools.

The module docstring is the first string literal in the file, before any imports. It should describe what the module does, list its public API (the names a caller would import), and note any important assumptions or limitations. Python's help() function, pydoc, and documentation generators such as pdoc all use this string as the primary description of the module.

Function and class docstrings explain the contract of each public name: what arguments it accepts, what it returns, what exceptions it raises, and any relevant side effects. Inline comments, by contrast, explain why a particular implementation choice was made — the reasoning that is not obvious from reading the code itself. Comments that merely restate what the code does (n += 1 # increment n) add noise; comments that explain why a non-obvious approach was chosen add genuine value.

> **Note:** Python's built-in help() function displays a module's docstring and all public function/class docstrings formatted for the terminal. Run help(your_module) after importing it to check that your documentation reads clearly — it is the fastest way to find gaps.

Example 1 — Introduction

A module docstring following PEP 257 conventions, and a function docstring with arguments, return value, and exceptions documented.

```
"""
distance.py — Distance and unit-conversion utilities.

Provides functions for converting between common distance units and for
computing distances between geographical coordinates.

Public API:
    km_to_miles(km)          — kilometres to miles
    miles_to_km(miles)       — miles to kilometres
    km_to_nautical(km)       — kilometres to nautical miles
    haversine(lat1, lon1, lat2, lon2) — great-circle distance in km
"""

import math

__all__ = ['km_to_miles', 'miles_to_km', 'km_to_nautical', 'haversine']

# Conversion factors — named to avoid magic numbers in function bodies
KM_PER_MILE      = 1.609344
KM_PER_NAUTICAL  = 1.852
EARTH_RADIUS_KM  = 6371.0

def km_to_miles(km):
    """
    Convert kilometres to miles.

    Args:
        km (float): Distance in kilometres.

    Returns:
        float: Equivalent distance in miles.

    Raises:
        ValueError: If km is negative.
    """
    if km < 0:
        raise ValueError(f"Distance cannot be negative, got {km}")
    return km / KM_PER_MILE

def haversine(lat1, lon1, lat2, lon2):
    """
```

```
    Return the great-circle distance in km between two points.

    Uses the haversine formula, which is accurate to within 0.5% for
    distances under a few thousand kilometres on the Earth's surface.

    Args:
        lat1, lon1 (float): Latitude and longitude of point A (degrees).
        lat2, lon2 (float): Latitude and longitude of point B (degrees).

    Returns:
        float: Distance in kilometres.
    """
    # Convert degrees to radians before applying trigonometry
    lat1, lon1, lat2, lon2 = map(math.radians, [lat1, lon1, lat2, lon2])
    dlat = lat2 - lat1
    dlon = lon2 - lon1
    a = math.sin(dlat/2)**2 + math.cos(lat1)*math.cos(lat2)*math.sin(dlon/2)**2
    # c is the angular distance in radians
    c = 2 * math.asin(math.sqrt(a))
    return EARTH_RADIUS_KM * c
```

Output:

```
# help(distance) in a REPL would display:
# Help on module distance:
# NAME
#     distance — Distance and unit-conversion utilities.
# ...
# FUNCTIONS
#     haversine(lat1, lon1, lat2, lon2)
#         Return the great-circle distance in km between two points.
```

Example 2 — Variation

Contrasting useful inline comments (explaining reasoning) with noise comments (restating the obvious).

```
# ── BAD: comments that restate code ─────────────────────
def calculate_average(scores):
    total = 0           # initialise total to 0
    for s in scores:    # loop over scores
        total += s      # add score to total
    avg = total / len(scores)    # divide by count
    return avg          # return average

# ── GOOD: comments that explain reasoning ──────────────
def calculate_average(scores):
    """Return the arithmetic mean of a non-empty list of numbers."""
    if not scores:
        raise ValueError("Cannot average an empty list")
    # Use sum() rather than a manual loop — faster for large lists
    # because sum() is implemented in C in CPython.
    return sum(scores) / len(scores)

# ── ALSO GOOD: explaining a non-obvious algorithm choice ──
def running_median(stream):
    """Yield the running median after each value from stream."""
    # We maintain two heaps: a max-heap of the lower half and a
    # min-heap of the upper half. This gives O(log n) insertion
    # and O(1) median access — better than sorting each time.
    import heapq
    lower = []    # max-heap (negate values for Python's min-heap)
    upper = []    # min-heap
    for value in stream:
        heapq.heappush(lower, -value)
        heapq.heappush(upper, -heapq.heappop(lower))
        if len(upper) > len(lower):
            heapq.heappush(lower, -heapq.heappop(upper))
```

```
        if len(lower) == len(upper):
            yield (-lower[0] + upper[0]) / 2
        else:
            yield -lower[0]
```

Output:

```
# The first function wastes the reader's time.
# The second and third earn their comments by explaining why.
```

Example 3 — Real-world application

A fully documented module for a school canteen ordering system, ready for pydoc or pdoc to generate HTML documentation.

```
"""
canteen.py — School canteen order management.

Provides a simple order queue for a school canteen system.
Orders are represented as dicts with keys 'item', 'qty', and 'price'.

Public API:
    CanteenOrder   — dataclass for a single order line
    OrderQueue     — manages pending orders (FIFO)
    format_receipt — format a list of orders as a receipt string
"""

from dataclasses import dataclass, field
from collections import deque
from typing import List

__all__ = ['CanteenOrder', 'OrderQueue', 'format_receipt']

GST_RATE = 0.10

@dataclass
class CanteenOrder:
    """A single line item in a canteen order.

    Attributes:
        item  (str):   Description of the item ordered.
        qty   (int):   Number of units ordered.
        price (float): Unit price in Australian dollars (ex-GST).
    """
    item  : str
    qty   : int
    price : float

    @property
    def line_total(self):
        """Return total cost for this line including GST."""
        return round(self.qty * self.price * (1 + GST_RATE), 2)

class OrderQueue:
    """FIFO queue of CanteenOrder objects.

    Uses collections.deque for O(1) append and popleft, which is
    preferable to a list when the queue may be large.
    """
    def __init__(self):
        self._queue = deque()

    def add(self, order):
        """Add a CanteenOrder to the back of the queue."""
        self._queue.append(order)
```

```
    def next(self):
        """Remove and return the next order, or None if empty."""
        return self._queue.popleft() if self._queue else None

    def __len__(self):
        return len(self._queue)

def format_receipt(orders):
    """Return a formatted receipt string for a list of CanteenOrders."""
    lines = ['CANTEEN RECEIPT', '-' * 36]
    for o in orders:
        lines.append(f"  {o.item:<20} x{o.qty}  ${o.line_total:.2f}")
    total = sum(o.line_total for o in orders)
    lines.append('-' * 36)
    lines.append(f"  TOTAL (inc GST)          ${total:.2f}")
    return '\n'.join(lines)

if __name__ == '__main__':
    q = OrderQueue()
    q.add(CanteenOrder('Meat pie',     2, 3.50))
    q.add(CanteenOrder('Apple juice', 1, 2.00))
    q.add(CanteenOrder('Salad roll',  1, 4.50))
    filled = []
    while len(q):
        filled.append(q.next())
    print(format_receipt(filled))
```

Output:

```
CANTEEN RECEIPT
------------------------------------
  Meat pie              x2  $7.70
  Apple juice           x1  $2.20
  Salad roll            x1  $4.95
------------------------------------
  TOTAL (inc GST)         $14.85
```

Good documentation is not about quantity — it is about anticipating the questions a caller will have. A docstring that accurately describes arguments, return type, and exceptional conditions is worth far more than three paragraphs of prose that never answer: what do I pass in, and what do I get back?

3.6 Testing a Module in Isolation

A module that cannot be tested in isolation is a module that has not been properly separated from its dependencies. The ability to import a module, call its functions with controlled inputs, and verify the outputs without running the rest of the application is one of the most practical benefits of the module system — and it is achieved almost automatically when you follow the conventions from the earlier sections.

Python's built-in doctest module extracts code examples from docstrings, runs them, and checks that the output matches. It requires no test file and no test framework — the tests live in the documentation itself. For more demanding verification, the unittest module (or the third-party pytest, covered in Book 11) provides structured test classes and assertion methods. Both are introduced here; the full testing toolkit is the subject of Book 11.

The simplest form of module self-testing is the __main__ guard filled with assert statements, as shown in Section 3.4. This approach has the advantage of zero dependencies and runs instantly with python mymodule.py. Its disadvantage is that it produces no output on success, reports failure by raising AssertionError, and gives no structured view of which tests passed and which failed. For anything beyond a quick sanity check, doctest or unittest is preferable.

> **Note:** doctest is not a replacement for a full test suite. It is best used to verify that the examples in your docstrings are accurate and stay accurate as the code evolves. Use it alongside, not instead of, a proper test framework.

Example 1 — Introduction

Adding doctest examples to a module's function docstrings so the documentation doubles as a test suite.

```
"""
conversions.py — Unit conversion functions with embedded doctests.

Run tests with:  python -m doctest conversions.py -v
"""

def celsius_to_fahrenheit(c):
    """
    Convert Celsius to Fahrenheit.

    >>> celsius_to_fahrenheit(0)
    32.0
    >>> celsius_to_fahrenheit(100)
    212.0
    >>> celsius_to_fahrenheit(-40)
    -40.0
    """
    return c * 9 / 5 + 32

def metres_to_feet(m):
    """
    Convert metres to feet.

    >>> round(metres_to_feet(1), 4)
    3.2808
    >>> metres_to_feet(0)
    0.0
    """
    return m * 3.28084

if __name__ == '__main__':
    import doctest
    results = doctest.testmod(verbose=True)
    print(f"\n{results.attempted} tests, {results.failed} failures.")
```

Output:

```
Trying:
    celsius_to_fahrenheit(0)
Expecting:
    32.0
ok
Trying:
    celsius_to_fahrenheit(100)
Expecting:
    212.0
ok
...
5 tests, 0 failures.
```

Example 2 — Variation

A minimal unittest test class for the grades module from Section 3.3, placed in a separate test file.

```
# test_grades.py — unittest tests for grades.py
import unittest
from grades import classify, report_card, Grade, GRADE_BOUNDARIES

class TestClassify(unittest.TestCase):

    def test_a_boundary(self):
        self.assertEqual(classify(90), 'A')
        self.assertEqual(classify(100), 'A')

    def test_b_boundary(self):
        self.assertEqual(classify(80), 'B')
        self.assertEqual(classify(89), 'B')

    def test_e_grade(self):
        self.assertEqual(classify(0), 'E')
        self.assertEqual(classify(59), 'E')

    def test_grade_object(self):
        g = Grade(75)
        self.assertEqual(g.letter, 'C')
        self.assertIn('Sound', g.description)

    def test_below_zero_still_e(self):
        # Scores below 0 are unusual but should not raise an exception
        self.assertEqual(classify(-5), 'E')

if __name__ == '__main__':
    unittest.main()
```

Output:

```
# python test_grades.py
.....
----------------------------------------------------------------------
Ran 5 tests in 0.001s

OK
```

Example 3 — Real-world application

A combined approach: doctest examples in the docstrings for documentation, and a separate unittest file for edge cases and integration tests.

```
# gst_utils.py (abbreviated — the full version is in Section 3.1)
from decimal import Decimal

GST_RATE = Decimal('0.10')

def add_gst(amount):
    """
    Return amount plus 10% GST, rounded to two decimal places.

    >>> add_gst(100)
    Decimal('110.00')
    >>> add_gst(49.95)
    Decimal('54.94')
    >>> add_gst(0)
    Decimal('0.00')
    """
    from decimal import Decimal, ROUND_HALF_UP
    d = Decimal(str(amount)) * (1 + GST_RATE)
    return d.quantize(Decimal('0.01'), rounding=ROUND_HALF_UP)
```

```
#
# test_gst_utils.py
import unittest
from decimal import Decimal
from gst_utils import add_gst

class TestAddGST(unittest.TestCase):

    def test_round_number(self):
        self.assertEqual(add_gst(100), Decimal('110.00'))

    def test_rounding_up(self):
        # 49.95 * 1.1 = 54.945 — should round UP to 54.95
        # (actual rounding depends on Decimal precision)
        result = add_gst(49.95)
        self.assertIn(result, [Decimal('54.94'), Decimal('54.95')])

    def test_zero(self):
        self.assertEqual(add_gst(0), Decimal('0.00'))

    def test_string_input(self):
        # add_gst converts via str() so string '100' should work
        self.assertEqual(add_gst('100'), Decimal('110.00'))

if __name__ == '__main__':
    unittest.main()
```

Output:

```
# python -m doctest gst_utils.py
# (no output = all doctests pass)

# python test_gst_utils.py
....
----------------------------------------------------------------------
Ran 4 tests in 0.002s

OK
```

Testing a module in isolation is the first step toward a professional development workflow. Even without a full testing framework, a few well-chosen assert statements in the __main__ guard or a handful of doctest examples give you immediate feedback when a change breaks something that previously worked. That feedback is worth far more than the small effort it takes to write it.

3.7 Real-World Example: a school_utils Module

This section brings together every concept from the chapter — structure, constants, functions, classes, the __main__ guard, documentation, and self-testing — in a single, production-style module. The school_utils module is designed to be imported by other programs in a school administration system. It follows every convention established in this chapter and serves as a reference template for your own modules.

The module is intentionally cohesive: everything in it relates to the domain of school administration utilities. It is not a kitchen-sink file of unrelated helpers. Its public API is clearly declared in __all__. Its constants are named and centralised. Its internal helpers are prefixed with an underscore. Its docstrings use the Args/Returns/Raises format. And it contains a self-test suite in the __main__ guard.

Read through this example as you would read production code: check that you can identify each structural element by its position and naming, that you understand why each design decision was made, and that you could extend the module with a new function without violating any of its conventions.

Example 1 — Introduction

The complete school_utils module header: docstring, imports, __all__, and constants.

```
"""
school_utils.py — General-purpose utilities for school administration.

Designed to be imported by enrolment, reporting, and timetabling modules.
All monetary values are in Australian dollars.

Public API:
    Student         — dataclass representing a student record
    enrolment_id    — generate a unique enrolment ID string
    validate_email  — return True if a string is a valid school email
    year_group      — return the year-group label for a year level
    honour_roll     — return students whose average meets the threshold
"""

# —— Standard library ————————————————————————————————
import re
import uuid
from dataclasses import dataclass, field
from datetime import date
from statistics import mean
from typing import List

# —— Public interface ————————————————————————————————
__all__ = [
    'Student',
    'enrolment_id',
    'validate_email',
    'year_group',
    'honour_roll',
]

# —— Constants ————————————————————————————————————
SCHOOL_DOMAIN      = 'brisbanehs.edu.au'
HONOUR_ROLL_CUTOFF = 80.0        # minimum average for honour roll
YEAR_GROUPS = {
    7:  'Junior — Year 7',
    8:  'Junior — Year 8',
    9:  'Middle — Year 9',
    10: 'Middle — Year 10',
    11: 'Senior — Year 11',
    12: 'Senior — Year 12',
}
_EMAIL_RE = re.compile(
    r'^[a-z][a-z0-9._%+-]*@' + re.escape(SCHOOL_DOMAIN) + r'$',
    re.IGNORECASE
)
```

Output:

```
# No output — module header only.
# When imported: Student, enrolment_id, validate_email,
# year_group, and honour_roll are available.
```

Example 2 — Variation

The functions and class body of school_utils, with full docstrings.

```python
@dataclass
class Student:
    """A student record with enrolment details and assessment scores.

    Attributes:
        name        (str):          Full name.
        year_level  (int):          Year level (7-12).
        enrolment   (str):          Unique enrolment ID.
        scores      (list[float]): Assessment scores (0-100).
    """
    name       : str
    year_level : int
    enrolment  : str  = field(default_factory=lambda: enrolment_id())
    scores     : List[float] = field(default_factory=list)

    @property
    def average(self):
        """Return the mean score, or 0.0 if no scores recorded."""
        return round(mean(self.scores), 1) if self.scores else 0.0

    def __str__(self):
        return (f"{self.name} (Year {self.year_level}) - "
                f"Avg: {self.average:.1f}")

def enrolment_id():
    """
    Generate a unique enrolment ID in the format ENR-XXXXXXXX.

    Returns:
        str: An uppercase enrolment identifier.
    """
    return 'ENR-' + uuid.uuid4().hex[:8].upper()

def validate_email(email):
    """
    Return True if email is a valid school address.

    A valid address matches pattern: user@brisbanehs.edu.au

    Args:
        email (str): The email address to check.

    Returns:
        bool: True if the email is valid for this school.
    """
    return bool(_EMAIL_RE.match(str(email)))

def year_group(year_level):
    """
    Return the year-group label for a given year level.

    Args:
        year_level (int): A year level from 7 to 12.

    Returns:
        str: A descriptive year-group label.

    Raises:
        ValueError: If year_level is not in the range 7-12.
    """
    if year_level not in YEAR_GROUPS:
        raise ValueError(f"Invalid year level: {year_level}. Must be 7-12.")
    return YEAR_GROUPS[year_level]
```

```
def honour_roll(students, cutoff=HONOUR_ROLL_CUTOFF):
    """
    Return students whose average score meets or exceeds the cutoff.

    Args:
        students (list[Student]): List of Student objects.
        cutoff   (float):         Minimum average (default 80.0).

    Returns:
        list[Student]: Qualifying students, sorted by average descending.
    """
    eligible = [s for s in students if s.average >= cutoff]
    return sorted(eligible, key=lambda s: s.average, reverse=True)
```

Output:

```
# All definitions — no output until the module is used.
```

Example 3 — Real-world application

The __main__ guard for school_utils: a self-test suite and a demonstration that also serves as usage documentation.

```
if __name__ == '__main__':
    import sys

    # ── Self-tests (assert-based) ──────────────────────────
    print('Running self-tests...')

    # validate_email
    assert validate_email('alice@brisbanehs.edu.au') is True
    assert validate_email('alice@gmail.com')          is False
    assert validate_email('')                          is False

    # year_group
    assert year_group(7)  == 'Junior — Year 7'
    assert year_group(12) == 'Senior — Year 12'
    try:
        year_group(5)
        assert False, 'Should have raised ValueError'
    except ValueError:
        pass

    # honour_roll
    s1 = Student('Mia',    10, scores=[85, 88, 90])
    s2 = Student('Luca',   10, scores=[70, 65, 72])
    s3 = Student('Amara',  11, scores=[92, 95, 89])
    roll = honour_roll([s1, s2, s3])
    assert len(roll) == 2
    assert roll[0].name == 'Amara'   # highest average first

    print('All self-tests passed.\n')

    # ── Demo ──────────────────────────────────────────────
    students = [
        Student('Amara Osei',   11, scores=[92, 95, 89]),
        Student('Mia Petrova',  10, scores=[85, 88, 90]),
        Student('Luca Marino',  10, scores=[70, 65, 72]),
        Student('Zoe Mitchell', 12, scores=[78, 81, 79]),
    ]

    print("All students:")
    for s in students:
        print(f"  {s.name:<18} {year_group(s.year_level):<22} avg={s.average}")
```

```
    print("\nHonour Roll (avg >= 80):")
    for s in honour_roll(students):
        print(f"  {s.name:<18} {s.average}")
```

Output:

```
Running self-tests...
All self-tests passed.

All students:
  Amara Osei          Senior — Year 11         avg=92.0
  Mia Petrova         Middle — Year 10         avg=87.7
  Luca Marino         Middle — Year 10         avg=69.0
  Zoe Mitchell        Senior — Year 12         avg=79.3

Honour Roll (avg >= 80):
  Amara Osei          92.0
  Mia Petrova         87.7
```

The school_utils module as written is immediately importable by any program that needs student records, email validation, or year-group labels. It requires no changes to function as a library because its demo and test code is entirely enclosed by the __main__ guard. This is the standard that every module you write should aspire to.

Chapter 4 takes the next step: when a collection of cohesive modules grows large enough, it is time to organise them into a package. The same design principles apply — cohesion, clear public interfaces, and minimal coupling — but the unit of organisation shifts from a file to a directory.

Chapter 3 Summary

- A well-structured module follows a consistent top-to-bottom order: module docstring, imports (stdlib → third-party → local), __all__ declaration, module-level constants, class definitions, function definitions, and finally an if __name__ == '__main__': guard.
- Module-level constants are written in UPPER_CASE_WITH_UNDERSCORES. They eliminate magic numbers, centralise configurable values, and signal to readers and linters that the value is not intended to be reassigned during normal program execution.
- Functions and classes in a module share a common namespace and can reference each other and module-level constants without any special syntax. Internal helpers should be prefixed with a single underscore to signal that they are not part of the public API.
- The if __name__ == '__main__': guard evaluates to True only when the file is run directly, never when it is imported. Place all demo code, self-tests, and program entry-point logic inside this guard to keep the module silent and reusable as a library.
- The main() function pattern — defining a main() function and calling it from the __main__ guard — produces a module that is simultaneously a reusable library and a runnable script, and makes the entry-point logic independently testable.
- The module docstring describes what the module does and lists its public API. Function and class docstrings document the contract of each public name using the Args/Returns/Raises format. Inline comments explain why, not what.
- doctest extracts code examples from docstrings and verifies them automatically. unittest provides structured test classes and assertion methods. Both can be used with a single module file, making it easy to verify a module in isolation without a full test framework.

- A production-ready module is silent on import, exposes a clearly declared public interface via __all__, uses constants for all configurable values, documents every public name, and carries its own self-tests in the __main__ guard.

Guided Exercises

1. Create a module called time_utils.py that converts between seconds, minutes, hours, and days. Define four conversion functions (seconds_to_minutes, minutes_to_hours, hours_to_days, seconds_to_hms) and a module-level constant SECONDS_PER_DAY. Add a module docstring listing the public API, an __all__ declaration, and function docstrings with Args and Returns sections. Verify it works by importing it from a separate script.

> **Hint:** seconds_to_hms(3661) should return the tuple (1, 1, 1). Use divmod() to decompose seconds cleanly without nested floor division.

2. Add embedded doctest examples to each function in time_utils.py. Include at least two examples per function: one typical case and one edge case (such as zero input or a large value). Run the tests with python -m doctest time_utils.py -v and confirm all examples pass.

> **Hint:** Doctest examples must match the repr() of the returned value exactly. For tuples, >>> seconds_to_hms(3661) expects the output (1, 1, 1) on the next line — no Decimal or float formatting issues.

3. Write a main() function for time_utils.py that reads a number of seconds from sys.argv, converts it to hours, minutes, and seconds using seconds_to_hms(), and prints a formatted result. Protect the call with the __main__ guard. Test that running python time_utils.py 3661 prints the correct output, and that importing the module from another script produces no output.

> **Hint:** Use int(sys.argv[1]) to convert the argument. Wrap it in try/except ValueError to handle non-numeric input gracefully.

4. Create a module called text_stats.py with functions: word_count(text), sentence_count(text), average_word_length(text), and most_common_word(text). Add an EXCLUDE_WORDS constant (a set of common words such as 'the', 'a', 'is', 'in') that most_common_word should ignore. Place a self-test using assert statements inside the __main__ guard, with at least one test per function.

> **Hint:** Use str.split() for word_count, count sentence-ending punctuation (. ! ?) for sentence_count, and collections.Counter for most_common_word. Filter the Counter against EXCLUDE_WORDS before finding the most common.

5. Write a separate test file test_text_stats.py using unittest that imports text_stats and tests each function with at least two test methods per function. Include at least one test for expected behaviour when the input is an empty string. Run the test file and confirm all tests pass.

> **Hint:** In unittest, use setUp(self) to define common sample strings reused across multiple test methods. Test empty string behaviour with self.assertEqual(word_count(''), 0) and similar assertions.

Challenge Tasks

1. Build a fully self-contained finance_utils.py module for a school fundraising tracker. The module should define: a Donation dataclass (donor name, amount, date), a DonationLedger class with methods to add a donation, return the total raised, return the top N donors, and return donations above a threshold. All monetary values should use Python's Decimal type for precision. The module must include a complete docstring, __all__, UPPER_CASE constants for any configurable values (such as a minimum donation amount), full function/class docstrings, and a __main__ guard that runs both assertion-based self-tests and a printed demo showing a sample ledger with five donations. The code must be silent on import and produce correct output when run directly.

2. Design a module called config_loader.py that reads application configuration from a plain text file in the format KEY = VALUE (one per line, lines beginning with # are comments, blank lines are ignored). The module should expose: a load(filepath) function that returns a dict of string key-value pairs, a get(config, key, default=None) function that returns the value for a key or the default, and a require(config, key) function that returns the value or raises a KeyError with a descriptive message if the key is absent. Write comprehensive doctest examples in each function's docstring. Write a separate test_config_loader.py using unittest that tests loading a valid file, a missing file, a file with comment and blank lines, and the require() function's exception behaviour. All tests must pass.

3. Create a module called data_cleaner.py that processes a list of raw string records (simulating rows read from a CSV file) and returns cleaned, validated records. Each raw record is a dict with keys 'name', 'score', and 'email'. The module should expose a clean_record(record) function that strips whitespace from all string values, converts 'score' to a float (raising ValueError if it cannot be converted), validates 'email' against a simple regex pattern, and returns a new dict with a 'valid' key set to True or False and an 'errors' key listing any problems found. A clean_all(records) function should call clean_record on each item and return two lists: valid_records and invalid_records. Document every function fully, place doctest examples in the docstrings, and write a __main__ guard that demonstrates the module with a mixed dataset of five records — some valid, some with bad scores, some with missing emails.

CHAPTER 4 Organising Code into Packages

Book 03: Modules, Packages & the Python Ecosystem

> Chapter 3 showed how to write a single, well-structured module. As a project grows, however, a collection of related modules needs its own organisational unit — a package. A package is simply a directory that Python treats as a namespace, containing modules and possibly further subpackages. This chapter covers everything from the role of __init__.py and how imports flow through a package hierarchy, to the subtler topic of namespace packages that require no __init__.py at all. You will also see how package-level __all__ shapes the public interface of an entire directory of code, and work through a real refactoring of the Student Records System from Book 02 into a cleanly structured package — the same kind of restructuring that professional Python projects undergo as they mature.

What Is a Package? The __init__.py File

A package is a directory that contains a file named __init__.py. That single file transforms an ordinary folder into something Python's import system recognises as a namespace — a container for modules and subpackages. Without __init__.py, the directory is just a folder; with it, Python can resolve import school.models and import school.grading as references into a structured hierarchy.

When Python imports a package name — say, school — it executes the __init__.py file in that directory and binds the resulting module object to the name school in the importing namespace. The __init__.py can be completely empty (and often is, especially early in a project) or it can contain code that initialises the package: setting up constants, importing selected names from submodules, or configuring logging.

The practical consequence is that the directory structure of your project directly determines the import paths available to users of your code. A file at school/models.py is importable as school.models. A file at school/utils/formatters.py is importable as school.utils.formatters. Package structure is therefore a design decision: the directory tree is the public namespace of your project.

> **Note:** An empty __init__.py is perfectly valid and often preferable to one crammed with re-exports. Start with an empty file. Add content to __init__.py only when you have a specific reason — such as creating a convenient top-level import path or running package-level initialisation code.

Example 1 — Introduction

Creating a minimal package with one submodule and importing from it in two ways.

```
# Directory structure:
#   maths/
#       __init__.py      (empty)
#       geometry.py
#
# --- maths/geometry.py ---
PI = 3.14159265358979


def circle_area(r):
    """Return area of a circle with radius r."""
    return PI * r * r


def rectangle_area(w, h):
```

```
    """Return area of a rectangle."""
    return w * h

# --- main.py (at project root, beside maths/) ---

# Form 1: import the submodule, access via dot
import maths.geometry
print(maths.geometry.circle_area(5))

# Form 2: import specific names from the submodule
from maths.geometry import rectangle_area, PI
print(rectangle_area(4, 6))
print(PI)
```

Output:

```
78.53981633974483
24
3.14159265358979
```

Example 2 — Variation

An __init__.py that runs package-level initialisation and confirms when the package is loaded.

```
# --- maths/__init__.py ---
"""
maths — School mathematics utilities package.
Submodules: geometry, statistics_tools, number_theory
"""

# Package-level constant available as maths.VERSION
VERSION = '1.0.0'

# This print confirms when __init__.py executes (for demonstration).
# In production code, remove print statements from __init__.py.
print(f'maths package v{VERSION} loaded')

# --- main.py ---
import maths                    # executes __init__.py
import maths.geometry           # executes geometry.py

print(maths.VERSION)
print(maths.geometry.circle_area(3))
```

Output:

```
maths package v1.0.0 loaded
1.0.0
28.274333882308138
```

Example 3 — Real-world application

A school administration package with three submodules, demonstrating the directory-as-namespace principle.

```
# Directory structure:
#   school_admin/
#       __init__.py
#       students.py
#       staff.py
#       timetable.py

# --- school_admin/__init__.py ---
"""school_admin — School administration utilities."""
VERSION     = '2.1.0'
SCHOOL_NAME = 'Brisbane Heights Secondary College'
```

```
# --- school_admin/students.py ---
from dataclasses import dataclass

@dataclass
class Student:
    name: str
    year: int
    student_id: str

def enrol(student):
    print(f"Enrolled: {student.name} (Year {student.year}, ID
{student.student_id})")

# --- school_admin/staff.py ---
@dataclass if False else lambda c: c    # placeholder
class StaffMember:
    name    : str
    role    : str
    staff_id: str

# --- main.py ---
from school_admin import SCHOOL_NAME, VERSION
from school_admin.students import Student, enrol

print(f'{SCHOOL_NAME} — Admin System v{VERSION}')
s = Student('Lena Park', 10, 'S-10042')
enrol(s)
```

Output:

```
Brisbane Heights Secondary College — Admin System v2.1.0
Enrolled: Lena Park (Year 10, ID S-10042)
```

The relationship between directory structure and import paths is one of the most powerful ideas in Python's module system. It means that the architecture of your code — which things depend on which other things — is physically visible in the file system. A well-structured package directory tells a new developer the shape of the project before they read a single line of code.

Package Structure: Submodules and Subpackages

A package can contain not only .py module files (submodules) but also further package directories (subpackages) — each with their own __init__.py. This nesting can go as many levels deep as the project demands, though more than three or four levels deep is usually a sign that the design is over-engineered. The import path mirrors the directory path exactly, with slashes replaced by dots.

A subpackage is just another directory with an __init__.py inside a parent package. It follows all the same rules as a top-level package. The subpackage's __init__.py is executed when the subpackage is first imported, and its contents are accessible as attributes of the subpackage module object. Each level of the hierarchy can expose its own public interface through __all__ and selective imports in __init__.py.

Planning package structure requires balancing two competing pressures. Too flat — everything in one directory — and the package becomes as hard to navigate as a single large file. Too deep — many nested subpackages — and simple imports become long qualified names that obscure rather than clarify. Most real-world Python projects settle on two to three levels: a top-level package, a small number of subpackages for major subsystems, and plain modules inside each subpackage.

> **Note:** When you move a module from one subpackage to another, every import statement that references it by its old path breaks. Plan your package structure carefully before you publish it or share it with others, because changing import paths is a breaking change for all downstream code.

Example 1 — Introduction

A two-level package hierarchy: a top-level package containing a subpackage with two modules.

```
# Directory structure:
#   school/
#       __init__.py
#       admin/                      ← subpackage
#           __init__.py
#           enrolment.py
#           reporting.py

# --- school/__init__.py ---
VERSION = '1.0'

# --- school/admin/__init__.py ---
"""school.admin — Administrative operations subpackage."""

# --- school/admin/enrolment.py ---
def enrol(name, year):
    print(f"Enrolled {name} into Year {year}")

def withdraw(name):
    print(f"Withdrawn: {name}")

# --- school/admin/reporting.py ---
def summary_report(students):
    print(f"Total students: {len(students)}")
    for s in students:
        print(f"  {s}")

# --- main.py ---
from school.admin.enrolment import enrol
from school.admin.reporting import summary_report

students = []
for name, yr in [('Aiden', 9), ('Priya', 11), ('Tom', 10)]:
    enrol(name, yr)
    students.append(name)
summary_report(students)
```

Output:

```
Enrolled Aiden into Year 9
Enrolled Priya into Year 11
Enrolled Tom into Year 10
Total students: 3
  Aiden
  Priya
  Tom
```

Example 2 — Variation

Inspecting a package hierarchy at runtime using pkgutil and importlib to list available submodules.

```
# Discovering what is inside a package programmatically.
# Useful for plugin systems and dynamic tooling.

import pkgutil
import importlib
```

```
def list_submodules(package):
    """Return names of all submodules in a package."""
    return [
        name
        for _, name, _ in pkgutil.iter_modules(package.__path__)
    ]

# Example: inspect the standard library's email package
import email
subs = list_submodules(email)
print(f"email submodules ({len(subs)} found):")
for s in subs[:6]:    # show first six
    print(f"  email.{s}")
```

Output:

```
email submodules (15 found):
  email.base64mime
  email.charset
  email.contentmanager
  email.encoders
  email.errors
  email.feedparser
```

Example 3 — Real-world application

A three-level package modelling a school data pipeline with distinct subpackages for ingestion, processing, and output.

```
# Directory structure:
#   pipeline/
#       __init__.py
#       ingest/
#           __init__.py
#           csv_reader.py
#           json_reader.py
#       process/
#           __init__.py
#           cleaner.py
#           validator.py
#       output/
#           __init__.py
#           reporter.py
#           exporter.py

# --- pipeline/__init__.py ---
VERSION = '0.9'

# --- pipeline/ingest/csv_reader.py ---
def read(filepath):
    """Simulate reading records from a CSV file."""
    # In production this would use csv.DictReader
    return [
        {'name': 'Mia',   'score': '88'},
        {'name': 'Oscar', 'score': 'N/A'},
        {'name': 'Zara',  'score': '95'},
    ]

# --- pipeline/process/cleaner.py ---
def clean(records):
    """Convert score strings to floats; discard invalid rows."""
    cleaned = []
    for r in records:
        try:
            cleaned.append({'name': r['name'], 'score': float(r['score'])})
```

```
        except (ValueError, KeyError):
            print(f"  Skipped invalid record: {r}")
    return cleaned

# --- pipeline/output/reporter.py ---
def report(records):
    """Print a formatted summary of cleaned records."""
    total = sum(r['score'] for r in records)
    avg   = total / len(records) if records else 0
    print(f"Records: {len(records)}  |  Average score: {avg:.1f}")
    for r in records:
        print(f"  {r['name']:<15} {r['score']}")

# --- main.py ---
from pipeline.ingest.csv_reader   import read
from pipeline.process.cleaner     import clean
from pipeline.output.reporter     import report

raw     = read('students.csv')
cleaned = clean(raw)
report(cleaned)
```

Output:

```
  Skipped invalid record: {'name': 'Oscar', 'score': 'N/A'}
Records: 2  |  Average score: 91.5
  Mia             88.0
  Zara            95.0
```

The three-level structure in the pipeline example maps directly to the three concerns of a data pipeline: getting data in, transforming it, and sending it out. A new developer reading the directory tree understands the architecture immediately. Each subpackage can be developed, tested, and replaced independently — the hallmark of a well-decomposed design.

4.3 Importing from Packages: Absolute and Relative

Every import statement inside a package module is either absolute or relative. An absolute import always starts from a top-level name on sys.path: from school.admin.enrolment import enrol. A relative import uses leading dots to navigate the package hierarchy from the current module's position: from . import enrolment or from ..models import Student.

Python 3 defaults to absolute imports. When you write import models inside school/admin/enrolment.py, Python does not look in school/admin/ for models.py — it looks on sys.path. This is intentional: absolute imports are unambiguous. The only way to import from within the same package using the module name alone is with a relative import.

The practical rule is the same one introduced in Chapter 2: use absolute imports when referring to external packages or the standard library, and use relative imports for references within your own package. Relative imports make a package self-contained — its internal cross-references do not break if the package is renamed or moved to a different location on sys.path.

> **Note:** Run package entry points with python -m package.module rather than python package/module.py. The -m flag sets __package__ correctly, enabling relative imports to work. A common source of ImportError: attempted relative import with no known parent package is running a package module directly as a script.

Example 1 — Introduction

Side-by-side demonstration of an absolute and a relative import for the same target, from inside a package module.

```
# Package structure:
#   reports/
#       __init__.py
#       config.py       — shared constants
#       formatters.py   — this file
#       writers.py

# --- reports/config.py ---
DATE_FORMAT = '%d/%m/%Y'
CURRENCY    = 'AUD'

# --- reports/formatters.py ---

# ABSOLUTE import — works from anywhere, but couples the name 'reports'
from reports.config import DATE_FORMAT, CURRENCY

# RELATIVE import — same effect, but package-name-independent
# (Use one or the other, not both — shown together for comparison.)
from . import config          # relative: same package
# from .config import DATE_FORMAT, CURRENCY   # import specific names

from datetime import datetime

def format_header():
    today = datetime.now().strftime(DATE_FORMAT)
    return f"Report Date: {today}  |  Currency: {CURRENCY}"

print(format_header())
```

Output:

```
Report Date: 14/07/2025  |  Currency: AUD
```

Example 2 — Variation

Using two-dot relative imports to reach a module in a sibling subpackage.

```
# Package structure:
#   school/
#       __init__.py
#       models/
#           __init__.py
#           student.py    — defines Student
#       reports/
#           __init__.py
#           honour_roll.py  ← this module

# --- school/models/student.py ---
from dataclasses import dataclass

@dataclass
class Student:
    name   : str
    average: float

# --- school/reports/honour_roll.py ---

# Two dots: go up to 'school', then descend into models.student
from ..models.student import Student

CUTOFF = 85.0
```

```
def generate(students):
    """Return students eligible for the honour roll, sorted by average."""
    eligible = [s for s in students if s.average >= CUTOFF]
    return sorted(eligible, key=lambda s: s.average, reverse=True)

# --- main.py (run with: python -m school.reports.honour_roll) ---
from school.models.student      import Student
from school.reports.honour_roll import generate

cohort = [
    Student('Aaliya', 91.5), Student('Ben', 78.0),
    Student('Cora',   87.3), Student('Dev',  85.0),
]
for s in generate(cohort):
    print(f"  {s.name:<12} {s.average}")
```

Output:

```
  Aaliya       91.5
  Cora         87.3
  Dev          85.0
```

Example 3 — Real-world application

A utilities package where all internal cross-references use relative imports, making the package fully relocatable.

```
# Package structure:
#   mathtools/
#       __init__.py
#       _validators.py   — internal only
#       algebra.py
#       geometry.py
#       statistics.py

# --- mathtools/_validators.py ---
def require_positive(value, name):
    if value <= 0:
        raise ValueError(f"{name} must be positive, got {value}")

def require_non_empty(seq, name):
    if not seq:
        raise ValueError(f"{name} must not be empty")

# --- mathtools/geometry.py ---
import math
from ._validators import require_positive   # relative: same package

__all__ = ['circle_area', 'sphere_volume', 'cylinder_volume']

def circle_area(r):
    require_positive(r, 'radius')
    return math.pi * r ** 2

def sphere_volume(r):
    require_positive(r, 'radius')
    return (4/3) * math.pi * r ** 3

def cylinder_volume(r, h):
    require_positive(r, 'radius')
    require_positive(h, 'height')
    return math.pi * r ** 2 * h

# --- mathtools/statistics.py ---
```

```
from ._validators import require_non_empty    # same relative import style

__all__ = ['mean', 'variance']

def mean(data):
    require_non_empty(data, 'data')
    return sum(data) / len(data)

def variance(data):
    require_non_empty(data, 'data')
    m = mean(data)
    return sum((x - m) ** 2 for x in data) / len(data)

# --- main.py ---
from mathtools.geometry   import circle_area, sphere_volume
from mathtools.statistics import mean, variance

print(f"Circle area (r=4) : {circle_area(4):.3f}")
print(f"Sphere vol  (r=3) : {sphere_volume(3):.3f}")
data = [72, 85, 91, 68, 79, 83]
print(f"Mean      : {mean(data):.1f}")
print(f"Variance  : {variance(data):.2f}")
```

Output:

```
Circle area (r=4) : 50.265
Sphere vol  (r=3) : 113.097
Mean      : 79.7
Variance  : 57.56
```

The mathtools package demonstrates an important pattern: a single shared internal module (_validators.py) used by all sibling modules through relative imports. If the package is renamed from mathtools to school_maths, not one import path inside the package needs to change. That is the value of relative imports for intra-package references.

__init__.py: What to Put In It and What to Avoid

The __init__.py file is the public face of a package. When a developer writes import school or from school import Student, Python executes __init__.py and makes its contents available as attributes of the school package. This means __init__.py is the right place to curate a package's public API — selecting which names should be directly accessible at the package level, rather than requiring users to know the exact submodule where each name lives.

The most common and useful content of __init__.py is a set of selective re-exports: importing names from submodules so that users can write from school import Student instead of from school.models.student import Student. This shortens import paths for callers while preserving the internal structure of the package. Combined with a __all__ list, it gives you precise control over what the package exposes.

What to avoid in __init__.py is equally important. Avoid importing submodules that are slow to load or have heavy dependencies, because __init__.py is executed every time the package is imported, even if the user only needs a lightweight part. Avoid executing code with side effects (file I/O, network calls, print statements). Avoid importing names that are not part of the public API — doing so makes them appear public even if they are not intended to be.

> **Note:** Circular imports in __init__.py are particularly difficult to debug because __init__.py is the first file executed when the package is imported. If __init__.py imports from submodule A, and submodule A

imports from the package, the package's __init__.py is still being executed and the package object is incomplete. Keep __init__.py imports minimal and simple to avoid this class of problem.

Example 1 — Introduction

An __init__.py that re-exports selected names from submodules to create a clean top-level API.

```
# Package structure:
#   shapes/
#       __init__.py        ← curates the public API
#       circle.py
#       rectangle.py
#       triangle.py

# --- shapes/circle.py ---
import math
class Circle:
    def __init__(self, radius): self.radius = radius
    @property
    def area(self): return math.pi * self.radius ** 2
    def __repr__(self): return f'Circle(r={self.radius})'

# --- shapes/rectangle.py ---
class Rectangle:
    def __init__(self, w, h): self.w, self.h = w, h
    @property
    def area(self): return self.w * self.h
    def __repr__(self): return f'Rectangle({self.w}x{self.h})'

# --- shapes/__init__.py ---
"""shapes — 2-D geometry classes."""

# Re-export the classes users will actually import.
# After this, callers write: from shapes import Circle
# instead of:               from shapes.circle import Circle
from .circle    import Circle
from .rectangle import Rectangle

__all__ = ['Circle', 'Rectangle']

# --- main.py ---
from shapes import Circle, Rectangle   # clean top-level import

shapes = [Circle(5), Rectangle(4, 7)]
for s in shapes:
    print(f"{s}  area={s.area:.2f}")
```

Output:

```
Circle(r=5)  area=78.54
Rectangle(4x7)  area=28.00
```

Example 2 — Variation

Comparing a bloated __init__.py (importing everything eagerly) with a lean one (minimal, purposeful re-exports).

```
# ── BLOATED __init__.py — avoid this ──────────────────────
# Imports everything from every submodule, including internals.
# This pollutes the package namespace and slows every import.
from .circle    import *
from .rectangle import *
from .triangle  import *
from .utils     import *    # internal helpers now appear public
```

```
# ── LEAN __init__.py — prefer this ──────────────────────────
"""shapes — 2-D geometry classes. Public: Circle, Rectangle, Triangle."""

from .circle    import Circle
from .rectangle import Rectangle
from .triangle  import Triangle

__all__ = ['Circle', 'Rectangle', 'Triangle']

# Internal helpers (shapes/utils.py) are available as shapes.utils
# to anyone who needs them, but they do not appear in the top-level
# namespace and are not advertised in __all__.

# ── Demonstrating the difference in practice ─────────────────
# import shapes
# dir(shapes)   with BLOATED: dozens of internal names visible
# dir(shapes)   with LEAN:    only Circle, Rectangle, Triangle + dunders
```

Output:

```
# The lean version produces a clean, predictable namespace.
# The bloated version exposes internals and makes the API unclear.
```

Example 3 — Real-world application

A notifications package whose __init__.py exposes a single factory function, hiding the internal class hierarchy from callers.

```
# Package structure:
#   notifications/
#       __init__.py
#       _email.py
#       _sms.py
#       _push.py

# --- notifications/_email.py ---
class EmailNotification:
    def send(self, recipient, message):
        print(f"[EMAIL] To: {recipient} | {message}")

# --- notifications/_sms.py ---
class SMSNotification:
    def send(self, recipient, message):
        print(f"[SMS]   To: {recipient} | {message}")

# --- notifications/_push.py ---
class PushNotification:
    def send(self, recipient, message):
        print(f"[PUSH]  To: {recipient} | {message}")

# --- notifications/__init__.py ---
"""
notifications — Multi-channel notification utilities.

Public API:
    create(channel) — return a notification object for the given channel.
    Supported channels: 'email', 'sms', 'push'
"""

from ._email import EmailNotification
from ._sms   import SMSNotification
from ._push  import PushNotification

__all__ = ['create']   # only the factory is public
```

```
_CHANNELS = {
    'email': EmailNotification,
    'sms':   SMSNotification,
    'push':  PushNotification,
}

def create(channel):
    """Return a notification object for the named channel."""
    cls = _CHANNELS.get(channel.lower())
    if cls is None:
        supported = ', '.join(_CHANNELS)
        raise ValueError(f"Unknown channel {channel!r}. Choose: {supported}")
    return cls()

# --- main.py ---
from notifications import create

for channel in ('email', 'sms', 'push'):
    n = create(channel)
    n.send('student@school.edu.au', 'Assignment due tomorrow')
```

Output:

```
[EMAIL] To: student@school.edu.au | Assignment due tomorrow
[SMS]   To: student@school.edu.au | Assignment due tomorrow
[PUSH]  To: student@school.edu.au | Assignment due tomorrow
```

The notifications package exposes exactly one name at the top level: create(). The three internal classes are imported inside __init__.py (so the factory can use them) but are not listed in __all__ and are not part of the documented API. A caller who writes from notifications import EmailNotification will succeed — Python does not enforce __all__ on explicit imports — but they are relying on an undocumented internal and should expect no stability guarantees.

4.5 Namespace Packages: Packages Without __init__.py

Python 3.3 introduced namespace packages (PEP 420): directories that Python treats as packages even without an __init__.py file. The mechanism allows a single logical package to be split across multiple directories on sys.path — useful for large codebases where different teams contribute to the same top-level namespace, or for installing package components in separate locations.

In practice, most projects never need true namespace packages. They matter most in two scenarios: plugin architectures where third parties contribute to a shared namespace (for example, several separately installed packages all providing submodules under the name myapp.plugins), and corporate codebases where a single logical package is stored in multiple source repositories and assembled by the build system.

The visible difference between a regular package and a namespace package is the absence of __init__.py. When Python cannot find __init__.py in a directory that otherwise looks like a package, it creates a namespace package object whose __path__ is a list of all matching directories found anywhere on sys.path. Importing a submodule from any of those directories then works transparently.

> **Note:** If you add an __init__.py to any directory in a namespace package, that directory becomes a regular package and Python stops searching other directories on sys.path for that package name. Do not mix __init__.py and namespace package conventions within the same package name.

Example 1 — Introduction

A namespace package: two directories without __init__.py that together form one importable package name.

```
# Imagine two separate source trees, both on sys.path:
#
# /source_a/
#     myapp/                (no __init__.py — namespace package)
#         core.py
#
# /source_b/
#     myapp/                (no __init__.py — namespace package)
#         extras.py
#
# Both /source_a and /source_b are on sys.path.

# --- /source_a/myapp/core.py ---
def hello():
    return "Hello from myapp.core"

# --- /source_b/myapp/extras.py ---
def greet(name):
    return f"Greetings, {name}, from myapp.extras"

# --- main.py ---
# Python merges both directories under the single name 'myapp'
from myapp.core   import hello
from myapp.extras import greet

print(hello())
print(greet('Aria'))

import myapp
print(myapp.__path__)     # shows both source directories
```

Output:

```
Hello from myapp.core
Greetings, Aria, from myapp.extras
_NamespacePath(['/source_a/myapp', '/source_b/myapp'])
```

Example 2 — Variation

Detecting at runtime whether a package is a regular package or a namespace package.

```
import importlib
import types

def package_type(name):
    """Return a description of how Python resolved the named package."""
    try:
        mod = importlib.import_module(name)
    except ImportError:
        return f"{name}: not found"

    if not hasattr(mod, '__file__') or mod.__file__ is None:
        # Namespace packages have __file__ == None
        return f"{name}: namespace package  (__path__={list(mod.__path__)})"
    if mod.__file__.endswith('__init__.py'):
        return f"{name}: regular package    (__file__={mod.__file__})"
    return f"{name}: module              (__file__={mod.__file__})"

# Test against a few standard library names
for pkg in ['email', 'json', 'xml.etree', 'encodings']:
    print(package_type(pkg))
```

Output:

```
email: regular package    (__file__=.../email/__init__.py)
json: regular package     (__file__=.../json/__init__.py)
xml.etree: regular package (__file__=.../xml/etree/__init__.py)
encodings: regular package (__file__=.../encodings/__init__.py)
```

Example 3 — Real-world application

A plugin architecture using namespace packages: core functionality and third-party plugins share the same top-level name without coordinating a central __init__.py.

```
# Core package (installed separately, no __init__.py):
#   /installed/
#       gradebook/
#           engine.py
#           reporter.py
#
# Plugin package (also installed separately, also no __init__.py):
#   /plugins/
#       gradebook/
#           csv_exporter.py
#           pdf_exporter.py
#
# Both /installed and /plugins are on sys.path.
# Python merges them: import gradebook.engine AND
# import gradebook.csv_exporter both resolve correctly.

# --- /installed/gradebook/engine.py ---
def compute_grade(scores):
    avg = sum(scores) / len(scores) if scores else 0
    return 'A' if avg >= 90 else 'B' if avg >= 80 else 'C'

# --- /installed/gradebook/reporter.py ---
def report(name, grade):
    print(f"Student: {name}  Grade: {grade}")

# --- /plugins/gradebook/csv_exporter.py ---
def export(records, path):
    print(f"Exporting {len(records)} records to {path} (CSV)")

# --- main.py ---
from gradebook.engine       import compute_grade
from gradebook.reporter     import report
from gradebook.csv_exporter import export    # from the plugin

students = [('Mei', [92, 88, 95]), ('Rafi', [74, 79, 71])]
records  = []
for name, scores in students:
    grade = compute_grade(scores)
    report(name, grade)
    records.append({'name': name, 'grade': grade})
export(records, 'results.csv')
```

Output:

```
Student: Mei  Grade: A
Student: Rafi  Grade: C
Exporting 2 records to results.csv (CSV)
```

Namespace packages are an advanced feature that most projects never need. Understanding them matters because you will encounter them in large codebases and when working with frameworks that support plugin extension. For any project you control entirely, regular packages with __init__.py remain the clearer, more predictable choice.

Package-Level __all__

Just as a module uses __all__ to declare its public API, a package's __init__.py can define __all__ to control what from package import * exports. Package-level __all__ is the combined public interface of the entire package — the names a caller gets when they use the wildcard import form.

Without __all__ in __init__.py, from package import * imports only the names that were explicitly placed in __init__.py's namespace (by assignments or re-export imports). It does not automatically include all submodules. This is a common source of confusion: after import mypackage, mypackage.submodule is only accessible if __init__.py imported it or if the caller explicitly imports the submodule.

The combination of selective re-exports in __init__.py and a well-curated __all__ list is the standard pattern for professional Python packages. It gives callers a flat, memorable import surface (from mypackage import ThingA, ThingB) while preserving the ability to organise implementation code into whatever internal submodule structure makes sense.

> **Note:** Package-level __all__ only affects the wildcard import form (from package import *). It does not prevent explicit imports of anything the package contains. If you want to truly hide an internal submodule, prefix its filename with an underscore and document clearly that it is private.

Example 1 — Introduction

A package whose __init__.py defines __all__ and re-exports selected names from three submodules.

```
# Package structure:
#   validators/
#       __init__.py
#       strings.py
#       numbers.py
#       dates.py

# --- validators/strings.py ---
import re
_EMAIL = re.compile(r'^[^@\s]+@[^@\s]+\.[^@\s]+$')
def is_email(s): return bool(_EMAIL.match(s))
def is_non_empty(s): return bool(s and s.strip())

# --- validators/numbers.py ---
def is_positive(n):
    try: return float(n) > 0
    except (TypeError, ValueError): return False
def is_integer(n):
    try: int(n); return True
    except (TypeError, ValueError): return False

# --- validators/dates.py ---
from datetime import datetime
def is_date(s, fmt='%d/%m/%Y'):
    try: datetime.strptime(s, fmt); return True
    except (ValueError, TypeError): return False

# --- validators/__init__.py ---
"""validators — Input validation functions for enrolment forms."""

from .strings import is_email, is_non_empty
from .numbers import is_positive, is_integer
from .dates   import is_date

__all__ = ['is_email', 'is_non_empty', 'is_positive', 'is_integer', 'is_date']
```

```
# --- main.py ---
from validators import *    # imports exactly the five names in __all__

print(is_email("student@school.edu.au"))  # True
print(is_positive(-5))                    # False
print(is_date("25/12/2025"))              # True
```

Output:

```
True
False
True
```

Example 2 — Variation

Showing that without __all__, from package import * does not automatically expose submodules.

```
# Package: toolbox/
#   __init__.py  (no __all__ defined, and no submodule imports)
#   hammer.py
#   wrench.py

# --- toolbox/__init__.py (minimal, no re-exports) ---
VERSION = '1.0'

# --- toolbox/hammer.py ---
def hit(): return 'Bang!'

# --- main.py ---
from toolbox import *

# VERSION was bound in __init__.py, so it is available:
print(VERSION)          # '1.0'

# hammer was NOT imported in __init__.py, so it is NOT available:
try:
    print(hammer.hit())
except NameError as e:
    print(f'NameError: {e}')

# To access hammer you must import it explicitly:
import toolbox.hammer
print(toolbox.hammer.hit())

# Or add this to __init__.py:
# from . import hammer
# from .hammer import hit
```

Output:

```
1.0
NameError: name 'hammer' is not defined
Bang!
```

Example 3 — Real-world application

A reporting package that exposes a version string, a registry of available formats, and a single generate() entry point through __init__.py.

```
# Package structure:
#   reporting/
#       __init__.py
#       _formats/
#           __init__.py
#           text_fmt.py
```

```
#           csv_fmt.py
#           html_fmt.py

# --- reporting/_formats/text_fmt.py ---
def render(records):
    lines = ['=== REPORT ==='
             ] + [f'  {r["name"]}: {r["score"]}' for r in records]
    return '\n'.join(lines)

# --- reporting/_formats/csv_fmt.py ---
def render(records):
    rows = ['name,score'] + [f'{r["name"]},{r["score"]}' for r in records]
    return '\n'.join(rows)

# --- reporting/__init__.py ---
"""reporting — Multi-format report generation."""

from ._formats import text_fmt, csv_fmt

VERSION = '1.2'

_FORMATS = {'text': text_fmt, 'csv': csv_fmt}

__all__ = ['VERSION', 'AVAILABLE_FORMATS', 'generate']

AVAILABLE_FORMATS = tuple(_FORMATS.keys())

def generate(records, fmt='text'):
    """Render records in the named format. Use AVAILABLE_FORMATS to list
options."""
    if fmt not in _FORMATS:
        raise ValueError(f"Unknown format {fmt!r}. Choose:
{AVAILABLE_FORMATS}")
    return _FORMATS[fmt].render(records)

# --- main.py ---
from reporting import VERSION, AVAILABLE_FORMATS, generate

print(f"reporting v{VERSION} — formats: {AVAILABLE_FORMATS}")
data = [{'name': 'Ivy', 'score': 91}, {'name': 'Leo', 'score': 76}]
print(generate(data, "text"))
print()
print(generate(data, "csv"))
```

Output:

```
reporting v1.2 — formats: ('text', 'csv')
=== REPORT ===
  Ivy: 91
  Leo: 76

name,score
Ivy,91
Leo,76
```

The reporting package's __init__.py acts as an API gateway: it hides the _formats subpackage (prefixed with underscore), exposes only the three names listed in __all__, and provides a single generate() entry point that dispatches to format-specific renderers. Callers never need to know that text_fmt or csv_fmt exist.

Real-World Example: Restructuring the SRS into a Package

The Student Records System (SRS) built in Book 02, Chapter 10 was a collection of related modules: models.py, store.py, persistence/csv_store.py, persistence/json_store.py, operations.py, reports.py, and a command-line entry point. That structure, while functional, lived in a flat directory. This section refactors it into a proper package hierarchy — the kind of restructuring that real projects undergo as they grow from prototype to maintainable codebase.

The refactoring follows three principles: group modules by subsystem (data model, persistence, business logic, presentation), expose a clean top-level API through __init__.py, and use relative imports throughout so the package can be installed or moved without breaking internal references. The public interface shrinks: callers import from srs, not from srs.persistence.csv_store.

This restructuring is not just cosmetic. It brings three practical benefits: each subsystem can be developed and tested independently; the package can be distributed as a proper installable unit (Chapter 9); and new persistence formats or report styles can be added inside the appropriate subpackage without touching any other part of the codebase.

Example 1 — Introduction

The before and after directory structure, and the new package's __init__.py defining its top-level API.

```
# ── BEFORE: flat module collection ──────────────────────────
# srs/
#   models.py
#   store.py
#   operations.py
#   reports.py
#   cli.py

# ── AFTER: structured package ────────────────────────────────
# srs/
#   __init__.py           ← package API gateway
#   models/
#       __init__.py
#       student.py        ← Student dataclass
#       course.py         ← Course dataclass
#       errors.py         ← SRSError hierarchy
#   persistence/
#       __init__.py
#       csv_store.py      ← CSV read/write
#       json_store.py     ← JSON read/write
#   operations/
#       __init__.py
#       enrolment.py      ← enrol/withdraw logic
#       grading.py        ← grade calculation
#   reports/
#       __init__.py
#       summary.py        ← summary report
#       honour_roll.py    ← honour roll report
#   cli.py                ← command-line entry point

# --- srs/__init__.py ---
"""
srs — Student Records System.

Public API:
    Student, Course                    — data model classes
    SRSError, RecordNotFoundError      — exception types
    enrol, withdraw, assign_grade      — operations
    summary_report, honour_roll        — reports
"""
```

```python
from .models.student    import Student
from .models.course     import Course
from .models.errors     import SRSError, RecordNotFoundError
from .operations.enrolment import enrol, withdraw
from .operations.grading   import assign_grade
from .reports.summary      import summary_report
from .reports.honour_roll  import honour_roll

__all__ = [
    'Student', 'Course',
    'SRSError', 'RecordNotFoundError',
    'enrol', 'withdraw', 'assign_grade',
    'summary_report', 'honour_roll',
]
```

Output:

```
# After this __init__.py, callers write:
# from srs import Student, enrol, summary_report
# instead of:
# from srs.models.student import Student
# from srs.operations.enrolment import enrol
```

Example 2 — Variation

The models and errors submodules using relative imports and clean dataclass definitions.

```python
# --- srs/models/errors.py ---
"""SRS exception hierarchy."""

class SRSError(Exception):
    """Base exception for all SRS errors."""

class RecordNotFoundError(SRSError):
    """Raised when a requested record does not exist."""
    def __init__(self, record_type, identifier):
        super().__init__(f"{record_type} not found: {identifier!r}")
        self.record_type = record_type
        self.identifier  = identifier

class DuplicateRecordError(SRSError):
    """Raised when an insert would create a duplicate record."""

# --- srs/models/student.py ---
from dataclasses import dataclass, field
from typing import List

# Relative import: errors.py is a sibling in srs/models/
from .errors import SRSError

@dataclass
class Student:
    student_id : str
    name       : str
    year_level : int
    scores     : List[float] = field(default_factory=list)

    @property
    def average(self):
        return round(sum(self.scores)/len(self.scores), 1) if self.scores else
0.0

    def add_score(self, score):
        if not 0 <= score <= 100:
            raise SRSError(f"Score must be 0-100, got {score}")
```

```
        self.scores.append(score)

# --- srs/models/course.py ---
from dataclasses import dataclass

@dataclass
class Course:
    course_id : str
    name      : str
    year_level: int
    capacity  : int = 30
```

Output:

```
# srs/models/ now contains three clean, cohesive modules:
#   errors.py    — exception hierarchy only
#   student.py   — Student dataclass + business rules
#   course.py    — Course dataclass
```

Example 3 — Real-world application

The operations and reports subpackages, and a main.py that uses only the clean top-level API.

```
# --- srs/operations/enrolment.py ---
from ..models.student import Student
from ..models.errors  import RecordNotFoundError

# Simulated in-memory store (a real system would use persistence/)
_students = {}

def enrol(student_id, name, year_level):
    """Add a new student to the records."""
    s = Student(student_id, name, year_level)
    _students[student_id] = s
    print(f"Enrolled: {s.name} [{s.student_id}] Year {s.year_level}")
    return s

def withdraw(student_id):
    """Remove a student from the records."""
    if student_id not in _students:
        raise RecordNotFoundError('Student', student_id)
    s = _students.pop(student_id)
    print(f"Withdrawn: {s.name}")

# --- srs/operations/grading.py ---
from ..models.errors import RecordNotFoundError
from .enrolment import _students

def assign_grade(student_id, score):
    if student_id not in _students:
        raise RecordNotFoundError('Student', student_id)
    _students[student_id].add_score(score)

# --- srs/reports/summary.py ---
from ..operations.enrolment import _students

def summary_report():
    hdr = "{:<20} {:>4} {:>6}".format("Name", "Year", "Avg")
    print(hdr)
    print("-" * 34)
    for s in sorted(_students.values(), key=lambda x: x.name):
        print(f"{s.name:<20} {s.year_level:>4} {s.average:>6.1f}")

# --- srs/reports/honour_roll.py ---
from ..operations.enrolment import _students
```

```
CUTOFF = 80.0

def honour_roll():
    eligible = [s for s in _students.values() if s.average >= CUTOFF]
    print(f"Honour Roll (avg >= {CUTOFF}):")
    for s in sorted(eligible, key=lambda x: x.average, reverse=True):
        print(f"  {s.name:<20} {s.average:.1f}")

# --- main.py (at project root, beside srs/) ---
from srs import enrol, assign_grade, summary_report, honour_roll
from srs import RecordNotFoundError

enrol('S001', 'Amara Osei',   11)
enrol('S002', 'Ben Whitmore', 10)
enrol('S003', 'Chloe Nguyen', 11)

for sid, scores in [('S001', [92,88,95]), ('S002',[74,79,71]),
('S003',[85,90,88])]:
    for sc in scores:
        assign_grade(sid, sc)

print()
summary_report()
print()
honour_roll()

try:
    withdraw = __import__('srs').withdraw
    withdraw('S999')
except RecordNotFoundError as e:
    print(f"\nCaught: {e}")
```

Output:

```
Enrolled: Amara Osei [S001] Year 11
Enrolled: Ben Whitmore [S002] Year 10
Enrolled: Chloe Nguyen [S003] Year 11

Name                     Year    Avg
----------------------------------
Amara Osei                 11   91.7
Ben Whitmore               10   74.7
Chloe Nguyen               11   87.7

Honour Roll (avg >= 80.0):
  Amara Osei              91.7
  Chloe Nguyen            87.7

Caught: Student not found: 'S999'
```

The refactored SRS demonstrates the full package design cycle: a structured directory tree that mirrors the application's subsystems, relative imports that make every internal reference explicit and portable, an __init__.py that curates a flat public API, and a main.py that uses only that API — completely unaware of the internal structure behind it. Adding a new report or a new persistence format now requires creating one new file in the appropriate subpackage, with no changes to any existing module.

Chapter 5 steps away from project structure and surveys the Python standard library — the vast collection of ready-made modules that ship with every Python installation and handle everything from file paths and dates to statistics, regular expressions, and network protocols.

Chapter 4 Summary

- A package is a directory containing an __init__.py file. The directory structure directly determines the import paths available to users: a file at school/admin/enrolment.py is importable as school.admin.enrolment.
- Python executes __init__.py when the package is first imported. An empty __init__.py is valid and often preferable to one that eagerly imports everything. Add content to __init__.py only for selective re-exports, version strings, or initialisation code that every caller needs.
- Subpackages are package directories nested inside a parent package, each with their own __init__.py. The import path mirrors the directory path with slashes replaced by dots. Most projects need no more than two or three levels of nesting.
- Use absolute imports (from school.models import Student) for external packages and the standard library. Use relative imports (from .models import Student, from ..utils import helper) for references within your own package, making the package relocatable.
- A well-designed __init__.py re-exports selected names from submodules so callers can write from mypackage import ThingA rather than from mypackage.subpackage.module import ThingA. Combined with __all__, this gives precise control over the package's public interface.
- Namespace packages (PEP 420, Python 3.3+) are directories without __init__.py that Python merges across multiple locations on sys.path. They enable plugin architectures and split-repository packages, but most projects should use regular packages.
- Package-level __all__ in __init__.py controls what from package import * exports. Without __all__, the wildcard import only includes names explicitly placed in __init__.py's namespace — it does not automatically expose submodules.
- The Student Records System refactoring demonstrates the full package design cycle: group modules by subsystem, use relative imports throughout, expose a curated flat API via __init__.py, and ensure callers depend only on that API rather than on internal paths.

Guided Exercises

1. Create a package called geometry/ with an __init__.py and three submodules: shapes.py (containing Circle and Rectangle classes with area and perimeter properties), units.py (containing mm_to_cm, cm_to_m, and m_to_km conversion functions), and constants.py (containing PI and GOLDEN_RATIO). In __init__.py, re-export Circle, Rectangle, and the three conversion functions. Add __all__ listing all five names. Verify that from geometry import Circle, mm_to_cm works without knowing the internal submodule structure.

Hint: Start with empty __init__.py files and confirm the imports work from a test script at the project root. Then add the re-exports to geometry/__init__.py one by one, testing after each addition.

2. Add a subpackage geometry/advanced/ containing a polygon.py module with a regular_polygon_area(sides, side_length) function. Import this function from the geometry/advanced/ level and confirm it is accessible as geometry.advanced.polygon.regular_polygon_area. Then re-export it through geometry/__init__.py so it is also available as from geometry import regular_polygon_area.

Hint: Create geometry/advanced/__init__.py as an empty file first. The relative import in polygon.py that accesses anything in the parent geometry/ package needs two leading dots: from .. import constants.

3. Demonstrate the effect of __all__ in a package's __init__.py. Create a package tools/ with two submodules: strings.py and numbers.py, each containing three functions. In tools/__init__.py, re-export all six functions but set __all__ to include only three of them (mixed from both submodules). In a test script, use from tools import * and confirm that only the three listed names are bound, while the other three require explicit import.

Hint: After from tools import *, call dir() or check for each name with name in dir() to verify exactly which names were imported by the wildcard.

4. Convert the flat collection of modules from a previous exercise (or from the grades/gst_utils modules built in Chapter 3) into a package. Create a school/ directory with __init__.py, then move the modules inside. Update all import statements in your test scripts to use the new package paths. Ensure the modules use relative imports to reference each other, and that the package is silent when imported from an external script.

Hint: The key change is converting import grades into from . import grades (inside the package) or from school import grades (from outside). Confirm that python -m school.module_name still runs the __main__ guard.

5. Build a minimal plugin system using a namespace package. Create two separate directories (plugins_core/ and plugins_extra/) and add both to sys.path manually using sys.path.insert(). In plugins_core/widgets/ place a button.py module, and in plugins_extra/widgets/ place a slider.py module (neither directory has __init__.py). From a main script, import from widgets.button and from widgets.slider and confirm both work. Print widgets.__path__ to show that Python merged both directories.

Hint: Use sys.path.insert(0, '/path/to/plugins_core') and sys.path.insert(0, '/path/to/plugins_extra') before any widget imports. Check that neither widgets/ directory contains an __init__.py — that is what makes it a namespace package.

Challenge Tasks

1. Design and implement a complete mathtools package with the following structure: a top-level mathtools/ package; a subpackage mathtools/algebra/ containing polynomial.py (a Polynomial class supporting addition, evaluation, and string representation) and equations.py (functions quadratic_roots(a, b, c) and linear_root(m, c)); a subpackage mathtools/geometry/ containing shapes.py and vectors.py (a Vector2D class with addition, dot product, and magnitude); and a subpackage mathtools/statistics/ containing descriptive.py (mean, median, mode, standard_deviation) and distributions.py (normal_pdf, uniform_pdf). All internal references must use relative imports. mathtools/__init__.py must re-export the most commonly used names and define a VERSION constant. Write a main.py that imports only from mathtools (not from any internal submodule) and demonstrates at least one function or class from each subpackage.

2. Implement a package-based configuration system called appconfig/. The package should support three configuration sources: a built-in defaults module (appconfig/defaults.py), a file-based loader (appconfig/file_loader.py that reads KEY=VALUE text files), and an environment variable reader (appconfig/env_loader.py that reads variables with a specified prefix from os.environ). appconfig/__init__.py should expose a single Config class that merges all three sources in priority order (env vars override file values, which override defaults). The Config class should support dictionary-style access (config['KEY']) and attribute-style access (config.KEY). Write comprehensive tests in a separate test_appconfig.py file covering all three source types and the priority merging behaviour.

3. Refactor the complete gst_utils, grades, school_utils, and time_utils modules built across Chapters 1–3 of this book into a single package called school_toolkit/. Design a sensible subpackage structure (for example: school_toolkit/finance/, school_toolkit/academic/, school_toolkit/utils/). Use relative imports throughout. school_toolkit/__init__.py must expose a curated top-level API with a meaningful __all__. Each subpackage must have its own __init__.py re-exporting the names most likely to be needed. Write a showcase script main.py that imports only from school_toolkit (never from any internal submodule path) and demonstrates at least five distinct functions or classes from across the package. Every module must be silent on import and carry its own docstring.

CHAPTER 5 Python Standard Library Tour

Book 03: Modules, Packages & the Python Ecosystem

> Python ships with a vast collection of ready-made modules called the standard library — code written, tested, and maintained by the Python core development team that covers everything from file paths and dates to statistics, iterators, and higher-order functions. Using the standard library is not optional: it is the difference between professional Python and amateur Python. A developer who reaches for a custom linked-list implementation when collections.deque exists, or reimplements memoisation when functools.lru_cache is available, is doing more work to produce an inferior result. This chapter tours seven areas of the standard library most relevant to everyday programming: system interaction, numeric tools, dates and times, container types, itertools, functools, and the file-system utilities. Each section focuses on the functions and classes you will use repeatedly, with real-world examples drawn from school, finance, and data-processing contexts.

5.1 os, sys, and platform: System Interaction

The os module is Python's portable interface to the operating system. It provides functions for querying and manipulating the environment: the current working directory, environment variables, process information, and low-level file-system operations. The sys module exposes the Python interpreter's own runtime state: the argument list, the module search path, standard streams, and the version information. The platform module adds hardware and operating-system detection, useful when a program needs to behave differently on Windows, macOS, or Linux.

Together these three modules answer the questions: where am I running, what arguments was I given, and what does the environment look like? They are used in almost every non-trivial Python program and are the first place to look when you need to interact with the surrounding system rather than just with data in memory.

A key design principle behind these modules is portability: os.path.join('data', 'records', 'file.csv') produces the correct path separator on every platform, whereas hard-coding 'data/records/file.csv' breaks on Windows. The same principle applies to os.environ for environment variables and sys.executable for the Python binary path — always use the module, never hard-code system-specific values.

> **Note:** os.system() and os.popen() run shell commands but are considered legacy. For running external processes in modern Python, use the subprocess module instead — it gives better control over input/output, error handling, and security.

Example 1 — Introduction

Exploring the runtime environment using os, sys, and platform.

```
import os
import sys
import platform

# Current working directory and script location
print(f"CWD        : {os.getcwd()}")
print(f"Script     : {sys.argv[0]}")
print(f"Python     : {sys.version.split()[0]}")
```

```
# Platform information
print(f"OS         : {platform.system()} {platform.release()}")
print(f"Machine    : {platform.machine()}")
print(f"Processor  : {platform.processor() or 'unknown'}")

# Environment variables
home = os.environ.get('HOME') or os.environ.get('USERPROFILE', 'unknown')
print(f"Home dir   : {home}")

# sys.path — the module search path
print(f"sys.path has {len(sys.path)} entries")
print(f"First entry: {sys.path[0] or '(current dir)'}")
```

Output:

```
CWD        : /home/student/projects/school
Script     : demo.py
Python     : 3.12.3
OS         : Linux 6.5.0
Machine    : x86_64
Processor  : x86_64
Home dir   : /home/student
sys.path has 7 entries
First entry: (current dir)
```

Example 2 — Variation

Using os.environ for configuration and os.path for portable path construction.

```
import os

# Read configuration from environment variables with defaults
DATA_DIR  = os.environ.get('SRS_DATA_DIR',  'data')
LOG_LEVEL = os.environ.get('SRS_LOG_LEVEL', 'INFO')
MAX_ROWS  = int(os.environ.get('SRS_MAX_ROWS', '1000'))

print(f"Data dir  : {DATA_DIR}")
print(f"Log level : {LOG_LEVEL}")
print(f"Max rows  : {MAX_ROWS}")

# Build portable paths — os.path.join uses the right separator
students_csv = os.path.join(DATA_DIR, 'students', 'records.csv')
backup_dir   = os.path.join(DATA_DIR, 'backups', '2025')
print(f"Students  : {students_csv}")
print(f"Backup dir: {backup_dir}")

# Check existence before opening
if os.path.isfile(students_csv):
    print("File exists — ready to load")
else:
    print("File not found — using defaults")

# List contents of a directory (if it exists)
if os.path.isdir(DATA_DIR):
    entries = os.listdir(DATA_DIR)
    print(f"{DATA_DIR}/ contains {len(entries)} items")
```

Output:

```
Data dir  : data
Log level : INFO
Max rows  : 1000
Students  : data/students/records.csv
Backup dir: data/backups/2025
File not found — using defaults
data/ contains 3 items
```

Example 3 — Real-world application

A startup diagnostics function that reports the runtime environment — useful at the top of a long-running server script.

```
import os
import sys
import platform
from datetime import datetime

def print_startup_info(app_name, version):
    """Print a formatted startup banner with environment details."""
    now = datetime.now().strftime('%d/%m/%Y %H:%M:%S')
    sep = '=' * 55
    print(sep)
    print(f"  {app_name} v{version}")
    print(f"  Started : {now}")
    print(sep)
    print(f"  Python  : {sys.version.split()[0]}")
    print(f"  OS      : {platform.system()} {platform.release()}")
    print(f"  CWD     : {os.getcwd()}")
    print(f"  PID     : {os.getpid()}")

    # Report key environment variables
    env_keys = ['VIRTUAL_ENV', 'PYTHONPATH', 'HOME']
    for key in env_keys:
        val = os.environ.get(key, '(not set)')
        print(f"  {key:<14}: {val}")
    print(sep)

print_startup_info('Student Records System', '2.1.0')
```

Output:

```
=======================================================
  Student Records System v2.1.0
  Started : 14/07/2025 09:31:02
=======================================================
  Python        : 3.12.3
  OS            : Linux 6.5.0
  CWD           : /home/student/srs
  PID           : 18472
  VIRTUAL_ENV   : /home/student/srs/.venv
  PYTHONPATH    : (not set)
  HOME          : /home/student
=======================================================
```

The os and sys modules are also the standard tools for writing scripts that behave differently based on their environment — reading data directories from environment variables rather than hard-coding paths, adjusting behaviour based on the operating system, and gracefully handling missing configuration. Every production Python application uses at least some of these patterns.

math, statistics, random: Numeric Tools

The math module provides the mathematical functions defined by the C standard library: trigonometric and hyperbolic functions, logarithms, rounding variants (floor, ceil, trunc), power and exponential functions, and a handful of constants including pi, e, tau, and inf. It operates on Python floats and is significantly faster than reimplementing these functions in pure Python.

The statistics module, added in Python 3.4 and substantially expanded in later versions, provides descriptive statistics for numeric data: mean, median, mode, variance, standard deviation, and more. Unlike math, which operates on individual numbers, statistics operates on sequences. It handles edge cases correctly (such as the two-arg form of median_low for even-length sequences) and uses Python's Fraction and Decimal types internally to avoid floating-point rounding errors where possible.

The random module generates pseudo-random numbers using the Mersenne Twister algorithm. It provides uniform random floats, random integers in a range, random choices from a sequence, and shuffling in place. For cryptographic applications — generating tokens, passwords, or keys — use the secrets module instead: random is not cryptographically secure.

> **Note:** random.seed() sets the initial state of the random number generator so that a sequence of random calls produces the same values on every run. This is essential for reproducible testing and simulation. Use random.seed(42) or any integer at the start of a script that needs reproducible random output.

Example 1 — Introduction

Key functions from math and statistics applied to a set of student scores.

```
import math
import statistics

scores = [72, 85, 91, 68, 79, 83, 91, 55, 88, 76]

# math functions on individual values
print(f"sqrt(2)        : {math.sqrt(2):.6f}")
print(f"log10(1000)    : {math.log10(1000):.1f}")
print(f"ceil(79.3)     : {math.ceil(79.3)}")
print(f"floor(79.9)    : {math.floor(79.9)}")
print(f"pi             : {math.pi:.6f}")

# statistics functions on the scores list
print(f"\nMean       : {statistics.mean(scores):.2f}")
print(f"Median    : {statistics.median(scores):.1f}")
print(f"Mode      : {statistics.mode(scores)}")
print(f"Std Dev   : {statistics.stdev(scores):.2f}")
print(f"Variance  : {statistics.variance(scores):.2f}")
print(f"Min/Max   : {min(scores)} / {max(scores)}")
```

Output:

```
sqrt(2)       : 1.414214
log10(1000)   : 3.0
ceil(79.3)    : 80
floor(79.9)   : 79
pi            : 3.141593

Mean     : 78.80
Median   : 81.00
Mode     : 91
Std Dev  : 11.32
Variance : 128.18
Min/Max  : 55 / 91
```

Example 2 — Variation

Using random to simulate a quiz with random questions and a random selection from a pool.

```
import random

# Seed for reproducible output
random.seed(42)

QUESTIONS = [
    ('What is 7 x 8?',            '56'),
```

```
    ('What is 12 squared?',       '144'),
    ('What is sqrt(144)?',        '12'),
    ('What is 15% of 200?',       '30'),
    ('How many sides on a hexagon?', '6'),
    ('What is 2 to the power 10?',    '1024'),
]

# Select 3 random questions without replacement
quiz = random.sample(QUESTIONS, k=3)

print("Mini Quiz — answer each question:")
for i, (question, answer) in enumerate(quiz, 1):
    print(f"  Q{i}: {question}  [Answer: {answer}]")

# Simulate a dice roll and a random score in a range
dice    = random.randint(1, 6)
score   = random.uniform(50.0, 100.0)
print(f"\nDice roll    : {dice}")
print(f"Random score: {score:.1f}")

# Shuffle a list of student names in place
names = ['Aria', 'Ben', 'Cora', 'Dev', 'Eva']
random.shuffle(names)
print(f"Shuffled     : {names}")
```

Output:

```
Mini Quiz — answer each question:
  Q1: What is 2 to the power 10?  [Answer: 1024]
  Q2: What is 15% of 200?  [Answer: 30]
  Q3: What is sqrt(144)?  [Answer: 12]

Dice roll    : 1
Random score: 74.4
Shuffled     : ['Cora', 'Dev', 'Ben', 'Aria', 'Eva']
```

Example 3 — Real-world application

A grade statistics report combining math and statistics for a year-level cohort.

```
import math
import statistics

COHORT = {
    'Year 9':  [72, 85, 63, 91, 78, 55, 82, 69, 88, 74],
    'Year 10': [80, 77, 92, 68, 84, 91, 73, 87, 79, 95],
    'Year 11': [88, 76, 94, 82, 91, 85, 79, 90, 83, 87],
}

def cohort_report(cohort):
    """Print a statistical summary for each year level."""
    HDR = '{:<10} {:>6} {:>6} {:>6} {:>6} {:>6}'.format(
        'Year', 'Mean', 'Median', 'StdDev', 'Min', 'Max'
    )
    print(HDR)
    print("-" * 46)
    for year, scores in cohort.items():
        mean   = statistics.mean(scores)
        median = statistics.median(scores)
        sd     = statistics.stdev(scores)
        lo, hi = min(scores), max(scores)
        row = '{:<10} {:>6.1f} {:>6.1f} {:>6.1f} {:>6} {:>6}'.format(
            year, mean, median, sd, lo, hi
        )
        print(row)
```

```
    # Correlation between year level and mean score
    years  = [int(y.split()[1]) for y in cohort]
    means  = [statistics.mean(s) for s in cohort.values()]
    corr   = statistics.correlation(years, means)
    print(f"\nCorrelation (year vs mean): {corr:.3f}")

    # Normal approximation: percentage within 1 SD of overall mean
    all_scores = [s for scores in cohort.values() for s in scores]
    overall_mean = statistics.mean(all_scores)
    overall_sd   = statistics.stdev(all_scores)
    within_1sd = sum(
        1 for s in all_scores
        if abs(s - overall_mean) <= overall_sd
    )
    pct = within_1sd / len(all_scores) * 100
    print(f"Within 1 SD of mean ({overall_mean:.1f}): {pct:.0f}% of students")

cohort_report(COHORT)
```

Output:

```
Year         Mean Median StdDev    Min     Max
----------------------------------------------
Year 9       75.7   76.5    9.8     55      91
Year 10      82.6   83.5    8.0     68      95
Year 11      85.5   86.5    5.1     76      94

Correlation (year vs mean): 0.999
Within 1 SD of mean (81.3): 67% of students
```

The statistics module's correlation() function (added in Python 3.10) and the NormalDist class are worth knowing as they make many data analysis tasks straightforward without requiring NumPy or Pandas. For Book 09's data analysis work, these will serve as a bridge between pure Python and full-scale data science toolkits.

5.3 datetime, calendar, and zoneinfo: Dates and Times

The datetime module provides four main types: date (year, month, day), time (hour, minute, second, microsecond), datetime (combined date and time), and timedelta (a duration). These types are immutable and support arithmetic: adding a timedelta to a date produces a new date, and subtracting two datetimes produces a timedelta. The module also includes timezone-aware variants that carry timezone information alongside the date-time value.

The calendar module provides utilities for working with calendars: testing whether a year is a leap year, computing the number of days in a month, generating text or HTML calendar representations, and iterating over the weeks of a given month. It is less commonly used than datetime but indispensable when building timetabling or scheduling functionality.

The zoneinfo module (added in Python 3.9) gives access to the IANA time zone database, replacing the older third-party pytz library for most purposes. A timezone-aware datetime created with ZoneInfo('Australia/Brisbane') correctly handles UTC offsets and will automatically apply daylight saving time rules for regions that observe it.

> **Note:** A naive datetime (one without timezone information) and a timezone-aware datetime cannot be compared or subtracted directly — Python raises TypeError. Always work consistently with either all-naive or all-aware datetimes within a single codebase. For any application that spans time zones, prefer aware datetimes from the start.

Example 1 — Introduction

Creating dates, computing durations, and formatting output with datetime.

```
from datetime import date, datetime, timedelta

# Create dates
today       = date.today()
school_start = date(2025, 1, 28)    # first day of school
school_end   = date(2025, 12, 5)    # last day of school

# Duration as timedelta
school_year = school_end - school_start
print(f"School year duration: {school_year.days} days")

# Days remaining until end of school year
remaining = school_end - today
print(f"Days remaining       : {remaining.days}")

# Arithmetic with timedelta
two_weeks = timedelta(weeks=2)
report_due = today + two_weeks
print(f"Report due           : {report_due.strftime('%A, %d %B %Y')}")

# Parsing a date string
excursion = datetime.strptime('14/08/2025', '%d/%m/%Y').date()
print(f"Excursion            : {excursion.strftime('%d %B %Y')}")

# Day of the week (0=Monday, 6=Sunday)
days = ['Mon','Tue','Wed','Thu','Fri','Sat','Sun']",
print(f"Excursion falls on   : {days[excursion.weekday()]}")
```

Output:

```
School year duration: 311 days
Days remaining      : 144
Report due          : Monday, 28 July 2025
Excursion           : 14 August 2025
Excursion falls on  : Thu
```

Example 2 — Variation

Using calendar to build a term planner and identify school weeks.

```
import calendar
from datetime import date

# Is a year a leap year?
print(f"2024 leap year: {calendar.isleap(2024)}")
print(f"2025 leap year: {calendar.isleap(2025)}")

# Number of days in a month
for month in range(1, 7):
    _, days = calendar.monthrange(2025, month)
    name = calendar.month_name[month]
    print(f"  {name:<12}: {days} days")

# Text calendar for a single month
print()
print(calendar.month(2025, 8))    # August 2025

# Find all Mondays in Term 3 (July 14 - Sep 19, 2025)
term3_start = date(2025, 7, 14)
term3_end   = date(2025, 9, 19)
from datetime import timedelta
mondays = []
```

```
d = term3_start
while d <= term3_end:
    if d.weekday() == 0:   # Monday
        mondays.append(d)
    d += timedelta(days=1)
print(f"Term 3 Mondays: {len(mondays)}")
print(f"First: {mondays[0]}  Last: {mondays[-1]}")
```

Output:

```
2024 leap year: True
2025 leap year: False
  January     : 31 days
  February    : 28 days
  March       : 31 days
  April       : 30 days
  May         : 31 days
  June        : 30 days

    August 2025
Mo Tu We Th Fr Sa Su
             1  2  3
 4  5  6  7  8  9 10
...
Term 3 Mondays: 10
First: 2025-07-14  Last: 2025-09-15
```

Example 3 — Real-world application

A timezone-aware event scheduler using zoneinfo, showing times in both Brisbane and London.

```
from datetime import datetime
from zoneinfo import ZoneInfo

BRISBANE = ZoneInfo('Australia/Brisbane')
LONDON   = ZoneInfo('Europe/London')
UTC      = ZoneInfo('UTC')

def schedule_event(name, year, month, day, hour, minute, tz):
    """Create a timezone-aware event and display in multiple zones."""
    local = datetime(year, month, day, hour, minute, tzinfo=tz)
    utc   = local.astimezone(UTC)
    bne   = local.astimezone(BRISBANE)
    lon   = local.astimezone(LONDON)

    print(f"Event    : {name}")
    print(f"Local    : {local.strftime('%d/%m/%Y %H:%M %Z')}")
    print(f"UTC      : {utc.strftime('%d/%m/%Y %H:%M %Z')}")
    print(f"Brisbane : {bne.strftime('%d/%m/%Y %H:%M %Z')}")
    print(f"London   : {lon.strftime('%d/%m/%Y %H:%M %Z')}")
    print()

# Online coding competition — hosted in Brisbane
schedule_event('QLD Schools Coding Cup',
               2025, 9, 10, 9, 0, BRISBANE)

# International webinar — hosted in London
schedule_event('Global EdTech Summit',
               2025, 11, 5, 14, 0, LONDON)
```

Output:

```
Event    : QLD Schools Coding Cup
Local    : 10/09/2025 09:00 AEST
UTC      : 10/09/2025 23:00 UTC
Brisbane : 10/09/2025 09:00 AEST
London   : 10/09/2025 00:00 BST
```

```
Event     : Global EdTech Summit
Local     : 05/11/2025 14:00 GMT
UTC       : 05/11/2025 14:00 UTC
Brisbane : 06/11/2025 00:00 AEST
London    : 05/11/2025 14:00 GMT
```

Date and time handling is one of the areas where beginners most often write their own code unnecessarily. String manipulation and manual day-counting are fragile; the datetime module handles leap years, month boundaries, and timedelta arithmetic correctly by design. Commit the strftime/strptime format codes to memory — they appear in almost every date-handling task.

5.4 collections: Counter, defaultdict, OrderedDict, namedtuple, deque

The collections module provides specialised container types that extend or refine Python's built-in dict, list, and tuple. Each type solves a specific pattern that would otherwise require boilerplate code: counting occurrences, handling missing dictionary keys gracefully, maintaining insertion order explicitly, naming tuple fields, or appending and removing from both ends of a sequence efficiently.

Counter is a dict subclass designed for counting hashable objects. It supports arithmetic operations (adding two Counters, subtracting, finding the intersection) and the most_common() method that returns elements sorted by frequency. defaultdict eliminates the common if key not in d: d[key] = [] pattern by accepting a callable that constructs the default value for any missing key. namedtuple creates tuple subclasses whose fields can be accessed by name as well as by index, making code that returns structured data more readable without the overhead of a full class.

deque (double-ended queue) supports O(1) append and remove from both ends, unlike a list where inserting or removing at position 0 is O(n). This makes deque the correct choice for queues (FIFO), stacks (LIFO), and sliding-window algorithms. OrderedDict is largely superseded by regular dicts in Python 3.7+ (which preserve insertion order), but it still provides the move_to_end() method and equality comparisons that consider order.

> **Note:** Counter.most_common(n) with no argument returns all elements sorted by count. Counter arithmetic respects signs: subtraction yields counts with positive results only, dropping zero and negative values. Use Counter.subtract() to allow negative counts.

Example 1 — Introduction

Counter and defaultdict solving common grouping and tallying problems.

```
from collections import Counter, defaultdict

# ── Counter ──────────────────────────────────────────
# Count word frequencies in a passage
passage = ('the quick brown fox jumps over the lazy dog '
           'the fox ran quickly over the hill')
words   = passage.split()
freq    = Counter(words)

print("Top 5 words:")
for word, count in freq.most_common(5):
    print(f"  {word:<10} {count}")

# Counter arithmetic
c1 = Counter(a=4, b=2, c=0)
c2 = Counter(a=1, b=3, d=5)
```

```python
print(f"c1 + c2 : {dict(c1 + c2)}")
print(f"c1 & c2 : {dict(c1 & c2)}")   # minimum of each

# ── defaultdict ──────────────────────────────────────
# Group students by year level without key-existence checks
enrolments = [
    ('Mia', 10), ('Leo', 9), ('Zara', 10),
    ('Sam', 9),  ('Ivy', 11), ('Kai', 10),
]
by_year = defaultdict(list)
for name, year in enrolments:
    by_year[year].append(name)   # no KeyError, list created automatically

for year in sorted(by_year):
    print(f"Year {year}: {by_year[year]}")
```

Output:

```
Top 5 words:
  the        4
  fox        2
  over       2
  quick      1
  brown      1
c1 + c2 : {'a': 5, 'b': 5, 'd': 5}
c1 & c2 : {'a': 1, 'b': 2}
Year 9: ['Leo', 'Sam']
Year 10: ['Mia', 'Zara', 'Kai']
Year 11: ['Ivy']
```

Example 2 — Variation

namedtuple and deque for structured data and efficient queue operations.

```python
from collections import namedtuple, deque

# ── namedtuple ──────────────────────────────────────
# A lightweight record type — fields accessible by name
Student = namedtuple('Student', ['name', 'year', 'average'])

cohort = [
    Student('Aaliya', 11, 91.5),
    Student('Ben',    10, 74.2),
    Student('Chloe',  11, 87.3),
    Student('Dev',    10, 85.0),
]

# Access by name (readable) or index (backward-compatible with tuples)
s = cohort[0]
print(f"{s.name} Year {s.year}  avg={s.average}")
print(f"Index access: {s[0]}, {s[2]}")

# Sort by average descending — works like a tuple
top = sorted(cohort, key=lambda s: s.average, reverse=True)
for s in top:
    print(f"  {s.name:<10} {s.average}")

# ── deque ──────────────────────────────────────
# O(1) append and popleft — ideal for a FIFO work queue
queue = deque()
for task in ['Mark essays', 'Email parents', 'Update rolls']:
    queue.append(task)          # add to right end

while queue:
    print(f"Processing: {queue.popleft()}")  # remove from left end
```

```
# maxlen creates a sliding window (bounded deque)
recent = deque(maxlen=3)
for score in [72, 85, 91, 68, 79]:
    recent.append(score)
    print(f"  Window: {list(recent)}")
```

Output:

```
Aaliya Year 11  avg=91.5
Index access: Aaliya, 91.5
  Aaliya     91.5
  Chloe      87.3
  Dev        85.0
  Ben        74.2
Processing: Mark essays
Processing: Email parents
Processing: Update rolls
  Window: [72]
  Window: [72, 85]
  Window: [72, 85, 91]
  Window: [85, 91, 68]
  Window: [91, 68, 79]
```

Example 3 — Real-world application

A canteen sales analytics report using Counter to rank items and defaultdict to group sales by day.

```
from collections import Counter, defaultdict
from datetime import date

# Simulated sales log: (date, item, qty)
SALES = [
    (date(2025, 7, 14), 'Meat pie',     3),
    (date(2025, 7, 14), 'Apple juice', 5),
    (date(2025, 7, 14), 'Salad roll',  2),
    (date(2025, 7, 15), 'Meat pie',     4),
    (date(2025, 7, 15), 'Sausage roll',7),
    (date(2025, 7, 15), 'Apple juice', 3),
    (date(2025, 7, 16), 'Salad roll',  6),
    (date(2025, 7, 16), 'Meat pie',     2),
    (date(2025, 7, 16), 'Sausage roll',4),
]

# Total units sold per item
item_totals = Counter()
daily_sales = defaultdict(Counter)

for day, item, qty in SALES:
    item_totals[item]      += qty
    daily_sales[day][item] += qty

print("=== Item Rankings ===")
for item, total in item_totals.most_common():
    print(f"  {item:<16} {total:>3} units")

print("\n=== Daily Breakdown ===")
for day in sorted(daily_sales):
    print(f"  {day.strftime('%A %d/%m')}:")
    for item, qty in daily_sales[day].most_common():
        print(f"    {item:<16} {qty}")
```

Output:

```
=== Item Rankings ===
  Sausage roll      11 units
  Apple juice        8 units
```

```
  Meat pie          9 units
  Salad roll        8 units

=== Daily Breakdown ===
  Monday 14/07:
    Apple juice      5
    Meat pie         3
    Salad roll       2
  Tuesday 15/07:
    Sausage roll     7
    Meat pie         4
    Apple juice      3
  Wednesday 16/07:
    Salad roll       6
    Sausage roll     4
    Meat pie         2
```

The collections types are the standard answer to a broad class of Python patterns. Whenever you find yourself writing boilerplate to initialise dictionary values, count occurrences, or manage a FIFO queue, the appropriate collections type almost certainly exists and is faster, more readable, and better tested than a hand-rolled solution.

5.5 itertools: Combinations, chain, islice, and groupby

The itertools module provides a collection of iterator-building functions that operate lazily — they produce values one at a time rather than constructing entire sequences in memory. This makes them efficient for large datasets and infinite sequences alike. The module is divided roughly into infinite iterators (count, cycle, repeat), finite iterators (chain, islice, compress, dropwhile, takewhile, zip_longest), and combinatorial iterators (combinations, permutations, product, combinations_with_replacement).

chain() flattens an arbitrary number of iterables into a single sequence without creating an intermediate list. islice() provides slicing for iterators that do not support the standard slice syntax. groupby() groups consecutive elements that share the same key function value — it works like SQL's GROUP BY but requires the input to be sorted by the same key first. These three functions appear in almost every non-trivial data-processing pipeline.

The combinatorial functions (combinations, permutations, product) generate mathematical sequences that would be tedious and error-prone to write manually. combinations('ABCD', 2) yields all 2-element combinations; permutations('ABCD', 2) yields all 2-element ordered arrangements; product([0,1], repeat=3) yields all 3-bit binary strings. These are indispensable for algorithm problems, quiz generators, and testing frameworks that need to enumerate all cases.

> **Note:** groupby() only groups consecutive equal-key elements. If the input is not sorted by the key, elements with the same key value that are separated in the sequence will appear as separate groups. Always sort the input by the groupby key before calling groupby().

Example 1 — Introduction

chain and islice for working with multiple iterables and lazy slicing.

```
import itertools

# — chain ──────────────────────────────────────
# Combine multiple lists without creating a merged list first
year9  = ['Aria', 'Ben', 'Cora']
```

```
year10 = ['Dev', 'Eva']
year11 = ['Finn', 'Grace', 'Hana', 'Ivan']

all_students = list(itertools.chain(year9, year10, year11))
print(f"All students: {all_students}")
print(f"Count: {len(all_students)}")

# chain.from_iterable when you have a list of lists
groups = [year9, year10, year11]
flat = list(itertools.chain.from_iterable(groups))
print(f"Flat (same): {flat}")

# — islice ──────────────────────────────────────
# Slice any iterable - useful for generators and file objects
def natural_numbers():
    """Infinite generator of natural numbers."""
    n = 1
    while True:
        yield n
        n += 1

# Take first 5, then the next 5 from the infinite stream
gen = natural_numbers()
first_five = list(itertools.islice(gen, 5))
next_five  = list(itertools.islice(gen, 5))
print(f"First five: {first_five}")
print(f"Next five : {next_five}")
```

Output:

```
All students: ['Aria', 'Ben', 'Cora', 'Dev', 'Eva', 'Finn', 'Grace', 'Hana',
'Ivan']
Count: 9
Flat (same): ['Aria', 'Ben', 'Cora', 'Dev', 'Eva', 'Finn', 'Grace', 'Hana',
'Ivan']
First five: [1, 2, 3, 4, 5]
Next five : [6, 7, 8, 9, 10]
```

Example 2 — Variation

groupby for summarising sorted data, and combinatorial functions for generating test cases.

```
import itertools

# — groupby ──────────────────────────────────────
# Group students by year level - MUST be sorted by key first
students = [
    ('Aria', 10), ('Ben', 9), ('Cora', 10),
    ('Dev',  9),  ('Eva', 11),('Finn', 9),
]
students.sort(key=lambda s: s[1])    # sort by year level

for year, group in itertools.groupby(students, key=lambda s: s[1]):
    names = [s[0] for s in group]
    print(f"Year {year}: {names}")

# — combinations, permutations, product ──────────────
subjects = ['Maths', 'English', 'Science']

# All 2-subject combinations (order does not matter)
print("\n2-subject combinations:")
for combo in itertools.combinations(subjects, 2):
    print(f"  {combo[0]} + {combo[1]}")

# All ordered pairs (for round-robin scheduling)
```

```
print("\nRound-robin matchups:")
teams = ['Brisbane', 'Sydney', 'Melbourne']
for a, b in itertools.permutations(teams, 2):
    print(f"  {a} vs {b}")

# Cartesian product - all combinations of two attributes
colours = ['Red', 'Blue']
sizes   = ['S', 'M', 'L']
print("\nShirt variants:")
for colour, size in itertools.product(colours, sizes):
    print(f"  {colour} {size}")
```

Output:

```
Year 9: ['Ben', 'Dev', 'Finn']
Year 10: ['Aria', 'Cora']
Year 11: ['Eva']

2-subject combinations:
  Maths + English
  Maths + Science
  English + Science

Round-robin matchups:
  Brisbane vs Sydney
  Brisbane vs Melbourne
  Sydney vs Brisbane
  Sydney vs Melbourne
  Melbourne vs Brisbane
  Melbourne vs Sydney

Shirt variants:
  Red S
  Red M
  Red L
  Blue S
  Blue M
  Blue L
```

Example 3 — Real-world application

A lazy data-processing pipeline using chain, islice, and groupby to analyse a school attendance log.

```
import itertools
from collections import namedtuple

Record = namedtuple('Record', ['date', 'student', 'status'])

# Simulated attendance records (would normally come from a file)
ATTENDANCE = [
    Record('2025-07-14', 'Aria',  'Present'),
    Record('2025-07-14', 'Ben',   'Absent'),
    Record('2025-07-14', 'Cora',  'Present'),
    Record('2025-07-15', 'Aria',  'Present'),
    Record('2025-07-15', 'Ben',   'Present'),
    Record('2025-07-15', 'Cora',  'Absent'),
    Record('2025-07-16', 'Aria',  'Absent'),
    Record('2025-07-16', 'Ben',   'Present'),
    Record('2025-07-16', 'Cora',  'Present'),
]

# Sort records by date, then group by date
sorted_records = sorted(ATTENDANCE, key=lambda r: r.date)

print("Daily Attendance Summary:")
for day, group in itertools.groupby(sorted_records, key=lambda r: r.date):
```

```
        day_records = list(group)
        present = sum(1 for r in day_records if r.status == 'Present')
        absent  = sum(1 for r in day_records if r.status == 'Absent')
        print(f"  {day}  Present: {present}  Absent: {absent}")

# Use islice to preview just the first 2 records from each day
print("\nFirst 2 records per day (preview):")
for day, group in itertools.groupby(sorted_records, key=lambda r: r.date):
    preview = list(itertools.islice(group, 2))
    print(f"  {day}: {[r.student for r in preview]}")
```

Output:

```
Daily Attendance Summary:
  2025-07-14  Present: 2  Absent: 1
  2025-07-15  Present: 2  Absent: 1
  2025-07-16  Present: 2  Absent: 1

First 2 records per day (preview):
  2025-07-14: ['Aria', 'Ben']
  2025-07-15: ['Aria', 'Ben']
  2025-07-16: ['Aria', 'Ben']
```

The itertools functions are composable: the output of chain() can be fed directly into groupby(), and the output of groupby() can be fed into islice(). Building up a pipeline of lazy iterators this way processes arbitrarily large datasets with constant memory usage — the data flows through one element at a time rather than being materialised all at once.

functools: partial, lru_cache, reduce, and wraps

The functools module provides higher-order functions — tools for working with and transforming other functions. It is the standard library's contribution to functional programming in Python, complementing the built-ins map(), filter(), and zip(). (See Chapter 14 of Think, Code, Create for lambda functions and closures, which pair naturally with functools.)

partial() fixes some arguments of a function, producing a new callable with a shorter signature. This is more readable than wrapping a function in a lambda purely to pin an argument. lru_cache() is a decorator that caches the return value of a function based on its arguments, so repeated calls with the same arguments return the cached result without re-executing the function body. For computationally expensive or frequently repeated calculations — especially recursive ones — lru_cache is one of the highest-value optimisations available in the standard library.

reduce() applies a binary function cumulatively to a sequence, reducing it to a single value. It is the generalised form of sum(), min(), and max(), and is used when the accumulation logic is more complex than those built-ins support. wraps() is used inside decorator definitions to preserve the __name__, __doc__, and other metadata of the wrapped function, ensuring that tools like help() and debuggers show the original function's information rather than the wrapper's.

> **Note:** lru_cache requires that all function arguments be hashable, because it uses a tuple of the arguments as the cache key. Functions that accept lists, dicts, or other mutable types cannot be decorated with lru_cache directly — convert them to tuples or frozensets before calling the cached function.

Example 1 — Introduction

partial() fixing arguments to create specialised functions from a general one.

```
from functools import partial
```

```
def format_score(score, subject, width=6):
    """Format a score for display."""
    return f'{subject:<12} {score:>{width}.1f}'

# partial: fix 'subject' to create subject-specific formatters
fmt_maths   = partial(format_score, subject='Maths')
fmt_english = partial(format_score, subject='English')
fmt_science = partial(format_score, subject='Science', width=8)

scores = [('Maths', 87.5), ('English', 74.0), ('Science', 91.25)]
formatters = {'Maths': fmt_maths, 'English': fmt_english, 'Science':
fmt_science}

for subject, score in scores:
    print(formatters[subject](score))

# partial with built-in functions
import os
# Create a path-builder rooted at a specific directory
data_path = partial(os.path.join, '/home/student/data')
print(data_path("students", "records.csv"))
print(data_path("reports", "term3.txt"))
```

Output:

```
Maths          87.5
English        74.0
Science          91.2
/home/student/data/students/records.csv
/home/student/data/reports/term3.txt
```

Example 2 — Variation

lru_cache memoising a recursive Fibonacci function and a slow database-lookup simulation.

```
from functools import lru_cache
import time

# ── Classic example: memoised Fibonacci ──────────────────
@lru_cache(maxsize=None)    # unlimited cache
def fib(n):
    """Return the nth Fibonacci number (memoised)."""
    if n <= 1: return n
    return fib(n - 1) + fib(n - 2)

# Without cache: fib(35) makes ~29 million calls.
# With cache: each value is computed exactly once.
start = time.perf_counter()
result = fib(50)
elapsed = time.perf_counter() - start
print(f"fib(50) = {result}  ({elapsed*1000:.3f} ms)")
print(f"Cache info: {fib.cache_info()}")

# ── Practical example: caching a slow lookup ──────────
@lru_cache(maxsize=128)
def get_year_group(year_level):
    """Simulate a slow lookup (e.g. database call)."""
    time.sleep(0.05)   # simulated delay
    groups = {7:'Junior',8:'Junior',9:'Middle',
              10:'Middle',11:'Senior',12:'Senior'}
    return groups.get(year_level, 'Unknown')

# First calls are slow; repeated calls are instant
levels = [9, 10, 11, 9, 10, 11, 12, 9]
```

```
start = time.perf_counter()
for lv in levels:
    get_year_group(lv)   # only unique values hit the 'database'
elapsed = time.perf_counter() - start
print(f"8 lookups (4 unique): {elapsed*1000:.0f} ms
{get_year_group.cache_info()}")
```

Output:

```
fib(50) = 12586269025  (0.052 ms)
Cache info: CacheInfo(hits=48, misses=51, maxsize=None, currsize=51)
8 lookups (4 unique): 200 ms  CacheInfo(hits=4, misses=4, maxsize=128,
currsize=4)
```

Example 3 — Real-world application

reduce for complex accumulation, and wraps for a decorator that preserves function metadata.

```
from functools import reduce, wraps
import time

# ── reduce ───────────────────────────────────────────────
# Compute a weighted average where each subject has a different weight
results = [
    ('Maths',   88, 0.40),    # (subject, score, weight)
    ('English', 74, 0.30),
    ('Science', 91, 0.20),
    ('Art',     79, 0.10),
]

# reduce to accumulate weighted sum; separate reduce for total weight
weighted_sum  = reduce(lambda acc, r: acc + r[1] * r[2], results, 0.0)
total_weight  = reduce(lambda acc, r: acc + r[2],        results, 0.0)
weighted_avg  = weighted_sum / total_weight
print(f"Weighted average: {weighted_avg:.2f}")

# ── wraps ───────────────────────────────────────────────
# A timing decorator that preserves the wrapped function's metadata
def timed(func):
    """Decorator: print execution time of the wrapped function."""
    @wraps(func)   # without this, func.__name__ would be 'wrapper'
    def wrapper(*args, **kwargs):
        start  = time.perf_counter()
        result = func(*args, **kwargs)
        elapsed = time.perf_counter() - start
        print(f"  {func.__name__} took {elapsed*1000:.2f} ms")
        return result
    return wrapper

@timed
def load_records(filepath):
    """Load student records from a CSV file (simulated)."""
    time.sleep(0.02)   # simulated I/O delay
    return [{'name': 'Aria', 'score': 88}, {'name': 'Ben', 'score': 74}]

records = load_records('students.csv')
# wraps ensures these show the original function's metadata
print(f"Function name: {load_records.__name__}")
print(f"Docstring    : {load_records.__doc__.strip()}")
```

Output:

```
Weighted average: 83.50
  load_records took 20.14 ms
Function name: load_records
Docstring    : Load student records from a CSV file (simulated).
```

functools is one of the most practical modules in the standard library because it directly supports the patterns that experienced Python developers reach for daily: fixing arguments to create reusable callables, caching expensive computations, and building decorators that behave transparently. Learning these four functions pays dividends in almost every non-trivial Python project.

5.7 pathlib, shutil, and tempfile: File System Utilities

The pathlib module, introduced in Python 3.4, provides an object-oriented interface to file system paths. A Path object is not just a string — it understands path components, supports the / operator for joining paths, and has methods for reading and writing files, checking existence, iterating directory contents, and manipulating extensions and stems. It is the modern replacement for most of the os.path functions covered in Section 5.1. (Book 02, Chapter 9 covered pathlib in the context of file system navigation; this section goes deeper into reading, writing, and bulk file operations.)

The shutil module provides high-level file operations: copying a file or directory tree, moving or renaming files, deleting an entire directory tree, creating and extracting archives. These operations are not provided by os, which deals in low-level single-file and single-directory operations. shutil.copy() copies file content and permissions; shutil.copytree() recursively copies a directory; shutil.rmtree() deletes a directory and all its contents. These are the standard tools for build systems, deployment scripts, and file organisation utilities.

The tempfile module creates temporary files and directories that are guaranteed not to conflict with existing names and can be cleaned up automatically. NamedTemporaryFile and TemporaryDirectory are context managers: on exit from the with block, the temporary file or directory is deleted. This is essential for any program that needs scratch space without polluting the user's file system.

> **Note:** shutil.rmtree() deletes everything inside a directory without asking for confirmation. There is no undo. Always verify the path before calling it — a bug that constructs the wrong path can delete important data. Consider calling shutil.rmtree() only on paths that were themselves created by your program, such as temporary build directories.

Example 1 — Introduction

pathlib.Path for reading, writing, and inspecting files using the object-oriented API.

```
from pathlib import Path

# Create a Path object — the / operator joins path segments
data_dir = Path('data')
report   = data_dir / 'reports' / 'term3.txt'

print(f"Path      : {report}")
print(f"Parent    : {report.parent}")
print(f"Name      : {report.name}")
print(f"Stem      : {report.stem}")
print(f"Suffix    : {report.suffix}")
print(f"Exists?   : {report.exists()}")

# Write and read text with Path methods
tmp = Path('temp_demo.txt')
tmp.write_text("Line 1\nLine 2\nLine 3\n", encoding="utf-8")
print(f"Written   : {tmp.stat().st_size} bytes")

content = tmp.read_text(encoding='utf-8')
for i, line in enumerate(content.splitlines(), 1):
```

```
    print(f"  [{i}] {line}")

# List .txt files in the current directory
txts = list(Path('.').glob('*.txt'))
print(f"TXT files: {[p.name for p in txts]}")

tmp.unlink()   # delete the temp file
```

Output:

```
Path      : data/reports/term3.txt
Parent    : data/reports
Name      : term3.txt
Stem      : term3
Suffix    : .txt
Exists?   : False
Written   : 21 bytes
  [1] Line 1
  [2] Line 2
  [3] Line 3
TXT files: ['temp_demo.txt']
```

Example 2 — Variation

shutil for copying, moving, and archiving a directory of student reports.

```
import shutil
from pathlib import Path

# Create a sample directory structure to work with
src = Path('reports_src')
src.mkdir(exist_ok=True)
for name in ['term1.txt', 'term2.txt', 'term3.txt']:
    (src / name).write_text(f'Report: {name}', encoding='utf-8')

# Copy a single file
shutil.copy(src / 'term1.txt', 'term1_backup.txt')
print("Copied term1.txt to term1_backup.txt")

# Copy entire directory tree
dst = Path('reports_dst')
if dst.exists():
    shutil.rmtree(dst)
shutil.copytree(src, dst)
print(f"Copied tree: {[p.name for p in dst.iterdir()]}")

# Move (rename) a file
shutil.move(str(dst / 'term1.txt'), str(dst / 'term1_final.txt'))
print(f"After move: {sorted(p.name for p in dst.iterdir())}")

# Create a zip archive of the reports
archive = shutil.make_archive('reports_archive', 'zip', src)
print(f"Archive: {Path(archive).name}  ({Path(archive).stat().st_size} bytes)")

# Cleanup
shutil.rmtree(src)
shutil.rmtree(dst)
Path('term1_backup.txt').unlink()
Path('reports_archive.zip').unlink()
```

Output:

```
Copied term1.txt to term1_backup.txt
Copied tree: ['term1.txt', 'term2.txt', 'term3.txt']
After move: ['term1_final.txt', 'term2.txt', 'term3.txt']
Archive: reports_archive.zip  (642 bytes)
```

Example 3 — Real-world application

A report-processing pipeline that uses tempfile for scratch space and pathlib for all path operations.

```
import tempfile
import shutil
from pathlib import Path

def process_reports(source_dir, output_dir):
    """
    Process all .txt reports in source_dir:
    — Count words in each report
    — Save a summary to output_dir
    Uses a temporary directory for intermediate work.
    """
    source = Path(source_dir)
    output = Path(output_dir)
    output.mkdir(parents=True, exist_ok=True)

    with tempfile.TemporaryDirectory() as tmpdir:
        tmp = Path(tmpdir)
        print(f"Using temp dir: {tmp}")

        # Copy source files into temp dir for safe processing
        for report in source.glob('*.txt'):
            shutil.copy(report, tmp / report.name)

        # Process each copied file
        summaries = []
        for report in sorted(tmp.glob('*.txt')):
            text  = report.read_text(encoding='utf-8')
            words = len(text.split())
            lines = len(text.splitlines())
            summaries.append(f'{report.stem:<20} {words:>5} words  {lines:>3}
lines')

        # Write summary to output directory
        summary_path = output / 'processing_summary.txt'
        summary_text = 'Report Processing Summary\n' + '='*40 + '\n'
        summary_text += '\n'.join(summaries)
        summary_path.write_text(summary_text, encoding='utf-8')
        print(f"Summary written to {summary_path}")

    # TemporaryDirectory deleted automatically when with block exits
    print("Temp dir cleaned up.")
    return summary_path

# Demonstration with inline data
demo_src = Path('demo_reports')
demo_src.mkdir(exist_ok=True)
(demo_src/'maths_report.txt').write_text('This is the maths report. It covers
algebra and geometry.', encoding='utf-8')
(demo_src/'english_report.txt').write_text('The English report discusses
creative writing and grammar skills.', encoding='utf-8')

result = process_reports('demo_reports', 'output')
print(result.read_text(encoding='utf-8'))

shutil.rmtree('demo_reports')
shutil.rmtree('output')
```

Output:

```
Using temp dir: /tmp/tmpX7k2mN
Summary written to output/processing_summary.txt
Temp dir cleaned up.
```

```
Report Processing Summary
========================================
english_report           10 words    1 lines
maths_report              9 words    1 lines
```

The combination of pathlib, shutil, and tempfile covers the full range of file-system tasks a Python program typically needs: reading and writing individual files, copying and moving files in bulk, archiving and extracting, and managing temporary scratch space. Together with the os module from Section 5.1, they give you a complete, portable file-system toolkit without reaching for any third-party library.

Chapter 6 shifts from code organisation and standard library tools to the Python environment itself: virtual environments — isolated workspaces that keep each project's dependencies separate from the system Python and from each other.

Chapter 5 Summary

- The os module provides portable access to the operating system: current working directory, environment variables, file path construction, and process information. sys exposes the interpreter's runtime state (argv, path, version). platform provides hardware and OS detection for cross-platform code.
- math provides single-value mathematical functions (sqrt, log, ceil, floor, trig) and constants (pi, e, tau). statistics operates on sequences, providing mean, median, mode, stdev, variance, and correlation. random generates pseudo-random numbers; use secrets for cryptographic purposes.
- datetime.date, datetime.datetime, and datetime.timedelta cover date creation, arithmetic, and formatting. calendar provides leap-year testing, days-in-month, and calendar generation. zoneinfo (Python 3.9+) gives access to the IANA time zone database for timezone-aware datetimes.
- collections provides specialised containers: Counter for frequency counting with arithmetic, defaultdict for missing-key handling, namedtuple for lightweight named records, deque for O(1) double-ended operations and bounded sliding windows, and OrderedDict for order-sensitive dict comparisons.
- itertools produces lazy iterators: chain flattens multiple iterables, islice slices any iterator, groupby groups consecutive equal-key elements (requires sorted input), and the combinatorial functions — combinations, permutations, product — generate mathematical sequences without manual loops.
- functools provides higher-order tools: partial fixes arguments to create specialised callables, lru_cache memoises function results by argument for significant performance gains on repeated calls, reduce applies a binary function cumulatively, and wraps preserves wrapped function metadata in decorators.
- pathlib.Path provides an object-oriented file-system interface: path construction with /, reading and writing with read_text/write_text, globbing with glob/rglob, and inspection with stat/exists/is_file. shutil handles bulk operations: copy, copytree, move, rmtree, and make_archive.
- tempfile.TemporaryDirectory and NamedTemporaryFile are context managers that create scratch space guaranteed to be cleaned up when the with block exits, making them the safe choice for any program that needs temporary storage without polluting the user's file system.

Guided Exercises

1. Write a script that uses os and sys to print a formatted environment report: Python version, current working directory, number of entries in sys.path, all environment variables whose names start with 'PYTHON', and whether a data/ directory exists in the current working directory (creating it if not). Run it from two different directories and observe how the output changes.

Hint: Use os.environ.items() to iterate over all environment variables, and filter with key.startswith('PYTHON'). Use os.path.isdir('data') to check existence and os.makedirs('data', exist_ok=True) to create it.

2. Create a school assessment statistics tool. Given a dict mapping student names to lists of scores (at least 5 students, 4 scores each), compute and print a formatted table showing: mean, median, standard deviation, and the highest and lowest score for each student. At the bottom, print the overall cohort mean, correlation between student number and mean score (to simulate a class-position effect), and a count of students within one standard deviation of the cohort mean.

Hint: Use statistics.mean, statistics.median, statistics.stdev, and statistics.correlation. For the cohort-mean check, compute the cohort mean and stdev across all scores pooled together, then count each student whose individual mean falls within cohort_mean ± cohort_stdev.

3. Build a term planner using the datetime and calendar modules. Given a term start date, an end date, and a list of public holidays (as date objects), write functions that: (a) return all school days (Monday–Friday excluding holidays) as a sorted list; (b) return all weeks in the term as a list of (week_number, [school_days]) tuples; (c) print a formatted week-by-week calendar showing the week number, dates, and a note for any holiday. Test with Queensland Term 3 2025 (14 July – 19 September) and at least two public holidays.

Hint: Use a while loop incrementing by timedelta(days=1). Check weekday() < 5 for Mon–Fri. Store holidays in a set for O(1) lookup. Group into weeks by tracking when the weekday resets to Monday.

4. Use itertools to build a round-robin sports fixture generator. Given a list of team names, generate a complete fixture list where every team plays every other team exactly once at home and once away (i.e., all ordered pairs). Group the fixtures into rounds using itertools.islice so that each round contains n//2 matches (where n is the number of teams). Print each round with the home team and away team clearly labelled.

Hint: Use itertools.permutations(teams, 2) for all ordered pairs. To divide into rounds of size n//2, use a loop with itertools.islice on the iterator. Consider that a valid round-robin requires that no team appears twice in the same round — a full balanced round-robin algorithm is not required; grouping by slice is sufficient.

5. Write a directory backup utility using pathlib and shutil. The function backup(source_dir, backup_root) should: create a timestamped subdirectory inside backup_root (format: YYYYMMDD_HHMMSS), copy all files from source_dir into it (non-recursive), then create a .zip archive of the subdirectory using shutil.make_archive. Print a summary showing how many files were backed up, the archive path, and its size in KB. Use tempfile.TemporaryDirectory to test the function without touching the real file system.

Hint: Use datetime.now().strftime('%Y%m%d_%H%M%S') for the timestamp. Use Path.glob('*') with p.is_file() to find files. shutil.make_archive(base_name, 'zip', root_dir) creates the archive. The base_name should not include the .zip extension.

Challenge Tasks

1. Build a complete school timetable generator. The generator should: accept a list of subjects and a list of teachers (as namedtuples), use itertools.product to generate all valid (subject, teacher) pairings, then use random.sample to select one pairing per period (6 periods over 5 days = 30 periods total, ensuring no subject or teacher appears twice in the same day). Output the timetable as a formatted grid using the datetime and calendar modules to label each day with its date (starting from a given

Monday). Use functools.lru_cache to memoise any repeated day-label formatting calls. The timetable must be printed cleanly to the terminal with aligned columns.

2. Write a log file analyser using pathlib, itertools, and collections. The analyser should: accept a directory path and a date range (as date objects); use pathlib.Path.glob to find all .log files; use itertools.chain.from_iterable to lazily combine lines from all files without loading everything into memory; parse each line assuming the format YYYY-MM-DD HH:MM:SS LEVEL message; filter to the date range; use collections.Counter to count messages per log level (INFO, WARNING, ERROR); use itertools.groupby to group messages by date and level; and print a formatted daily summary table plus a bar chart of level frequencies (using ASCII block characters). Test with at least three simulated log files covering five days.

3. Create a data pipeline package called pipeline/ using the package structure from Chapter 4, with the following stages implemented as separate modules: pipeline/extract.py (reads CSV data from a directory using pathlib.glob, returns records as namedtuples), pipeline/transform.py (uses functools.reduce and collections.defaultdict to aggregate scores by student and compute statistics using the statistics module), pipeline/load.py (writes a summary CSV and a JSON manifest to an output directory using pathlib), and pipeline/report.py (uses itertools.groupby and collections.Counter to build a formatted console report). pipeline/__init__.py should expose a single run(source_dir, output_dir) function that chains all four stages. Include a __main__ guard in each module for standalone testing, and write a main.py that calls pipeline.run() with sample data.

CHAPTER 6 Virtual Environments

Book 03: Modules, Packages & the Python Ecosystem

> Every chapter so far has assumed that import works — that the modules you need are findable on sys.path and that your project's dependencies do not conflict with anyone else's. In practice, that assumption breaks the moment you work on more than one Python project at a time. Project A needs version 1.x of a library; Project B needs version 2.x; the system Python can hold only one. Virtual environments solve this problem by giving each project its own isolated Python installation with its own site-packages directory. This chapter covers everything you need to create, activate, populate, and reproduce virtual environments using Python's built-in venv module, the pip package manager, and the modern alternatives pipenv and poetry. By the end you will have a repeatable workflow for setting up any Python project from scratch with its dependencies precisely recorded and reproducible.

6.1 What Is a Virtual Environment and Why It Matters

When Python installs a third-party package, it places it in a directory called site-packages inside the Python installation. On a system with a single Python installation, every project shares the same site-packages. That means installing a newer version of a library for one project can silently break another project that depends on the older version. This is the dependency conflict problem, and it is the reason virtual environments exist.

A virtual environment is a self-contained directory tree that contains a Python interpreter, a pip executable, and its own site-packages directory, entirely separate from the system Python. When you activate a virtual environment, your shell's PATH is modified so that python and pip point into the environment's directory rather than the system installation. Every package you install goes into that environment's site-packages, leaving the system Python completely untouched.

The isolation cuts both ways: packages installed in the system Python are not visible inside the virtual environment (unless you pass --system-site-packages when creating it), and packages installed inside the environment are not visible to the system Python or to other environments. Each project gets a clean slate. This makes dependency conflicts impossible between projects and makes the environment's exact package set easy to capture and reproduce.

> **Note:** Never install third-party packages with pip into the system Python on macOS or Linux. Modern operating systems increasingly ship scripts that depend on specific versions of Python packages; pip-installing into system Python can break those scripts. Always work inside a virtual environment.

Example 1 — Introduction

Inspecting sys.path and sys.executable inside and outside a virtual environment to see what isolation means concretely.

```
# Run this script OUTSIDE a virtual environment (system Python)
import sys

print("=== System Python ===")
print(f"Executable : {sys.executable}")
print(f"Version    : {sys.version.split()[0]}")
print(f"site-pkgs  : {[p for p in sys.path if 'site-packages' in p]}")
```

```
# Now create and activate a virtual environment, then run again:
#   python -m venv .venv
#   source .venv/bin/activate           # macOS / Linux
#   .venv\Scripts\activate              # Windows
#   python inspect_env.py

# Inside the venv the output changes to:
# === Virtual Environment ===
# Executable : /home/student/myproject/.venv/bin/python
# Version    : 3.12.3
# site-pkgs  : ['/home/student/myproject/.venv/lib/python3.12/site-packages']

# The executable and site-packages path both point INSIDE .venv/
# — completely separate from the system installation.
```

Output:

```
=== System Python ===
Executable : /usr/bin/python3
Version    : 3.12.3
site-pkgs  : ['/usr/lib/python3/dist-packages',
              '/usr/local/lib/python3.12/dist-packages']
```

Example 2 — Variation

A concrete demonstration of the dependency conflict problem that virtual environments prevent.

```
# Scenario: two projects need incompatible versions of the same library.
#
# project_a/  — requires requests==2.28.0
# project_b/  — requires requests==2.31.0
#
# Without virtual environments:
#   pip install requests==2.28.0   # installs for project_a
#   pip install requests==2.31.0   # overwrites — project_a now broken
#
# With virtual environments:
#   cd project_a
#   python -m venv .venv
#   source .venv/bin/activate
#   pip install requests==2.28.0   # installed in project_a/.venv only
#   deactivate
#
#   cd ../project_b
#   python -m venv .venv
#   source .venv/bin/activate
#   pip install requests==2.31.0   # installed in project_b/.venv only
#
# Each project has exactly the version it needs.
# Changing one environment has zero effect on the other.

# Python code to confirm the isolation at runtime:
import importlib.metadata
try:
    ver = importlib.metadata.version('requests')
    print(f"requests version in this environment: {ver}")
except importlib.metadata.PackageNotFoundError:
    print("requests is not installed in this environment")
```

Output:

```
# In project_a's venv:
requests version in this environment: 2.28.0

# In project_b's venv:
requests version in this environment: 2.31.0
```

Example 3 — Real-world application

A diagnostic script that reports whether the current Python process is running inside a virtual environment and prints a summary of the active environment.

```
import sys
import os
from pathlib import Path

def check_environment():
    """Report whether the current Python is in a virtual environment."""
    # sys.base_prefix is the original Python installation.
    # sys.prefix is the active prefix — same as base_prefix when no
    # venv is active, different when inside a venv.
    in_venv = sys.prefix != sys.base_prefix

    if in_venv:
        venv_path = Path(sys.prefix)
        print("Virtual environment: ACTIVE")
        print(f"  Path      : {venv_path}")
        print(f"  Python    : {sys.executable}")
        # The VIRTUAL_ENV environment variable is set by activate
        venv_name = os.environ.get('VIRTUAL_ENV', str(venv_path))
        print(f"  Name      : {Path(venv_name).name}")
        # Count installed packages
        import importlib.metadata
        packages = list(importlib.metadata.packages_distributions())
        print(f"  Packages  : {len(packages)} installed")
    else:
        print("Virtual environment: NOT ACTIVE")
        print(f"  Using system Python: {sys.executable}")
        print("  Recommendation: activate a venv before installing packages.")

check_environment()
```

Output:

```
# When active:
Virtual environment: ACTIVE
  Path      : /home/student/srs_project/.venv
  Python    : /home/student/srs_project/.venv/bin/python
  Name      : .venv
  Packages  : 12 installed

# When not active:
Virtual environment: NOT ACTIVE
  Using system Python: /usr/bin/python3
  Recommendation: activate a venv before installing packages.
```

The check_environment() function is worth adding to the startup code of any script that requires specific packages. Running it at launch gives an immediate, clear message if the environment is not set up correctly, rather than a confusing ModuleNotFoundError several lines into execution.

6.2 Creating and Activating venvs with venv

Python's built-in venv module has been the standard tool for creating virtual environments since Python 3.3. It requires no installation and is available everywhere Python 3 is installed. The core workflow is three commands: create the environment, activate it, and deactivate it when you are done.

Creating a virtual environment copies (or symlinks) the Python interpreter into a new directory and sets up a fresh, empty site-packages. By convention the directory is named .venv (with a leading dot to signal that it is a project tool rather than source code) and lives at the project root. Some developers name it venv or env; the name does not matter to Python, but .venv is the most common convention and is recognised by default by many editors and CI systems.

Activation modifies the current shell session — specifically the PATH variable — so that python and pip resolve to the environment's copies. Deactivation reverses this change. Activation is shell-specific: the command is different on Windows Command Prompt, Windows PowerShell, macOS Terminal, and Linux bash/zsh. The venv module creates activation scripts for all these shells inside the environment's Scripts/ (Windows) or bin/ (macOS/Linux) directory.

> **Note:** Activation is a convenience, not a requirement. You can also run the environment's Python directly using its full path: .venv/bin/python script.py (macOS/Linux) or .venv\Scripts\python script.py (Windows). This is useful in automated scripts and CI pipelines where shell activation is awkward.

Example 1 — Introduction

Creating and activating a virtual environment: the complete workflow from terminal.

```
# — Step 1: Create the environment ──────────────────────────
# Run from your project directory
python -m venv .venv

# What this creates:
# .venv/
#   bin/              (macOS/Linux) or Scripts/ (Windows)
#     python         — copy or symlink of the Python interpreter
#     pip            — pip for this environment only
#     activate       — shell activation script
#   lib/
#     python3.12/
#       site-packages/   — where packages will be installed
#   pyvenv.cfg       — records the Python version and base prefix

# — Step 2: Activate ─────────────────────────────────────────
# macOS / Linux (bash or zsh):
source .venv/bin/activate

# Windows Command Prompt:
.venv\Scripts\activate.bat

# Windows PowerShell:
.venv\Scripts\Activate.ps1

# After activation, the prompt changes to show the venv name:
# (.venv) student@machine:~/srs_project$

# — Step 3: Verify ───────────────────────────────────────────
which python         # macOS/Linux: shows .venv/bin/python
where python         # Windows:     shows .venv\Scripts\python.exe
python --version     # confirms the venv's Python version

# — Step 4: Deactivate when done ─────────────────────────────
deactivate           # works on all platforms
```

Output:

```
# After source .venv/bin/activate:
(.venv) student@machine:~/srs_project$

# which python
/home/student/srs_project/.venv/bin/python

# python --version
```

```
Python 3.12.3

# After deactivate:
student@machine:~/srs_project$
```

Example 2 — Variation

Useful venv creation options: specifying a Python version, upgrading pip immediately, and creating without pip.

```
# ── Specify a Python version ──────────────────────────────────
# If multiple Python versions are installed, name the executable
python3.11 -m venv .venv-py311
python3.12 -m venv .venv-py312

# ── Upgrade pip immediately after creation ─────────────────────
# pip inside a new venv is often older than the latest release.
# The --upgrade-deps flag upgrades pip and setuptools automatically.
python -m venv .venv --upgrade-deps

# Or upgrade manually after activation:
python -m pip install --upgrade pip

# ── Create without pip (rare — for minimal environments) ───────
python -m venv .venv --without-pip

# ── Recreate a corrupted environment ───────────────────────────
# Delete and recreate from scratch; requirements.txt restores packages
rm -rf .venv              # macOS/Linux
rmdir /s /q .venv         # Windows
python -m venv .venv --upgrade-deps
pip install -r requirements.txt

# ── Check the pyvenv.cfg file that records the environment ─────
cat .venv/pyvenv.cfg
```

Output:

```
# pyvenv.cfg contents:
home = /usr/bin
include-system-site-packages = false
version = 3.12.3
executable = /usr/bin/python3.12
command = /usr/bin/python3.12 -m venv .venv
```

Example 3 — Real-world application

A project setup script that automates virtual environment creation and initial package installation.

```
#!/usr/bin/env python3
"""
setup_project.py — Automated project environment setup.

Run once after cloning a repository to create the venv and install
all dependencies from requirements.txt.

Usage: python setup_project.py
"""

import subprocess
import sys
from pathlib import Path

VENV_DIR    = Path('.venv')
REQ_FILE    = Path('requirements.txt')
```

```python
DEV_REQ     = Path('requirements-dev.txt')

def run(cmd, **kwargs):
    """Run a shell command, printing it first."""
    print(f"  $ {" ".join(cmd)}")
    subprocess.run(cmd, check=True, **kwargs)

def main():
    print("=== Project Setup ===")

    # 1. Create virtual environment
    if VENV_DIR.exists():
        print(f"  .venv already exists — skipping creation")
    else:
        print("Creating virtual environment...")
        run([sys.executable, '-m', 'venv', str(VENV_DIR), '--upgrade-deps'])

    # 2. Determine pip path (platform-aware)
    pip = VENV_DIR / ('Scripts/pip' if sys.platform == 'win32' else 'bin/pip')

    # 3. Install production dependencies
    if REQ_FILE.exists():
        print("Installing production dependencies...")
        run([str(pip), 'install', '-r', str(REQ_FILE)])
    else:
        print(f"  {REQ_FILE} not found — skipping")

    # 4. Install dev dependencies if present
    if DEV_REQ.exists():
        print("Installing development dependencies...")
        run([str(pip), 'install', '-r', str(DEV_REQ)])

    print("\nSetup complete.")
    if sys.platform == 'win32':
        print("  Activate with: .venv\\Scripts\\activate")
    else:
        print("  Activate with: source .venv/bin/activate")

if __name__ == '__main__':
    main()
```

Output:

```
=== Project Setup ===
Creating virtual environment...
  $ /usr/bin/python3 -m venv .venv --upgrade-deps
Installing production dependencies...
  $ .venv/bin/pip install -r requirements.txt
Successfully installed certifi-2024.2.2 charset-normalizer-3.3.2 ...
Installing development dependencies...
  $ .venv/bin/pip install -r requirements-dev.txt
Successfully installed iniconfig-2.0.0 pytest-8.1.1 ...

Setup complete.
  Activate with: source .venv/bin/activate
```

Automating environment setup with a script like this eliminates the most common onboarding failure mode: a new developer clones the repository and runs the main script, only to encounter a cascade of ModuleNotFoundError messages. One command creates the complete environment, and the project is immediately ready to run.

6.3 Installing Packages into a venv

With a virtual environment activated, pip install works exactly as it does without one — but packages are installed into the environment's site-packages rather than the system Python's. The pip executable that comes with the venv is a standard pip; every command and flag works identically. The only difference is the destination of what gets installed.

The most common pip commands are: pip install <package> to install the latest version, pip install <package>==<version> to install a specific version, pip install --upgrade <package> to upgrade to the latest, pip uninstall <package> to remove, pip list to show all installed packages, and pip show <package> to display detailed information about a specific one. Each command operates on the active environment only.

pip can install packages from several sources beyond PyPI: a local directory containing a setup.py or pyproject.toml (pip install ./mypackage), a Git repository URL (pip install git+https://github.com/user/repo), a wheel file (.whl), or a local .tar.gz archive. The flexibility makes pip useful not only for published packages but also for in-development packages and corporate packages hosted on private indexes.

> **Note:** pip install with no version specifier installs the latest available version. This is convenient but means that running the same command on two different dates may produce different results. For reproducible environments, always pin versions in requirements.txt (covered in Section 6.4) rather than relying on pip install <name> alone.

Example 1 — Introduction

The essential pip commands for managing packages inside an active virtual environment.

```
# All commands assume the virtual environment is activated.

# ── Install a package (latest version) ──────────────────
pip install requests

# ── Install a specific version ──────────────────────────
pip install requests==2.31.0

# ── Install multiple packages at once ───────────────────
pip install requests flask jinja2

# ── Upgrade an existing package ─────────────────────────
pip install --upgrade requests

# ── Uninstall a package ─────────────────────────────────
pip uninstall requests
pip uninstall requests -y     # skip the confirmation prompt

# ── List installed packages ─────────────────────────────
pip list

# ── Show details about a package ────────────────────────
pip show requests

# ── Check for outdated packages ─────────────────────────
pip list --outdated
```

Output:

```
# pip install requests
Collecting requests
  Downloading requests-2.31.0-py3-none-any.whl (62 kB)
```

```
Installing collected packages: certifi, charset-normalizer,
  idna, urllib3, requests
Successfully installed certifi-2024.2.2 ...

# pip show requests
Name: requests
Version: 2.31.0
Summary: Python HTTP for Humans.
Home-page: https://requests.readthedocs.io
Author: Kenneth Reitz
Location: /home/student/project/.venv/lib/python3.12/site-packages
Requires: certifi, charset-normalizer, idna, urllib3
Required-by:
```

Example 2 — Variation

Using pip from Python code — useful in setup scripts and CI pipelines that run without an activated shell.

```
# pip can be invoked programmatically via subprocess.
# This is the recommended approach when you cannot activate a venv
# in a shell script (e.g., in a Python-driven CI pipeline).

import subprocess
import sys
from pathlib import Path

def pip_install(packages, venv_dir='.venv'):
    """Install packages into the named venv using its pip."""
    venv = Path(venv_dir)
    pip  = venv / ('Scripts/pip' if sys.platform == 'win32' else 'bin/pip')
    if not pip.exists():
        raise FileNotFoundError(f"pip not found: {pip}. Is the venv created?")
    cmd = [str(pip), 'install'] + list(packages)
    result = subprocess.run(cmd, capture_output=True, text=True)
    if result.returncode != 0:
        print(result.stderr)
        raise RuntimeError(f"pip install failed with code {result.returncode}")
    return result.stdout

def pip_list(venv_dir='.venv'):
    """Return a dict of {package_name: version} for the named venv."""
    venv = Path(venv_dir)
    pip  = venv / ('Scripts/pip' if sys.platform == 'win32' else 'bin/pip')
    result = subprocess.run([str(pip), 'list', '--format=json'],
                            capture_output=True, text=True, check=True)
    import json
    return {p['name']: p['version'] for p in json.loads(result.stdout)}

# Example usage (venv must already exist)
# output = pip_install(['requests', 'python-dateutil'])
# packages = pip_list()
# print({k: v for k, v in packages.items() if k in ['requests', 'pip']})
```

Output:

```
# pip_install(['requests'])
Successfully installed certifi-2024.2.2 requests-2.31.0 ...

# pip_list() — filtered output:
{'requests': '2.31.0', 'pip': '24.0'}
```

Example 3 — Real-world application

A dependency audit script that checks whether required packages are installed and at an acceptable version.

```python
"""
check_deps.py — Verify that all required dependencies are satisfied.

Run this at startup to catch missing or outdated packages early,
before the application reaches the code that needs them.
"""

import importlib.metadata
import sys
from packaging.version import Version    # pip install packaging

REQUIRED = {
    'requests': '2.28.0',
    'python-dateutil': '2.8.0',
    'colorama': '0.4.0',
}

def check_dependencies(required):
    """
    Verify each required package is installed at the minimum version.
    Returns (ok, list_of_problems).
    """
    problems = []
    for package, min_ver in required.items():
        try:
            installed = importlib.metadata.version(package)
            if Version(installed) < Version(min_ver):
                problems.append(
                    f'  {package}: need >={min_ver}, have {installed}'
                )
        except importlib.metadata.PackageNotFoundError:
            problems.append(f'  {package}: NOT INSTALLED')
    return len(problems) == 0, problems

def main():
    ok, problems = check_dependencies(REQUIRED)
    if ok:
        print("All dependencies satisfied.")
    else:
        print("Dependency problems found:")
        for p in problems:
            print(p)
        print("\nFix with: pip install -r requirements.txt")
        sys.exit(1)

if __name__ == '__main__':
    main()
```

Output:

```
# When all packages are present:
All dependencies satisfied.

# When a package is missing or outdated:
Dependency problems found:
  requests: need >=2.28.0, have 2.25.1
  colorama: NOT INSTALLED

Fix with: pip install -r requirements.txt
```

Running a dependency check at startup is particularly valuable in educational and team settings, where collaborators may have set up their environments at different times. The script above exits with a non-zero code when requirements are not met, which CI pipelines can detect and fail on — preventing broken builds from reaching production.

6.4 requirements.txt: Capturing and Reproducing Dependencies

A requirements.txt file is a plain text list of Python packages and their version specifiers. It is the standard way to record a project's dependencies so that another developer — or an automated deployment system — can recreate the exact same environment with a single command: pip install -r requirements.txt. The -r flag tells pip to read package names from the file.

There are two philosophies for what to put in requirements.txt. The first is to pin exact versions (requests==2.31.0), which guarantees that every installation produces byte-for-byte identical environments — important for production systems. The second is to specify minimum or compatible versions (requests>=2.28.0 or requests~=2.28), which allows pip to install newer compatible versions — useful for libraries that want to avoid unnecessarily restricting their users. Most applications use pinned versions; most libraries use version ranges.

The pip freeze command outputs the exact version of every package currently installed in the active environment in a format suitable for requirements.txt. Running pip freeze > requirements.txt captures a complete snapshot. The result includes all transitive dependencies — the dependencies of your dependencies — which is what you want for a fully reproducible environment. Many teams maintain two files: requirements.txt (pinned production dependencies) and requirements-dev.txt (additional tools used only during development, such as pytest and linters).

> **Note:** pip freeze includes every package in the environment, including packages you installed incidentally as dependencies of other packages. For a cleaner requirements.txt that only lists your direct dependencies, consider using pip-compile from the pip-tools package, or the lock-file functionality of pipenv or poetry (Section 6.6).

Example 1 — Introduction

Generating, reviewing, and using a requirements.txt file.

```
# — Generate from the current environment ————————————
pip freeze > requirements.txt

# — Contents of requirements.txt (example) ————————————
# certifi==2024.2.2
# charset-normalizer==3.3.2
# idna==3.7
# requests==2.31.0
# urllib3==2.2.1

# — Install from requirements.txt ————————————————
pip install -r requirements.txt

# — Upgrade all packages and regenerate ——————————————
pip install --upgrade -r requirements.txt
pip freeze > requirements.txt   # capture the new versions

# — Install with verbose output ————————————————
pip install -r requirements.txt -v

# — Check what is already satisfied vs what needs installing —
pip install -r requirements.txt --dry-run
```

Output:

```
# pip install -r requirements.txt
Collecting certifi==2024.2.2
```

```
  Using cached certifi-2024.2.2-py3-none-any.whl (164 kB)
Collecting requests==2.31.0
  Using cached requests-2.31.0-py3-none-any.whl (62 kB)
...
Successfully installed certifi-2024.2.2 charset-normalizer-3.3.2
  idna-3.7 requests-2.31.0 urllib3-2.2.1
```

Example 2 — Variation

A production requirements.txt with pinned versions, a development requirements-dev.txt, and version specifier syntax.

```
# ── requirements.txt — production dependencies (pinned) ──────
# Install with: pip install -r requirements.txt
requests==2.31.0
python-dateutil==2.9.0
colorama==0.4.6

# ── requirements-dev.txt — development-only tools ───────────
# Install with: pip install -r requirements-dev.txt
# Includes production deps by reference:
-r requirements.txt
pytest==8.1.1
pytest-cov==5.0.0
black==24.4.2
flake8==7.0.0
mypy==1.9.0

# ── Version specifier syntax ─────────────────────────────────
# Exact version (recommended for applications):
requests==2.31.0

# Minimum version (common in library requirements):
requests>=2.28.0

# Compatible release — same as >=2.28.0, ==2.*
requests~=2.28

# Range:
requests>=2.28.0,<3.0.0

# Latest (no specifier — use with caution):
requests
```

Output:

```
# File structure in a typical project:
srs_project/
  .venv/
  requirements.txt          <- pinned production packages
  requirements-dev.txt      <- dev tools + -r requirements.txt
  src/
    srs/
      ...
  tests/
    ...
```

Example 3 — Real-world application

A Python script that generates a human-readable dependency report from requirements.txt, showing each package's purpose and whether it is up to date.

```
"""
dep_report.py — Human-readable dependency audit.

Reads requirements.txt and for each package prints its installed
```

```
version, a brief description, and whether a newer version exists.
"""

import importlib.metadata
import subprocess
import sys
from pathlib import Path

DESCRIPTIONS = {
    'requests'        : 'HTTP library for making web requests',
    'python-dateutil' : 'Powerful extensions to the datetime module',
    'colorama'        : 'Cross-platform coloured terminal text',
    'pytest'          : 'Testing framework',
    'black'           : 'Code formatter',
    'flake8'          : 'Style guide enforcement tool',
}

def parse_requirements(path='requirements.txt'):
    """Return a list of (name, version_spec) tuples from requirements.txt."""
    lines = Path(path).read_text(encoding='utf-8').splitlines()
    packages = []
    for line in lines:
        line = line.strip()
        if not line or line.startswith('#') or line.startswith('-r'):
            continue
        # Split on ==, >=, ~=, etc. — take just the package name
        import re
        match = re.match(r'([A-Za-z0-9_\-]+)', line)
        if match:
            packages.append((match.group(1), line))
    return packages

def report(req_file='requirements.txt'):
    """Print a formatted dependency report."""
    print(f"Dependency Report: {req_file}")
    print("=" * 60)
    for name, spec in parse_requirements(req_file):
        try:
            ver = importlib.metadata.version(name)
            desc = DESCRIPTIONS.get(name, '(no description)')
            print(f"  {name:<25} {ver:<12} {desc}")
        except importlib.metadata.PackageNotFoundError:
            print(f"  {name:<25} NOT INSTALLED")
    print("=" * 60)

if __name__ == '__main__':
    req = sys.argv[1] if len(sys.argv) > 1 else 'requirements.txt'
    report(req)
```

Output:

```
Dependency Report: requirements.txt
============================================================
  requests                  2.31.0       HTTP library for making web requests
  python-dateutil           2.9.0        Powerful extensions to the datetime
module
  colorama                  0.4.6        Cross-platform coloured terminal text
============================================================
```

Maintaining two requirements files — one for production, one for development — is the single most effective practice for keeping a Python project manageable over time. It makes onboarding clear (run this one command), deployment reliable (exact versions are pinned), and the development/production boundary explicit.

.gitignore and venv: Keeping the Environment Out of Version Control

A virtual environment directory contains thousands of files — the Python interpreter, compiled C extension modules, wheel caches, and every installed package. It can easily reach several hundred megabytes. None of this should be committed to version control. The environment is a build artefact, not source code: it can always be recreated from requirements.txt. Committing it wastes repository space, slows git operations, and frequently causes conflicts when developers on different operating systems check out the same repository.

The solution is a .gitignore file at the project root that lists the venv directory. Git will then refuse to track any file inside it. The .gitignore file itself should be committed — it is project configuration, not a build artefact. The convention of naming the virtual environment .venv is convenient here because many templates and IDE configurations already include .venv in their default .gitignore entries.

Beyond the virtual environment, a Python project's .gitignore should also exclude: compiled Python bytecode (__pycache__/, *.pyc, *.pyo), build and distribution directories (build/, dist/, *.egg-info/), test coverage reports (.coverage, htmlcov/), editor configuration that is specific to individual developers (.idea/, .vscode/ unless the team agrees to share it), and any files containing secrets or credentials.

> **Note:** Even if you accidentally commit the venv directory, git rm -r --cached .venv will stop tracking it without deleting it from your local file system. Add .venv to .gitignore before running git rm --cached so it stays untracked after the remove.

Example 1 — Introduction

A complete .gitignore file for a Python project, with each section explained.

```
# .gitignore for a Python project

# ── Virtual environments ──────────────────────────────
.venv/
venv/
env/
.env/

# ── Python bytecode cache ─────────────────────────────
__pycache__/
*.py[cod]
*$py.class

# ── Distribution / packaging ──────────────────────────
build/
dist/
*.egg-info/
.eggs/

# ── Testing and coverage ──────────────────────────────
.pytest_cache/
.coverage
htmlcov/
.tox/

# ── Type checker caches ───────────────────────────────
.mypy_cache/
.pytype/

# ── IDE and editor files ──────────────────────────────
.idea/
```

```
.vscode/
*.sublime-project
*.sublime-workspace

# — OS-generated files ──────────────────────────────────────
.DS_Store
Thumbs.db

# — Secrets and credentials (never commit these) ─────────────
.env
*.pem
secrets.json
config.local.py
```

Output:

```
# After adding .gitignore:
# git status will no longer show .venv/, __pycache__/,
# or any other excluded file.

# Verify a file is ignored:
# git check-ignore -v .venv
# .gitignore:4:.venv/    .venv
```

Example 2 — Variation

Checking what Git is tracking, removing an accidentally committed venv, and verifying the result.

```
# Check whether .venv is currently tracked by git
git ls-files .venv
# If this outputs files, the venv has been committed — fix it:

# Step 1: Add .venv/ to .gitignore (if not already there)
echo '.venv/' >> .gitignore

# Step 2: Remove the venv from git's index without deleting local files
git rm -r --cached .venv

# Step 3: Commit the removal
git add .gitignore
git commit -m "Remove .venv from tracking; add to .gitignore"

# Step 4: Verify .venv is now ignored
git status
# .venv/ should NOT appear in the output

# — Useful git commands for checking ignore status ──────────
# List all files git is currently tracking:
git ls-files

# Check if a specific path is ignored and why:
git check-ignore -v somefile.txt

# Show all ignored files in the current directory:
git status --ignored
```

Output:

```
# After git rm -r --cached .venv && git commit:
$ git status
On branch main
nothing to commit, working tree clean

$ git check-ignore -v .venv
.gitignore:4:.venv/    .venv
```

Example 3 — Real-world application

A project health checker that verifies .gitignore is present and contains the essential Python exclusions.

```
"""
check_gitignore.py — Verify that the project .gitignore is correctly
configured.
"""

from pathlib import Path

REQUIRED_PATTERNS = [
    '.venv/',
    '__pycache__/',
    '*.pyc',
    '.env',
    '*.egg-info/',
]

def check_gitignore(root='.'):
    """Check that .gitignore exists and contains essential patterns."""
    gi_path = Path(root) / '.gitignore'

    if not gi_path.exists():
        print("FAIL: .gitignore not found. Create one before committing.")
        return False

    content = gi_path.read_text(encoding='utf-8')
    lines   = {line.strip() for line in content.splitlines()}

    all_ok  = True
    print("Checking .gitignore...")
    for pattern in REQUIRED_PATTERNS:
        if pattern in lines:
            print(f"  OK  {pattern}")
        else:
            print(f"  MISSING: {pattern}")
            all_ok = False

    if all_ok:
        print("\n.gitignore is correctly configured.")
    else:
        print("\nAdd missing patterns to .gitignore.")
    return all_ok

if __name__ == '__main__':
    check_gitignore()
```

Output:

```
Checking .gitignore...
  OK  .venv/
  OK  __pycache__/
  OK  *.pyc
  MISSING: .env
  OK  *.egg-info/

Add missing patterns to .gitignore.
```

A correct .gitignore is not optional housekeeping — it is the difference between a repository that is fast, portable, and secure, and one that is bloated with build artefacts and at risk of exposing credentials. Set it up at project creation and check it into the repository in the first commit, before you install any packages.

6.5 pipenv and poetry: Modern Dependency Tools

Python's venv + pip workflow is powerful but requires manual coordination: create the environment, activate it, install packages, run pip freeze, commit requirements.txt. Two tools — pipenv and poetry — automate this coordination and add deterministic dependency resolution that plain pip lacks.

pipenv

pipenv combines venv and pip into one tool. It maintains two files: Pipfile (human-readable, with package names and version constraints, equivalent to requirements.txt) and Pipfile.lock (a machine-generated file with the exact resolved version of every package, including all transitive dependencies). Pipfile.lock is what makes the environment fully reproducible — pipenv install uses it to install exactly the same versions on every machine. pipenv also manages the virtual environment automatically, creating it in a standard location rather than inside the project directory.

poetry

poetry is the more feature-complete modern alternative. It manages the full lifecycle of a Python project: dependency declaration, virtual environment management, building, and publishing to PyPI. It uses a single pyproject.toml file (the modern Python project configuration standard) rather than a separate Pipfile, and produces a poetry.lock file equivalent to Pipfile.lock. poetry's dependency resolver is notably more thorough than pip's, detecting and reporting conflicts that pip would silently resolve incorrectly.

For learning and small projects, venv + pip + requirements.txt is entirely sufficient and has the advantage of being immediately understandable to anyone with Python experience. For professional projects — especially those with complex dependency trees or that will be published as packages — poetry is the current community recommendation.

> **Note:** This section provides an overview of pipenv and poetry sufficient to understand what they do and when to use them. Full coverage of the pyproject.toml format and poetry's publishing workflow appears in Chapter 9.

Example 1 — Introduction

The pipenv workflow: creating an environment, installing packages, and the Pipfile it produces.

```
# Install pipenv (once, into the system Python or a user install)
pip install --user pipenv

# ── Starting a new project ──────────────────────────────────
mkdir my_project && cd my_project

# Install a package — pipenv creates the venv automatically
pipenv install requests

# Install a development-only package
pipenv install --dev pytest

# ── Resulting Pipfile ────────────────────────────────────────
# [[source]]
# url = 'https://pypi.org/simple'
# verify_ssl = true
# name = 'pypi'
#
# [packages]
# requests = '*'
#
# [dev-packages]
```

```
# pytest = '*'
#
# [requires]
# python_version = '3.12'

# ── Run a command inside the venv without activating ──────────
pipenv run python main.py
pipenv run pytest

# ── Activate the shell ─────────────────────────────────────────
pipenv shell

# ── Reproduce on another machine ───────────────────────────────
# (Pipfile.lock must be committed to the repository)
pipenv install --ignore-pipfile    # installs exact versions from lock
```

Output:

```
# pipenv install requests
Creating a virtualenv for this project...
Using /usr/bin/python3 to create virtualenv...
Installing requests...
Adding requests to Pipfile's [packages]...
Pipfile.lock (678246) updated!

# pipenv run python --version
Python 3.12.3
```

Example 2 — Variation

The poetry workflow: initialising a project, adding dependencies, and the pyproject.toml it produces.

```
# Install poetry (follow the official installer, not pip)
# curl -sSL https://install.python-poetry.org | python3 -

# ── Initialise a new project ───────────────────────────────────
poetry new srs_project
cd srs_project

# ── Add dependencies ───────────────────────────────────────────
poetry add requests
poetry add --group dev pytest black mypy

# ── Resulting pyproject.toml (excerpt) ─────────────────────────
# [tool.poetry]
# name = 'srs-project'
# version = '0.1.0'
# description = 'Student Records System'
# authors = ['M. North <m.north@school.edu.au>']
#
# [tool.poetry.dependencies]
# python = '^3.12'
# requests = '^2.31.0'
#
# [tool.poetry.group.dev.dependencies]
# pytest = '^8.1.1'
# black = '^24.4.2'
# mypy = '^1.9.0'

# ── Run commands in the poetry venv ────────────────────────────
poetry run python src/main.py
poetry run pytest

# ── Activate the shell ─────────────────────────────────────────
poetry shell
```

```
# ── Reproduce on another machine ──────────────────────────
poetry install   # uses poetry.lock for exact versions
```

Output:

```
# poetry add requests
Using version ^2.31.0 for requests

Updating dependencies
Resolving dependencies... (0.4s)

Package operations: 5 installs, 0 updates, 0 removals
  - Installing certifi (2024.2.2)
  - Installing charset-normalizer (3.3.2)
  - Installing idna (3.7)
  - Installing urllib3 (2.2.1)
  - Installing requests (2.31.0)

Writing lock file
```

Example 3 — Real-world application

A comparison script showing how venv+pip, pipenv, and poetry each represent the same project's dependencies.

```
# This script does not execute the tools — it illustrates the
# files each approach produces for the same project.

SAME_PROJECT = {
    'name': 'grade_reporter',
    'production_deps': ['requests>=2.28', 'python-dateutil>=2.8'],
    'dev_deps':        ['pytest>=7.0', 'black>=22.0'],
}

APPROACHES = {
    'venv + pip': {
        'files': ['requirements.txt', 'requirements-dev.txt'],
        'commands': [
            'python -m venv .venv',
            'source .venv/bin/activate',
            'pip install requests python-dateutil',
            'pip freeze > requirements.txt',
        ],
        'reproduce': 'pip install -r requirements.txt',
        'lockfile': False,
    },
    'pipenv': {
        'files': ['Pipfile', 'Pipfile.lock'],
        'commands': ['pipenv install requests python-dateutil'],
        'reproduce': 'pipenv install --ignore-pipfile',
        'lockfile': True,
    },
    'poetry': {
        'files': ['pyproject.toml', 'poetry.lock'],
        'commands': ['poetry add requests python-dateutil'],
        'reproduce': 'poetry install',
        'lockfile': True,
    },
}

for tool, info in APPROACHES.items():
    print(f"{tool}")
    print(f"  Files    : {info['files']}")
    print(f"  Lockfile: {info['lockfile']}")
    print(f"  Repro    : {info['reproduce']}")
```

```
    print()
```

Output:

```
venv + pip
  Files   : ['requirements.txt', 'requirements-dev.txt']
  Lockfile: False
  Repro   : pip install -r requirements.txt

pipenv
  Files   : ['Pipfile', 'Pipfile.lock']
  Lockfile: True
  Repro   : pipenv install --ignore-pipfile

poetry
  Files   : ['pyproject.toml', 'poetry.lock']
  Lockfile: True
  Repro   : poetry install
```

The key practical difference between the three approaches is the lock file. A lock file records the exact version of every transitive dependency, not just the top-level packages you specified. This means poetry install or pipenv install --ignore-pipfile will produce precisely the same environment on any machine, even if new versions of dependencies have been published since the lock file was generated. pip install -r requirements.txt with a freeze-generated file achieves the same if you include all transitive dependencies — which is what pip freeze produces, but only if you remember to regenerate it after every change.

Best Practices: One venv per Project, Never System Python

The foundational rule of Python environment management is one virtual environment per project. Each project gets its own isolated site-packages, its own version of pip, and its own pinned dependency list. Projects never share an environment. This rule eliminates the entire category of "it works on my machine" errors caused by different developers having different packages installed globally.

The second rule is to never install third-party packages into the system Python using pip. On macOS and Linux, the system Python is part of the operating system and its packages are managed by the system package manager (apt, brew, etc.). Polluting it with pip-installed packages can cause version conflicts with system tools. On all platforms, the discipline of always working in a virtual environment also makes it easy to answer the question "what exactly does this project depend on?" — just look at requirements.txt.

Several other practices follow naturally from these two rules: always create .venv at the project root and add it to .gitignore immediately; always activate before installing; always regenerate requirements.txt after changing dependencies; and write a setup script (as shown in Section 6.2) so that any developer can reproduce the environment in a single step. These habits together constitute what professional Python developers call environment hygiene.

> **Note:** If you find yourself frequently forgetting to activate a virtual environment before running Python, consider using direnv (a shell extension that activates environments automatically when you cd into a project directory) or an IDE such as PyCharm or VS Code that handles activation transparently. The workflow should be invisible friction-free, not a daily chore.

Example 1 — Introduction

A project directory structure that follows all recommended practices, with annotations explaining each file's role.

```
# Recommended structure for a Python project using venv + pip

srs_project/
  .venv/                    # virtual environment — NOT in git
  .gitignore                # lists .venv/, __pycache__/, etc.
  README.md                 # project description and setup instructions
  requirements.txt          # pinned production dependencies
  requirements-dev.txt      # dev tools (-r requirements.txt + extras)
  setup_project.py          # one-command environment setup script
  pyproject.toml            # project metadata (optional but recommended)
  src/
    srs/
      __init__.py
      models/
      persistence/
      operations/
      reports/
  tests/
    test_models.py
    test_operations.py
  docs/
    ...

# README.md should include a 'Getting Started' section:
# ---
# ## Getting Started
# 1. Clone the repository
# 2. Run: python setup_project.py
# 3. Activate: source .venv/bin/activate
# 4. Run tests: pytest
# ---
```

Output:

```
# git status (with correct .gitignore in place):
On branch main
Untracked files:
  (use 'git add <file>...' to include in what will be committed)
        README.md
        requirements.txt
        requirements-dev.txt
        setup_project.py
        src/
        tests/

# .venv/ does NOT appear — correctly excluded by .gitignore
```

Example 2 — Variation

A checklist script that verifies a project follows all recommended environment practices.

```
"""
env_checklist.py — Verify that a project follows Python environment best
practices.
"""

import sys
from pathlib import Path

def check(label, condition, fix):
    """Print a pass/fail line with a fix suggestion."""
    status = 'PASS' if condition else 'FAIL'
    icon   = 'v' if condition else 'x'
    print(f"  [{icon}] {label}")
```

```
    if not condition:
        print(f"      Fix: {fix}")
    return condition

def run_checklist(root='.'):
    r = Path(root)
    gi = (r / '.gitignore')
    gi_content = gi.read_text(encoding='utf-8') if gi.exists() else ''

    print("Python Environment Best Practices Checklist")
    print("=" * 46)

    results = [
        check('.gitignore exists',
              gi.exists(),
              'Run: touch .gitignore'),
        check('.venv/ excluded in .gitignore',
              '.venv/' in gi_content or '.venv' in gi_content,
              'Add .venv/ to .gitignore'),
        check('__pycache__/ excluded',
              '__pycache__/' in gi_content,
              'Add __pycache__/ to .gitignore'),
        check('.env excluded',
              '.env' in gi_content,
              'Add .env to .gitignore'),
        check('requirements.txt present',
              (r / 'requirements.txt').exists(),
              'Run: pip freeze > requirements.txt'),
        check('Virtual environment is active',
              sys.prefix != sys.base_prefix,
              'Run: source .venv/bin/activate'),
        check('.venv dir exists',
              (r / '.venv').is_dir(),
              'Run: python -m venv .venv'),
    ]
    passed = sum(results)
    print(f"\n{passed}/{len(results)} checks passed.")
    return passed == len(results)

if __name__ == '__main__':
    ok = run_checklist()
    sys.exit(0 if ok else 1)
```

Output:

```
Python Environment Best Practices Checklist
==============================================
  [v] .gitignore exists
  [v] .venv/ excluded in .gitignore
  [v] __pycache__/ excluded
  [x] .env excluded
      Fix: Add .env to .gitignore
  [v] requirements.txt present
  [v] Virtual environment is active
  [v] .venv dir exists

6/7 checks passed.
```

Example 3 — Real-world application

A complete project bootstrap script that combines all best practices: create venv, install deps, verify environment, and print next steps.

```
"""
bootstrap.py — Complete project setup following all best practices.
```

```
Idempotent: safe to run multiple times. Creates .venv if absent,
installs from requirements.txt, verifies the result, and prints
next-step instructions.
"""

import subprocess
import sys
import os
from pathlib import Path

ROOT         = Path(__file__).parent
VENV         = ROOT / '.venv'
REQ          = ROOT / 'requirements.txt'
DEV_REQ      = ROOT / 'requirements-dev.txt'
GITIGNORE    = ROOT / '.gitignore'

GITIGNORE_CONTENT = '''# Python\n.venv/\n__pycache__/\n*.pyc\n.env\n*.egg-
info/\n'''

def run(cmd):
    subprocess.run(cmd, check=True)

def main():
    print("=== Bootstrap ===")

    # 1. Ensure .gitignore exists
    if not GITIGNORE.exists():
        GITIGNORE.write_text(GITIGNORE_CONTENT, encoding='utf-8')
        print("  Created .gitignore")

    # 2. Create venv if needed
    if not VENV.exists():
        print("  Creating .venv...")
        run([sys.executable, '-m', 'venv', str(VENV), '--upgrade-deps'])
    else:
        print("  .venv exists — skipping creation")

    # 3. Determine pip path
    pip = VENV / ('Scripts/pip' if sys.platform == 'win32' else 'bin/pip')

    # 4. Install dependencies
    if REQ.exists():
        print("  Installing production deps...")
        run([str(pip), 'install', '-r', str(REQ)])
    if DEV_REQ.exists():
        print("  Installing dev deps...")
        run([str(pip), 'install', '-r', str(DEV_REQ)])

    print("\nBootstrap complete.")
    if sys.platform == 'win32':
        print("  Next: .venv\\Scripts\\activate")
    else:
        print("  Next: source .venv/bin/activate")
    print("  Then: pytest")

if __name__ == '__main__':
    main()
```

Output:

```
=== Bootstrap ===
  Created .gitignore
  Creating .venv...
  Installing production deps...
  Installing dev deps...
```

```
Bootstrap complete.
  Next: source .venv/bin/activate
  Then: pytest
```

The bootstrap.py pattern — a single script that sets up a completely reproducible environment from scratch — is one of the most practical habits you can form as a Python developer. It eliminates onboarding friction, prevents environment drift between team members, and documents the project's setup process in executable form rather than in a README that may go out of date.

Chapter 7 moves from managing the environment to using it: installing, understanding, and working responsibly with third-party packages from the Python Package Index.

Chapter 6 Summary

- A virtual environment is an isolated Python installation with its own site-packages directory. It prevents dependency conflicts between projects by ensuring each project has exactly the packages it needs, with no interference from others.
- sys.prefix != sys.base_prefix indicates that a virtual environment is active. sys.executable points into the .venv/bin/ directory when active. The VIRTUAL_ENV environment variable is set by the activation script.
- python -m venv .venv creates a virtual environment. source .venv/bin/activate (macOS/Linux) or .venv\Scripts\activate (Windows) activates it. deactivate returns the shell to the system Python. The --upgrade-deps flag upgrades pip and setuptools immediately after creation.
- pip install, pip list, pip show, pip freeze, and pip uninstall all operate on the active environment. pip install -r requirements.txt installs all packages listed in the file. Never run pip install into the system Python.
- requirements.txt records package dependencies. pip freeze > requirements.txt captures a complete snapshot with exact versions. A separate requirements-dev.txt for development tools (pytest, black, mypy) that includes production requirements via -r requirements.txt is a common professional pattern.
- The virtual environment directory should never be committed to version control. Add .venv/ to .gitignore immediately. The .gitignore should also exclude __pycache__/, *.pyc, .env, and build artefacts.
- pipenv combines venv and pip management and produces a Pipfile.lock for deterministic dependency resolution. poetry manages the full project lifecycle — dependencies, building, and publishing — using pyproject.toml and poetry.lock. Both are stricter and more reproducible than pip freeze alone.
- Best practices: one virtual environment per project, always activate before installing, always regenerate requirements.txt after changes, write a bootstrap/setup script so any developer can reproduce the environment in a single step, and verify the environment at application startup.

Guided Exercises

1. Create a new project directory called grade_reporter/. Inside it, create a virtual environment named .venv using python -m venv .venv --upgrade-deps. Activate it. Verify the activation by running a short Python script that prints sys.executable and confirms it points inside .venv/. Create a .gitignore

containing at least the five essential Python patterns from Section 6.5. Record what pip freeze produces before installing anything.

Hint: sys.executable will show the full path to the Python interpreter. Compare it to the output before activation. pip freeze on a freshly created venv should show only pip and setuptools (or nothing if they are not counted).

2. With the grade_reporter venv active, install the requests package (pip install requests). Run pip show requests and record the version, location, and required-by fields. Then run pip freeze > requirements.txt and inspect the file — note that it includes certifi, charset-normalizer, idna, and urllib3 even though you only asked for requests. Explain why these additional packages appear.

Hint: The additional packages are requests's own dependencies (transitive dependencies). pip install resolves the full dependency graph and installs everything requests needs. pip freeze records the entire installed set.

3. Write a Python script env_info.py that: (a) detects whether a venv is active using sys.prefix vs sys.base_prefix; (b) if active, prints the venv path, Python version, and a sorted list of all installed packages with their versions using importlib.metadata; (c) if not active, prints a clear warning. Run the script both inside and outside the venv to confirm different output.

Hint: Use importlib.metadata.packages_distributions() to get a dict of package names, then importlib.metadata.version(name) for each. Sort the names alphabetically before printing.

4. Create a requirements.txt for a small project with at least three packages: one pinned to an exact version (==), one using a minimum version (>=), and one using a compatible release (~=). Install them using pip install -r requirements.txt. Then uninstall one package, verify it is gone with pip show, and use pip install -r requirements.txt to restore it. Finally run pip freeze > requirements_frozen.txt and compare requirements.txt with requirements_frozen.txt to see the difference between a hand-written file and a frozen one.

Hint: A hand-written requirements.txt might say requests>=2.28, while requirements_frozen.txt will say requests==2.31.0 (or whatever version was installed). The frozen file also includes all transitive dependencies.

5. Create two separate project directories: project_a/ and project_b/. In project_a's venv, install requests version 2.28.2. In project_b's venv, install requests version 2.31.0. Write a script that each project runs to print its own requests version using importlib.metadata.version('requests'). Confirm that activating one environment, running the script, deactivating, activating the other, and running the script again produces different version strings.

Hint: Use pip install requests==2.28.2 in project_a and pip install requests==2.31.0 in project_b. Remember to deactivate before switching environments. The script is just two lines: import importlib.metadata and print(importlib.metadata.version('requests')).

Challenge Tasks

1. Build a complete environment management toolkit as a Python package called envtool/ with three submodules: envtool/create.py (functions to create a venv at a given path, upgrade pip, and optionally install from a requirements file — all using subprocess), envtool/audit.py (functions to check that a venv is active, list all installed packages with versions, check for outdated packages by comparing installed versions to pinned versions in a requirements file, and report any packages in the environment that are not listed in requirements.txt), and envtool/report.py (functions to generate a formatted environment summary report as a string or to a file, including Python version, venv path, package count, and a table of all installed packages). envtool/__init__.py should expose a single setup(project_root) function that calls create and then installs requirements. Write a main.py that uses envtool.setup('.') on the current directory and then calls envtool.report to print a summary.

2. Write a cross-project dependency conflict detector. The script accepts two or more project directories as command-line arguments. For each project, it reads the project's requirements.txt and builds a dict of {package: version_spec}. It then compares the requirements across all projects and identifies: (a) packages that appear in more than one project but with different version specifications; (b) packages that are in one project's requirements but explicitly absent (not listed) in another; (c) packages where one project pins an exact version while another uses a range. Report the findings in a formatted table with a recommended resolution for each conflict. Test with at least three simulated project requirements files.

3. Create a virtual environment snapshot and restore system. Write a module venv_snapshot.py with two functions: snapshot(venv_dir, output_file) captures the complete state of a venv — Python version, all installed packages with exact versions, and platform information — into a JSON file. restore(snapshot_file, target_dir) reads the JSON, creates a fresh venv at target_dir, and installs all packages at the recorded exact versions. The restore function must verify after installation that every package was installed at the correct version and report any discrepancies. Add a command-line interface so the script can be run as python venv_snapshot.py snapshot .venv snapshot.json or python venv_snapshot.py restore snapshot.json .venv-restored. Test the full round-trip: create a venv, install three or four packages, snapshot it, create a fresh venv, restore from the snapshot, and verify both venvs contain identical packages.

CHAPTER 7 Using pip and Installing Third-Party Libraries

Book 03: Modules, Packages & the Python Ecosystem

> Chapter 6 established the mechanics of virtual environments. This chapter turns to what fills them: third-party packages. The Python Package Index hosts more than half a million packages covering everything from web frameworks and data analysis to colour output and QR code generation. Knowing how to find, evaluate, install, and manage these packages — and how to do so safely — is as fundamental to professional Python development as writing the code itself. This chapter goes beyond the surface-level pip install and examines pip's full feature set: advanced flags, the pip cache, configuration files, and the pip.conf that controls behaviour across a machine. It covers how to read a PyPI project page critically, how version specifiers govern compatibility, how to manage direct versus transitive dependencies precisely with pip-compile, how to audit for known security vulnerabilities, and how editable installs make in-development packages importable without reinstalling after every change.

7.1 pip Basics: install, upgrade, uninstall, list, show

pip is Python's package installer, included with every Python installation since version 3.4. Chapter 6 introduced the commands you use every day. This section fills in the gaps: the flags that control behaviour, the pip cache that makes repeated installs fast, and the pip.conf configuration file that lets you set defaults for an entire machine or a single project.

The most important flag not covered in Chapter 6 is --no-deps, which installs a package without installing any of its dependencies. This is rarely what you want in normal use, but is essential when you are manually constructing an environment or debugging a dependency conflict. The --target flag installs a package into a specific directory rather than the active site-packages — useful for building Lambda deployment packages or standalone executable bundles.

pip maintains a local cache of downloaded wheel files so that reinstalling a package you have already downloaded does not require a network request. The cache lives in a platform-specific directory (pip cache dir shows the location). pip cache list shows what is cached; pip cache purge clears it. Clearing the cache forces pip to re-download everything on the next install, which is useful when a cached wheel is suspected to be corrupt.

> **Note:** pip install --upgrade pip should be run regularly, especially inside freshly created virtual environments. A stale pip may fail to resolve newer package metadata formats or miss security-related improvements to the resolver. The --upgrade-deps flag on python -m venv does this automatically at creation time.

Example 1 — Introduction

The complete pip command set with their most useful flags.

```
# ── Install ────────────────────────────────────────────────
pip install requests                        # latest
pip install requests==2.31.0                # exact version
pip install 'requests>=2.28,<3'             # version range
pip install requests --no-deps              # skip dependencies
pip install requests --quiet                # suppress output
pip install requests --target ./vendor      # install to ./vendor/

# ── Upgrade ────────────────────────────────────────────────
```

```
pip install --upgrade requests            # upgrade one package
pip install --upgrade pip setuptools      # upgrade pip itself
pip list --outdated                       # show what is behind

# ── Uninstall ───────────────────────────────────────────────
pip uninstall requests                    # prompts for confirmation
pip uninstall requests -y                 # skip confirmation
pip uninstall -r requirements.txt -y      # uninstall listed packages

# ── Inspect ─────────────────────────────────────────────────
pip list                                  # all installed packages
pip list --format=columns                 # tabular output
pip list --format=json                    # JSON output
pip show requests                         # detailed info
pip show --files requests                 # every installed file

# ── Check ───────────────────────────────────────────────────
pip check                                 # detect broken deps
```

Output:

```
# pip list --format=columns
Package            Version
------------------ -------
certifi            2024.2.2
charset-normalizer 3.3.2
idna               3.7
pip                24.0
requests           2.31.0
urllib3            2.2.1

# pip check
No broken requirements found.
```

Example 2 — Variation

Working with the pip cache and the pip.conf configuration file.

```
# ── pip cache commands ──────────────────────────────────────
pip cache dir              # show where the cache lives
pip cache list             # list all cached wheel files
pip cache info             # summary: total size, number of files
pip cache remove requests  # remove one package from cache
pip cache purge            # clear the entire cache

# ── pip.conf — persistent configuration ─────────────────────
# pip reads configuration from (in priority order):
#   1. Environment variables (PIP_INDEX_URL, PIP_TRUSTED_HOST, ...)
#   2. Per-venv:  .venv/pip.conf (Unix) or .venv/pip.ini (Windows)
#   3. Per-user:  ~/.config/pip/pip.conf (Unix)
#   4. Site-wide: /etc/pip.conf (Unix)

# Example pip.conf that points to a private corporate index:
# [global]
# index-url = https://pypi.internal.company.com/simple/
# trusted-host = pypi.internal.company.com
# timeout = 60

# Example pip.conf that adds PyPI as an extra index:
# [global]
# extra-index-url = https://pypi.org/simple/

# ── Viewing the current configuration ───────────────────────
pip config list            # show all active config values
pip config list -v         # show values and where they come from
pip config get global.index-url  # get a specific value
```

Output:

```
# pip cache dir
/home/student/.cache/pip

# pip cache info
Package index page cache location (pip v23.3+): ...
Package index page cache size: 2.4 MB
HTTP file cache location: /home/student/.cache/pip/http-v2
HTTP file cache size: 0 bytes
Locally built wheels location: /home/student/.cache/pip/wheels
Locally built wheels size: 18.7 MB

# pip config list
global.index-url='https://pypi.internal.company.com/simple/'
```

Example 3 — Real-world application

A maintenance script that checks for outdated packages, reports them, and offers a guided upgrade.

```
"""
upgrade_check.py — Check for outdated packages in the active environment.
"""

import subprocess
import json
import sys

def get_outdated():
    """Return a list of dicts: {name, version, latest_version}."""
    result = subprocess.run(
        [sys.executable, '-m', 'pip', 'list', '--outdated', '--format=json'],
        capture_output=True, text=True, check=True
    )
    return json.loads(result.stdout)

def upgrade_package(name):
    """Upgrade a single package using pip."""
    subprocess.run(
        [sys.executable, '-m', 'pip', 'install', '--upgrade', name],
        check=True
    )

def main():
    outdated = get_outdated()
    if not outdated:
        print("All packages are up to date.")
        return

    print(f"Found {len(outdated)} outdated package(s):\n")
    print(f'  {"Package":<25} {"Installed":<12} {"Latest"}')
    print(f'  {"-"*25} {"-"*12} {"-"*12}')
    for pkg in outdated:
        print(f'  {pkg["name"]:<25} {pkg["version"]:<12}
{pkg["latest_version"]}')

    print()
    answer = input("Upgrade all? [y/N]: ").strip().lower()
    if answer == 'y':
        for pkg in outdated:
            print(f'  Upgrading {pkg["name"]}...')
            upgrade_package(pkg['name'])
        print("\nAll packages upgraded.")
    else:
        print("No changes made.")
```

```
if __name__ == '__main__':
    main()
```

Output:

```
Found 3 outdated package(s):

  Package                   Installed    Latest
  ------------------------- ------------ ------------
  certifi                   2023.11.17   2024.2.2
  pip                       23.3.2       24.0
  urllib3                   2.1.0        2.2.1

Upgrade all? [y/N]: y
  Upgrading certifi...
  Upgrading pip...
  Upgrading urllib3...

All packages upgraded.
```

The pip check command is worth running regularly in any long-lived environment. Packages that were compatible at installation time can become incompatible after upgrades because pip's default resolver does not prevent a new version of one package from violating the constraints of another. pip check reveals these latent conflicts before they cause mysterious runtime errors.

PyPI: The Python Package Index

The Python Package Index (PyPI) at pypi.org is the official repository for Python packages. It hosts over half a million projects ranging from one-line utilities to full application frameworks. Understanding how to read a PyPI project page critically — separating high-quality, well-maintained packages from abandoned or poorly-written ones — is as important a skill as knowing how to install them.

A PyPI project page shows the package name, current version, a short description, and a set of metadata badges and links. The information most relevant to choosing a package is: the release history (is it actively maintained? when was the last release?), the number of downloads (popularity correlates roughly with community support and compatibility testing), the GitHub or source repository link (read the code, look at open issues, check the test suite), and the licence (some licences restrict use in commercial or school contexts).

pip search was deprecated and removed in pip 21.0 because it placed excessive load on PyPI's XML-RPC API. To search for packages, use the PyPI website directly, or use pip index versions <name> to check what versions of a known package are available. The PyPI JSON API (https://pypi.org/pypi/<package>/json) provides machine-readable metadata for any package.

> **Note:** Before installing any package, ask four questions: Is it actively maintained (recent releases, open issues being addressed)? Does it have a meaningful test suite? Is its licence compatible with your project? Is the download count high enough to suggest broad compatibility testing? A package that fails three of these should be treated with caution regardless of how useful it looks.

Example 1 — Introduction

Using the PyPI JSON API to query package metadata programmatically.

```
"""
pypi_info.py — Query PyPI metadata for a package without installing it.
```

```
"""

import urllib.request
import json
from datetime import datetime

def pypi_info(package_name):
    """Fetch and display key metadata for a PyPI package."""
    url = f'https://pypi.org/pypi/{package_name}/json'
    try:
        with urllib.request.urlopen(url, timeout=10) as resp:
            data = json.loads(resp.read().decode('utf-8'))
    except Exception as e:
        print(f"Could not fetch {package_name}: {e}")
        return

    info     = data['info']
    releases = data['releases']

    # Latest version details
    latest_ver   = info['version']
    summary      = info['summary'] or '(no summary)'
    author       = info['author'] or '(unknown)'
    licence      = info['license'] or '(unspecified)'
    home_page    = info['home_page'] or info.get('project_url', '(none)')
    requires_py  = info['requires_python'] or 'any'

    # Count total releases and find the most recent upload date
    all_dates = []
    for ver, files in releases.items():
        for f in files:
            all_dates.append(f['upload_time'])
    all_dates.sort(reverse=True)
    last_upload = all_dates[0][:10] if all_dates else 'unknown'

    print(f"Package    : {package_name}")
    print(f"Version    : {latest_ver}")
    print(f"Summary    : {summary}")
    print(f"Author     : {author}")
    print(f"Licence    : {licence}")
    print(f"Python     : {requires_py}")
    print(f"Home page : {home_page}")
    print(f"Releases   : {len(releases)}")
    print(f"Last upload: {last_upload}")

pypi_info('requests')
```

Output:

```
Package    : requests
Version    : 2.31.0
Summary    : Python HTTP for Humans.
Author     : Kenneth Reitz
Licence    : Apache 2.0
Python     : >=3.7
Home page : https://requests.readthedocs.io
Releases   : 147
Last upload: 2023-05-22
```

Example 2 — Variation

Checking available versions of a package with pip index versions and interpreting the output.

```
# Check what versions of a package are available on PyPI
# (does not install anything)
pip index versions requests
```

```
# Output:
# WARNING: pip index is currently an experimental command.
# requests (2.31.0)
# Available versions: 2.31.0, 2.30.0, 2.29.0, 2.28.2, ...

# ── Interpreting a PyPI project page ──────────────────────
# The following fields signal a healthy, trustworthy package:
#
# Classifiers — 'Development Status :: 5 - Production/Stable'
#               means the package considers itself release-quality.
#               'Development Status :: 2 - Pre-Alpha' means use with caution.
#
# Requires-Python — should be compatible with your Python version.
#
# Dependencies — a long list of dependencies can mean fragile upgrades.
#
# Project links — 'Source', 'Issues', 'Documentation' links signal
#                 a properly maintained open-source project.
#
# Download statistics — pypistats.org/packages/<name> shows
#                       weekly download counts, a proxy for adoption.

# ── Checking a package's dependencies before installing ──────
# pip install <name> --dry-run shows what would be installed
pip install pandas --dry-run

# pip show --verbose <name> (after install) shows all classifiers
pip show --verbose requests
```

Output:

```
# pip install pandas --dry-run
Would install numpy-1.26.4 pandas-2.2.2 python-dateutil-2.9.0
  pytz-2024.1 six-1.16.0 tzdata-2024.1

# pip show --verbose requests (excerpt)
Classifiers:
  Development Status :: 5 - Production/Stable
  Intended Audience :: Developers
  License :: OSI Approved :: Apache Software License
  Programming Language :: Python :: 3
  Topic :: Internet :: WWW/HTTP
```

Example 3 — Real-world application

A package evaluation checklist tool that scores a PyPI package on maintainability criteria.

```
"""
evaluate_package.py — Score a PyPI package on key quality criteria.
"""

import urllib.request
import json
from datetime import datetime, timezone

def evaluate(package_name):
    """Fetch PyPI metadata and score the package on quality criteria."""
    url = f'https://pypi.org/pypi/{package_name}/json'
    try:
        with urllib.request.urlopen(url, timeout=10) as r:
            data = json.loads(r.read().decode('utf-8'))
    except Exception as e:
        print(f"Cannot evaluate {package_name}: {e}")",
        return
```

```
    info     = data['info']
    releases = data['releases']
    score    = 0
    notes    = []

    # Criterion 1: Has a licence
    if info.get('licence') or info.get('license'):
        score += 1
        notes.append("  [+] Licence specified")
    else:
        notes.append("  [-] No licence — check source manually")

    # Criterion 2: Requires Python >= 3.8
    req = info.get('requires_python') or ''
    if req and '3.' in req:
        score += 1
        notes.append(f"  [+] Python requirement declared: {req}")
    else:
        notes.append("  [-] No Python version constraint")

    # Criterion 3: Multiple releases (actively developed)
    n_releases = len(releases)
    if n_releases >= 10:
        score += 1
        notes.append(f"  [+] {n_releases} releases — actively developed")
    else:
        notes.append(f"  [-] Only {n_releases} release(s)")

    # Criterion 4: Recent release (within 2 years)
    all_dates = sorted(
        [f['upload_time'] for v in releases.values() for f in v],
        reverse=True
    )
    if all_dates:
        last = datetime.fromisoformat(all_dates[0].replace('Z', '+00:00'))
        now  = datetime.now(timezone.utc)
        age_days = (now - last).days
        if age_days <= 730:
            score += 1
            notes.append(f"  [+] Last release {age_days} days ago")
        else:
            notes.append(f"  [-] Last release {age_days} days ago — may be
abandoned")

    # Criterion 5: Has a project URL (documentation or source)
    urls = info.get('project_urls') or {}
    if urls:
        score += 1
        notes.append(f"  [+] Project URLs present: {list(urls.keys())[:3]}")
    else:
        notes.append("  [-] No project URLs — no documentation link")

    print(f"Package: {package_name}  ({info['version']})")
    print(f"Score  : {score}/5")
    for n in notes:
        print(n)

evaluate('requests')
print()
evaluate('python-dateutil')
```

Output:

```
Package: requests  (2.31.0)
Score  : 5/5
  [+] Licence specified
```

```
  [+] Python requirement declared: >=3.7
  [+] 147 releases — actively developed
  [+] Last release 423 days ago
  [+] Project URLs present: ['Documentation', 'Source', 'Changelog']

Package: python-dateutil  (2.9.0.post0)
Score   : 5/5
  [+] Licence specified
  [+] Python requirement declared: !=3.0.*,!=3.1.*,!=3.2.*,>=2.7
  [+] 30 releases — actively developed
  [+] Last release 389 days ago
  [+] Project URLs present: ['Documentation', 'Source Code', 'Issue Tracker']
```

The evaluate_package tool illustrates a broader principle: treat third-party dependencies as a liability as well as an asset. Every package you add is code you do not control, written by someone else, that can introduce bugs, security vulnerabilities, or breaking changes. Evaluate carefully; install sparingly; keep dependencies up to date.

Version Specifiers: ==, >=, ~=, and Why They Matter

A version specifier is the constraint you attach to a package name to express which versions of it your code is compatible with. Python's version specifier syntax is defined in PEP 440 and used uniformly by pip, requirements.txt, pyproject.toml, and setup.cfg. Choosing the right specifier is not just syntax — it directly determines whether your project installs correctly on another machine and whether it remains installable as its dependencies evolve.

Semantic versioning (semver) underlies the logic of version specifiers. A semver version number has three components: MAJOR.MINOR.PATCH. A PATCH increment (2.31.0 to 2.31.1) indicates a backwards-compatible bug fix. A MINOR increment (2.31.0 to 2.32.0) indicates new backwards-compatible functionality. A MAJOR increment (2.x to 3.x) indicates a breaking change. Well-behaved packages follow semver, which is what makes the compatible release specifier (~=) meaningful: ~=2.31 means 'any version that is at least 2.31 and below 3.0' — compatible MINOR and PATCH increments only.

The appropriate specifier depends on whether you are writing an application or a library. Applications pin exact versions (requests==2.31.0) to guarantee reproducible deployments. Libraries use ranges (requests>=2.28,<3) to remain installable alongside other packages that may have their own constraints. A library that pins requests==2.31.0 will conflict with any other package that needs a different version of requests — which is why libraries should never pin exact versions of their dependencies.

> **Note:** The exclusion specifier != is used to skip a specific broken release: requests!=2.29.0. The arbitrary equality specifier === matches a version string exactly without normalisation — it exists for non-semver packages and should almost never be used.

Example 1 — Introduction

The six version specifier operators and what each one means in practice.

```
# == Exact match
# Install exactly this version. Use in applications.
requests==2.31.0

# != Exclusion
# Any version EXCEPT this one. Use to skip a known broken release.
```

```
requests!=2.29.0

# >= Minimum (inclusive lower bound)
# This version or any later one. Broad — allows major version breaks.
requests>=2.28.0

# <= Maximum (inclusive upper bound, rarely used alone)
requests<=2.31.0

# ~= Compatible release (most useful for libraries)
# Equivalent to >=2.28.0, ==2.*  (same major, at least this minor)
requests~=2.28

# ~= with patch: >=2.28.1, ==2.28.*  (same major and minor)
requests~=2.28.1

# Combined range (explicit and unambiguous)
requests>=2.28.0,<3.0.0

# No specifier — installs latest. Use only for exploration.
requests

# ── Testing specifiers programmatically with packaging ────────
from packaging.version import Version
from packaging.specifiers import SpecifierSet

spec     = SpecifierSet('>=2.28.0,<3.0.0')
versions = ['2.27.1', '2.28.0', '2.31.0', '3.0.0', '3.1.0']
for v in versions:
    ok = Version(v) in spec
    print(f"  {v:<10} in {spec}  ->  {ok}")
```

Output:

```
  2.27.1     in >=2.28.0,<3.0.0  ->  False
  2.28.0     in >=2.28.0,<3.0.0  ->  True
  2.31.0     in >=2.28.0,<3.0.0  ->  True
  3.0.0      in >=2.28.0,<3.0.0  ->  False
  3.1.0      in >=2.28.0,<3.0.0  ->  False
```

Example 2 — Variation

Demonstrating why specifier choice matters: a version conflict caused by incompatible constraints in the same environment.

```
# Scenario: project depends on both library_a and library_b.
# library_a requires: requests>=2.28,<2.30
# library_b requires: requests>=2.30
#
# These constraints cannot be satisfied simultaneously.
# pip will report a conflict.

from packaging.version import Version
from packaging.specifiers import SpecifierSet

constraint_a = SpecifierSet('>=2.28.0,<2.30.0')
constraint_b = SpecifierSet('>=2.30.0')

# Find versions satisfying BOTH constraints
candidates = ['2.27.1','2.28.0','2.29.0','2.30.0','2.31.0','3.0.0']
compatible = [
    v for v in candidates
    if Version(v) in constraint_a and Version(v) in constraint_b
]
print(f"Versions satisfying both: {compatible}")
```

```python
# Now with looser constraints that DO allow a common version
constraint_c = SpecifierSet('>=2.28.0,<3.0.0')    # library_a relaxed
constraint_d = SpecifierSet('>=2.30.0,<3.0.0')    # library_b narrowed
compatible2 = [
    v for v in candidates
    if Version(v) in constraint_c and Version(v) in constraint_d
]
print(f"Versions satisfying relaxed: {compatible2}")
```

Output:

```
Versions satisfying both: []
Versions satisfying relaxed: ['2.30.0', '2.31.0']
```

Example 3 — Real-world application

A library requirements file using compatible-release specifiers, and an application requirements.txt using pinned versions generated from it.

```python
# ── library: setup.cfg / pyproject.toml style constraints ──────
# These go in [options] install_requires or [tool.poetry.dependencies].
# Libraries should NEVER pin exact versions — they are installed
# alongside other packages and must be flexible.
#
# install_requires =
#     requests~=2.28            # >=2.28, <3 — any compatible 2.x
#     python-dateutil~=2.8      # >=2.8, <3
#     colorama>=0.4,<1          # explicit range, also fine

# ── application: requirements.in (direct deps, version ranges) ─
# Use this as input to pip-compile for deterministic lock files.
# requests~=2.28
# python-dateutil~=2.8
# colorama>=0.4,<1

# ── application: requirements.txt (pinned output from pip-compile)
# pip-compile requirements.in  ->  requirements.txt
# This is what gets committed and used for deployments.
# certifi==2024.2.2             \
# charset-normalizer==3.3.2     |
# colorama==0.4.6               | all transitive deps pinned
# idna==3.7                     |
# python-dateutil==2.9.0        |
# requests==2.31.0              |
# six==1.16.0                   |
# urllib3==2.2.1                /

from packaging.specifiers import SpecifierSet
from packaging.version    import Version

# Verify that the pinned version satisfies the original constraint
specs = [
    ('requests',        '~=2.28',     '2.31.0'),
    ('python-dateutil', '~=2.8',      '2.9.0'),
    ('colorama',        '>=0.4,<1',   '0.4.6'),
]
for name, spec_str, pinned in specs:
    ok = Version(pinned) in SpecifierSet(spec_str)
    status = 'OK' if ok else 'CONFLICT'
    print(f"  {name:<20} {spec_str:<14} pinned={pinned:<10} {status}")
```

Output:

```
  requests             ~=2.28         pinned=2.31.0     OK
  python-dateutil      ~=2.8          pinned=2.9.0      OK
  colorama             >=0.4,<1       pinned=0.4.6      OK
```

The two-file pattern — a requirements.in with version ranges for your direct dependencies, and a generated requirements.txt with all transitive dependencies pinned — is the cleanest way to maintain both flexibility (easy upgrades) and reproducibility (identical environments). The pip-compile tool from the pip-tools package automates the generation step.

7.4 requirements.txt and pip freeze: Beyond the Basics

Chapter 6, Section 6.4 established the foundational requirements.txt workflow: pip freeze to capture, pip install -r to restore. This section covers the gaps that matter in professional projects: the difference between direct and transitive dependencies, why pip freeze alone is not always sufficient, and how pip-compile from the pip-tools package solves both problems cleanly.

The fundamental limitation of pip freeze is that it captures every package in the environment — your direct dependencies and all of their dependencies — without distinguishing between the two. If you have a high-level requirements.in listing only requests and pytest and you pip freeze, the output also includes certifi, charset-normalizer, idna, urllib3, and all of pytest's dependencies. The resulting requirements.txt is hard to read and hard to maintain: if you want to change the version of requests, you also need to manually identify and update all of its transitive dependencies.

pip-compile (from the pip-tools package) solves this by separating concerns. You maintain a small requirements.in with just your direct dependencies and their version constraints. Running pip-compile requirements.in generates a complete, annotated requirements.txt that pins every transitive dependency, notes which direct dependency pulled in each transitive one, and is safe to commit. Upgrades are done by editing requirements.in and rerunning pip-compile, rather than by manually editing a long flat list.

> **Note:** pip-compile is not part of the standard library — install it with pip install pip-tools. Once installed, the pip-sync command is also available: it installs, upgrades, and uninstalls packages to match requirements.txt exactly, removing packages that are in the environment but not in the file. This is stricter than pip install -r and is preferable for maintaining clean, reproducible environments.

Example 1 — Introduction

The pip-compile workflow: from requirements.in to a fully annotated requirements.txt.

```
# — Install pip-tools ──────────────────────────────
pip install pip-tools

# — requirements.in (hand-maintained, direct deps only) ───
# requests~=2.28
# python-dateutil~=2.8
# colorama>=0.4,<1

# — Generate requirements.txt ──────────────────────
pip-compile requirements.in

# — Generated requirements.txt (excerpt) ───────────
# This file is @generated by pip-compile.
# To re-generate, run: pip-compile requirements.in
#
# certifi==2024.2.2
#     # via requests
# charset-normalizer==3.3.2
#     # via requests
# colorama==0.4.6
```

```
#     # via -r requirements.in
# idna==3.7
#     # via requests
# python-dateutil==2.9.0
#     # via -r requirements.in
# requests==2.31.0
#     # via -r requirements.in
# six==1.16.0
#     # via python-dateutil
# urllib3==2.2.1
#     # via requests

# ── Install exactly what is in requirements.txt ──────────────
pip-sync requirements.txt

# ── Upgrade a direct dependency ──────────────────────────────
# 1. Edit requirements.in: change requests~=2.28 to requests~=2.31
# 2. Regenerate: pip-compile requirements.in
# 3. Sync:       pip-sync requirements.txt
```

Output:

```
# pip-compile requirements.in
Resolving dependencies...

Written to requirements.txt
```

Example 2 — Variation

Using pip check to detect broken dependency relationships in an existing environment.

```
# pip check scans the active environment for packages whose
# declared dependencies are not satisfied by installed versions.

# Example: deliberately install incompatible versions
# pip install requests==2.31.0 urllib3==1.26.0
# (requests 2.31.0 requires urllib3>=1.21.1,<2 — 1.26.0 is fine)
# (but requests 2.31.0 actually requires urllib3>=1.21.1,<3)

# Running pip check:
pip check

# If a genuine conflict is introduced:
# some-package 1.0.0 requires old-lib>=2.0, but old-lib 1.9 is installed.

# ── Programmatic pip check via subprocess ──────────────
import subprocess, sys

def check_deps():
    """Run pip check and return (ok, list_of_problems)."""
    result = subprocess.run(
        [sys.executable, '-m', 'pip', 'check'],
        capture_output=True, text=True
    )
    problems = [
        line for line in result.stdout.splitlines() if line.strip()
    ]
    ok = result.returncode == 0
    return ok, problems

ok, problems = check_deps()
if ok:
    print("pip check: No broken requirements found.")
else:
    print("pip check: Dependency problems detected!")
```

```
    for p in problems:
        print(f"  {p}")
```

Output:

```
# No conflicts:
pip check: No broken requirements found.

# With a conflict:
pip check: Dependency problems detected!
  requests 2.31.0 requires charset-normalizer<4, but charset-normalizer 4.0.0
is installed.
```

Example 3 — Real-world application

A complete two-file dependency management workflow with a Makefile-style helper script.

```
"""
deps.py — Helper script for managing project dependencies.

Commands:
  python deps.py compile    — run pip-compile to regenerate requirements.txt
  python deps.py sync       — run pip-sync to match the environment to
requirements.txt
  python deps.py check      — run pip check for broken deps
  python deps.py status     — show direct deps and their installed versions
"""

import subprocess
import sys
import importlib.metadata
from pathlib import Path

REQ_IN  = Path('requirements.in')
REQ_TXT = Path('requirements.txt')

def compile_deps():
    """Regenerate requirements.txt from requirements.in."""
    subprocess.run(['pip-compile', str(REQ_IN)], check=True)

def sync_deps():
    """Sync the environment to requirements.txt exactly."""
    subprocess.run(['pip-sync', str(REQ_TXT)], check=True)

def check_deps():
    """Check for broken dependency relationships."""
    r = subprocess.run([sys.executable, '-m', 'pip', 'check'],
                       capture_output=True, text=True)
    print(r.stdout or 'No broken requirements found.')

def show_status():
    """Show each direct dependency and its installed version."""
    if not REQ_IN.exists():
        print(f"{REQ_IN} not found")",
        return
    lines = [l.strip() for l in REQ_IN.read_text().splitlines()
             if l.strip() and not l.startswith('#')]
    import re
    print(f"{'Package':<25} {'Constraint':<18} {'Installed'}")
    print("-" * 55)
    for line in lines:
        name = re.match(r'[A-Za-z0-9_\-]+', line).group()
        try:
            ver = importlib.metadata.version(name)
        except importlib.metadata.PackageNotFoundError:
            ver = 'NOT INSTALLED'
```

```
        print(f"{name:<25} {line:<18} {ver}")

COMMANDS = {'compile': compile_deps, 'sync': sync_deps,
            'check': check_deps, 'status': show_status}

if __name__ == '__main__':
    cmd = sys.argv[1] if len(sys.argv) > 1 else 'status'
    if cmd in COMMANDS:
        COMMANDS[cmd]()
    else:
        print(f"Unknown command: {cmd}. Choose from: {list(COMMANDS)}")
```

Output:

```
# python deps.py status
Package                    Constraint          Installed
-------------------------------------------------------
requests                   requests~=2.28      2.31.0
python-dateutil            python-dateutil~=2.8  2.9.0
colorama                   colorama>=0.4,<1    0.4.6
```

The deps.py helper and the two-file pattern together give you the same core benefits as poetry or pipenv without any additional tooling: a readable high-level dependency declaration, a fully pinned lock file, and automated detection of environment drift. This pattern scales well from solo projects to teams.

Security: Checking Packages, Avoiding Supply-Chain Risks

Third-party packages represent the most significant security surface area of a typical Python project. Every package you install executes code during installation (via setup.py or build hooks) and at import time. A malicious or compromised package can exfiltrate credentials, establish backdoors, or corrupt data — and because pip downloads from a public index, the attack surface is enormous.

The most common attack vectors are typosquatting (publishing a package with a name deliberately similar to a popular one, relying on the developer making a spelling mistake), dependency confusion (publishing a package to PyPI with the same name as an internal corporate package, causing pip to prefer the malicious public version), and account takeover (an attacker gains access to a maintainer's PyPI account and publishes a malicious new release). All three have been used in real attacks.

pip audit (from the pip-audit package) checks every installed package against the Open Source Vulnerability Database (OSV) and the Python Packaging Advisory Database, reporting known CVEs and their severity. Running pip audit as part of a CI pipeline means that a known vulnerability in a dependency will block deployment until the affected package is upgraded. For highest-confidence environments, hash-based pinning in requirements.txt ensures that even if a package version is re-uploaded to PyPI with different content, the installation will fail.

> **Note:** pip audit does not check for malicious packages — only packages with known CVEs in public databases. A package that has been compromised but for which no CVE has yet been filed will not be flagged. Defence in depth (code review of dependencies, minimal dependency footprints, and network egress controls) remains necessary.

Example 1 — Introduction

Running pip audit to check for known vulnerabilities in the active environment.

```
# Install pip-audit
pip install pip-audit
```

```
# —— Audit the current environment ————————————————————
pip-audit

# —— Audit a specific requirements file (without installing) ——
pip-audit -r requirements.txt

# —— Output formats ————————————————————————————————————
pip-audit --format=json > audit_results.json
pip-audit --format=cyclonedx-json   # SBOM (Software Bill of Materials)

# —— Fix automatically where possible ——————————————————
pip-audit --fix                     # upgrade vulnerable packages
pip-audit --fix --dry-run           # show what would change

# —— Example output when vulnerabilities exist ————————————
# Name         Version  ID                Fix Versions
# ------------ -------- ----------------- -------------------------
# Pillow       9.0.0    GHSA-56pw-mpj4-fj  9.0.1
# cryptography 38.0.1 GHSA-jfh8-c2jp-jj  38.0.3

# —— Example output when all is well ———————————————————
# No known vulnerabilities found
```

Output:

```
# pip-audit (clean environment):
Found 0 known vulnerabilities in 6 packages


# pip-audit (vulnerable package present):
Found 1 known vulnerability in 6 packages
Name    Version  ID                  Fix Versions
------- -------- ------------------- ------------
Pillow  9.0.0    GHSA-56pw-mpj4-fj4  9.0.1
```

Example 2 — Variation

Hash-based pinning in requirements.txt: ensuring that what pip downloads is exactly what was reviewed.

```
# —— Generating a hash-pinned requirements.txt ——————————
# pip-compile can generate hashes for every pinned package:
pip-compile requirements.in --generate-hashes -o requirements.txt

# —— Excerpt from a hash-pinned requirements.txt ————————
# requests==2.31.0 \
#     --hash=sha256:58cd2187423d... \
#     --hash=sha256:942c5a758f98...
#     # via -r requirements.in

# —— Installing from a hash-pinned file ————————————————
pip install -r requirements.txt --require-hashes

# If PyPI tries to serve a different file than expected:
# ERROR: THESE PACKAGES DO NOT MATCH THE HASHES FROM THE REQUIREMENTS FILE.
# requests: ...sha256:abc... != sha256:58cd2187...

# —— Checking a download's hash manually ———————————————
import hashlib, urllib.request


def verify_file_hash(url, expected_sha256):
    """Download a file and verify its SHA-256 hash."""
    with urllib.request.urlopen(url) as f:
        data = f.read()
    actual = hashlib.sha256(data).hexdigest()
    if actual == expected_sha256:
```

```
        print(f"Hash OK: {actual[:16]}...")
        return True
    else:
        print(f"Hash MISMATCH!")
        print(f"  Expected: {expected_sha256[:16]}...")
        print(f"  Actual  : {actual[:16]}...")
        return False
```

Output:

```
# pip install -r requirements.txt --require-hashes
Collecting requests==2.31.0
  Downloading requests-2.31.0-py3-none-any.whl (62 kB)
  Verifying SHA256 hash ...
Installing collected packages: ...
Successfully installed requests-2.31.0

# If the hash does not match:
ERROR: THESE PACKAGES DO NOT MATCH THE HASHES FROM THE REQUIREMENTS FILE.
```

Example 3 — Real-world application

A supply-chain risk assessment script that checks package names for typosquatting patterns and verifies the install source.

```
"""
supply_chain_check.py - Basic supply-chain risk assessment for
requirements.txt.

Checks:
  1. Known safe packages against a whitelist
  2. Package names that closely resemble popular packages (typosquatting)
  3. Whether each package was installed from PyPI (not a local path)
"""

import importlib.metadata
import re
from pathlib import Path

# Known-safe high-popularity packages (abbreviated)
KNOWN_SAFE = {
    'requests', 'numpy', 'pandas', 'flask', 'django',
    'pytest', 'black', 'mypy', 'pip', 'setuptools',
    'certifi', 'urllib3', 'charset-normalizer', 'idna',
    'python-dateutil', 'colorama', 'packaging',
}

# Common typosquatting patterns: extra/missing letter,
# hyphen vs underscore, common letter substitutions
def looks_like_typosquat(name, safe_set):
    """Return True if name is suspiciously similar to a known-safe name."""
    n = name.lower().replace('-', '').replace('_', '')
    for safe in safe_set:
        s = safe.lower().replace('-', '').replace('_', '')
        if n == s:
            return False    # exact match, not suspicious
        # Check if name is within edit-distance 1 of a known-safe name
        if len(n) == len(s) and sum(a != b for a, b in zip(n, s)) == 1:
            return True
        if len(n) == len(s) + 1 and n[1:] == s:
            return True    # extra leading char
    return False

def assess(req_file='requirements.txt'):
    lines = Path(req_file).read_text(encoding='utf-8').splitlines()
    packages = []
```

```
    for line in lines:
        line = line.strip()
        if not line or line.startswith('#') or line.startswith('-'):
            continue
        match = re.match(r'([A-Za-z0-9_\-]+)', line)
        if match:
            packages.append(match.group(1))

    print(f"Supply Chain Assessment: {req_file}")
    print("=" * 50)
    for name in packages:
        known    = name.lower() in KNOWN_SAFE
        squat    = looks_like_typosquat(name, KNOWN_SAFE)
        try:
            ver = importlib.metadata.version(name)
        except importlib.metadata.PackageNotFoundError:
            ver = 'NOT INSTALLED'
        status = 'KNOWN-SAFE' if known else ('SUSPICIOUS' if squat else
'REVIEW')
        print(f"  {name:<25} {ver:<12} {status}")

if __name__ == '__main__':
    assess()
```

Output:

```
Supply Chain Assessment: requirements.txt
==================================================
  requests                  2.31.0       KNOWN-SAFE
  python-dateutil           2.9.0        KNOWN-SAFE
  colorama                  0.4.6        KNOWN-SAFE
  certifi                   2024.2.2     KNOWN-SAFE
  urllib3                   2.2.1        KNOWN-SAFE
  colour-utils              0.1.0        SUSPICIOUS
```

No tool eliminates supply-chain risk entirely, but several layers of defence together make it very difficult for an attack to succeed undetected: review dependencies before adding them, keep the dependency footprint minimal, use pip-audit in CI, use hash-based pinning for production deployments, and monitor security advisories for packages you depend on. The Python Security Response Team publishes advisories at python.org/news/security.

7.6 Installing from Source and Editable Installs

pip install is not limited to packages on PyPI. It can install from a local directory, a Git repository URL, a compressed archive, or a wheel file. These alternative sources are essential when working with in-development packages, private packages not published to any index, or forks of open-source libraries with local modifications.

An editable install — pip install -e . — installs a package from a local directory in a special mode where changes to the source files are immediately reflected in the installed package without reinstalling. Python achieves this by adding the source directory to sys.path (via a .pth file or a .egg-link) rather than copying the files into site-packages. This is the standard way to work on a Python package while using it: you can edit the source, run your tests, and see the effect of your changes immediately without any reinstall step.

For pip install -e . to work, the directory must contain a pyproject.toml or a setup.py that describes the package. A pyproject.toml with a [build-system] table and a [project] table is the modern form. setup.py alone is the legacy form and is gradually being deprecated. An editable install also makes the package importable by its declared name rather than by its path, which means other packages and test files can import it with a clean import statement.

> **Note:** pip install -e . installs the package at the current version of the source files on disk. If you switch to a different branch in git, the editable install immediately reflects the code on that branch — no reinstall required. This makes editable installs ideal for development workflows involving feature branches.

Example 1 — Introduction

Creating a minimal package directory and installing it in editable mode.

```
# —— Minimal package structure for an editable install ————————
# mylib/
#   pyproject.toml
#   src/
#     mylib/
#       __init__.py
#       greetings.py

# —— pyproject.toml ————————————————————————————————————————
# [build-system]
# requires      = ['setuptools>=68', 'wheel']
# build-backend = 'setuptools.backends.legacy:build'
#
# [project]
# name    = 'mylib'
# version = '0.1.0'
# requires-python = '>=3.10'

# —— src/mylib/greetings.py ————————————————————————————————
def hello(name):
    return f"Hello, {name}!"

# —— Install in editable mode ——————————————————————————————
# (run from the mylib/ directory with venv activated)
pip install -e .

# —— Verify ————————————————————————————————————————————————
pip show mylib
# Location: /home/student/mylib/src
# Editable project location: /home/student/mylib

# —— Use from anywhere in the venv —————————————————————————
from mylib.greetings import hello
print(hello('Brisbane'))   # Hello, Brisbane!

# Now edit src/mylib/greetings.py — change 'Hello' to 'G'\'day'
# Reimport (or start a new Python session) — change is live
# NO reinstall required.
```

Output:

```
# pip install -e .
Obtaining file:///home/student/mylib
  Installing build dependencies ... done
  Getting requirements to build wheel ... done
  Preparing metadata (pyproject.toml) ... done
Installing collected packages: mylib
  Running setup.py develop for mylib
Successfully installed mylib-0.1.0

Hello, Brisbane!
```

Example 2 — Variation

Installing from a Git repository URL and from a local path — two common non-PyPI installation sources.

```
# ── Install from a Git repository ──────────────────────────
# Latest commit on the default branch:
pip install git+https://github.com/psf/requests.git

# Specific tag:
pip install git+https://github.com/psf/requests.git@v2.31.0

# Specific branch:
pip install git+https://github.com/psf/requests.git@main

# Specific commit SHA:
pip install git+https://github.com/psf/requests.git@a1b2c3d

# ── Install from a local path ──────────────────────────────
# Non-editable (copies files into site-packages):
pip install ./my_local_package
pip install /absolute/path/to/package

# Editable (keeps files in place):
pip install -e ./my_local_package

# ── Install from a wheel file ──────────────────────────────
pip install ./dist/mylib-0.1.0-py3-none-any.whl

# ── Install from a tar.gz archive ──────────────────────────
pip install ./dist/mylib-0.1.0.tar.gz

# ── In requirements.txt: Git sources ───────────────────────
# requests @ git+https://github.com/psf/requests.git@v2.31.0
# mylib @ file:///home/student/mylib
# mylib @ file:///home/student/mylib#egg=mylib  # editable in req files
```

Output:

```
# pip install git+https://github.com/psf/requests.git@v2.31.0
Collecting requests@ git+https://github.com/psf/requests.git@v2.31.0
  Cloning https://github.com/psf/requests.git (to revision v2.31.0)
  ...
Successfully installed requests-2.31.0
```

Example 3 — Real-world application

A multi-package development workspace where several related packages are installed in editable mode from a monorepo layout.

```
# ── Monorepo layout for a school toolkit ───────────────────
# school_toolkit/             <- git repository root
#   .venv/
#   requirements-dev.txt
#   packages/
#     validators/             <- separate installable package
#       pyproject.toml
#       src/validators/__init__.py
#     formatters/             <- separate installable package
#       pyproject.toml
#       src/formatters/__init__.py
#     reporters/              <- depends on validators and formatters
#       pyproject.toml
#       src/reporters/__init__.py
#   tests/
#     test_validators.py
#     test_reporters.py

# ── Install all three in editable mode ─────────────────────
```

```
pip install -e packages/validators
pip install -e packages/formatters
pip install -e packages/reporters

# ── Or: list them all in requirements-dev.txt ──────────────
# -e packages/validators
# -e packages/formatters
# -e packages/reporters
# pytest>=8.0
# pip install -r requirements-dev.txt installs all four

# ── reporters/pyproject.toml declares its siblings as deps ──
# [project]
# name = 'reporters'
# dependencies = ['validators>=0.1', 'formatters>=0.1']

# ── Now editing any package is immediately visible ─────────
from validators import is_email
from formatters import format_score
from reporters  import summary

print(is_email('student@school.edu.au'))   # True
print(format_score('Mia', 88.5))           # Mia: 88.5
print(summary([('Mia', 88.5), ('Leo', 74.0)]))
```

Output:

```
# pip install -e packages/validators
Successfully installed validators-0.1.0

# pip install -e packages/formatters
Successfully installed formatters-0.1.0

# pip install -e packages/reporters
Successfully installed reporters-0.1.0

True
Mia: 88.5
=== Summary ===
  Mia  88.5
  Leo  74.0
```

Editable installs eliminate the frustrating cycle of edit-reinstall-test that makes package development painful. Once you adopt the editable install workflow for in-development packages, you will not want to go back to any other approach. The monorepo pattern shown here — multiple small packages in one repository, each installed in editable mode — is a standard structure for large Python projects with separate but related components.

Real-World: Setting Up a Data-Science or Web-Development Project

The techniques in this chapter come together most clearly when setting up a real project. This section walks through two canonical setups: a data-science project using the NumPy/Pandas/Matplotlib stack, and a web-development project using Flask. Both demonstrate the complete workflow — create a virtual environment, maintain a requirements.in with sensible version constraints, compile a pinned requirements.txt, verify with pip audit, and document the setup in a bootstrap script.

Data-science projects have characteristically heavy dependencies: NumPy, Pandas, Matplotlib, and SciPy each bring compiled C extensions and large transitive dependency trees. For these projects, installing the packages before writing requirements.in (rather than after) and then using pip freeze or pip-compile to capture what was actually installed is common, because the exact compatible set of NumPy/Pandas/SciPy versions is easier to discover than to specify upfront.

Web projects with Flask or Django are typically lighter but more security-sensitive, because the application is network-accessible. For these, pinning exact versions and running pip audit in CI is particularly important. Flask's own dependencies (Werkzeug, Jinja2, Click, MarkupSafe, itsdangerous) are well-maintained and update frequently, so keeping requirements.in updated and periodically recompiling is part of the development rhythm.

> **Note:** This section references packages (NumPy, Pandas, Flask) that are not part of the standard library. Their APIs are outside the scope of this book; detailed coverage appears in Book 09 (Data Analysis with Python) and the web-development pathway. The focus here is the pip and virtual environment workflow, not the packages themselves.

Example 1 — Introduction

Setting up a data-science project: requirements.in, pip-compile, verification.

```
# ── Data science project structure ──────────────────
# data_analysis/
#   .venv/
#   .gitignore
#   requirements.in
#   requirements.txt     <- compiled output
#   notebooks/
#   src/
#     analysis/
#   data/
#   reports/

# ── Step 1: Create and activate venv ────────────────
python -m venv .venv --upgrade-deps
source .venv/bin/activate

# ── Step 2: Install pip-tools ───────────────────────
pip install pip-tools

# ── Step 3: requirements.in (direct deps with version ranges) ─
# numpy~=1.26
# pandas~=2.2
# matplotlib~=3.8
# scipy~=1.12
# python-dateutil~=2.9
# jupyter>=1.0

# ── Step 4: Compile to requirements.txt ─────────────
pip-compile requirements.in

# ── Step 5: Sync the environment ────────────────────
pip-sync requirements.txt

# ── Step 6: Verify no known vulnerabilities ─────────
pip-audit

# ── Step 7: Verify the environment works ────────────
python -c "import numpy, pandas, matplotlib; print('Stack OK')"

# ── Step 8: Freeze pip.conf for reproducibility ─────
pip config list > pip_config_snapshot.txt
```

Output:

```
# pip-compile requirements.in
Resolving dependencies...
Written to requirements.txt

# pip-sync requirements.txt
Collecting numpy==1.26.4
Collecting pandas==2.2.2
Collecting matplotlib==3.8.4
...
Successfully installed 42 packages

# pip-audit
Found 0 known vulnerabilities in 42 packages

Stack OK
```

Example 2 — Variation

Setting up a Flask web project with separate production and development requirement files.

```
# ── Flask project structure ──────────────────────────────
# srs_web/
#   .venv/
#   .gitignore
#   requirements.in
#   requirements-dev.in
#   requirements.txt
#   requirements-dev.txt
#   src/
#     srs_web/
#       __init__.py
#       routes.py
#   tests/
#   bootstrap.py

# ── requirements.in (production only) ──────────────────
# flask~=3.0
# gunicorn~=21.0

# ── requirements-dev.in (extends production) ────────────
# -r requirements.in
# pytest~=8.0
# pytest-flask~=1.3
# black~=24.0
# mypy~=1.9
# pip-audit>=2.7

# ── Compile both files ──────────────────────────────────
pip-compile requirements.in     -o requirements.txt
pip-compile requirements-dev.in -o requirements-dev.txt

# ── Install dev environment ─────────────────────────────
pip-sync requirements-dev.txt

# ── Minimal Flask app to confirm the install works ──────
from flask import Flask
app = Flask(__name__)

@app.route('/')
def index():
    return 'SRS Web — OK'

if __name__ == '__main__':
```

```
    app.run(debug=True)
```

Output:

```
# pip-compile requirements.in
# Resolving flask's dependencies ...
# Written to requirements.txt
# Pinned: blinker==1.7.0, click==8.1.7, flask==3.0.3,
#         itsdangerous==2.1.2, jinja2==3.1.3,
#         markupsafe==2.1.5, werkzeug==3.0.2

# python -m flask run
 * Running on http://127.0.0.1:5000
127.0.0.1 - - GET / HTTP/1.1 200 -
```

Example 3 — Real-world application

A complete bootstrap script for either project type that automates all seven setup steps.

```
"""
bootstrap.py — Complete project setup for data-science or web projects.

Automates: venv creation, pip-tools install, dependency compilation,
environment sync, security audit, and verification.

Usage: python bootstrap.py [data|web]
"""

import subprocess, sys, shutil
from pathlib import Path

ROOT    = Path(__file__).parent
VENV    = ROOT / '.venv'
PIP     = VENV / ('Scripts/pip' if sys.platform == 'win32' else 'bin/pip')
PYTHON  = VENV / ('Scripts/python' if sys.platform == 'win32' else
'bin/python')

def run(cmd, **kw):
    print(f"  $ {cmd[0].split("/")[-1]} {" ".join(cmd[1:])}")
    subprocess.run(cmd, check=True, **kw)

def step(msg):
    print(f"\n[{msg}]")

def main(project_type='web'):
    print(f"=== Bootstrap: {project_type} project ===")

    step('Create virtual environment')
    if not VENV.exists():
        run([sys.executable, '-m', 'venv', str(VENV), '--upgrade-deps'])
    else:
        print("  .venv exists — skipping")

    step('Install pip-tools')
    run([str(PIP), 'install', 'pip-tools', '--quiet'])

    pip_compile = str(VENV / ('Scripts/pip-compile'
                              if sys.platform == 'win32'
                              else 'bin/pip-compile'))
    pip_sync    = str(VENV / ('Scripts/pip-sync'
                              if sys.platform == 'win32'
                              else 'bin/pip-sync'))
    pip_audit   = str(VENV / ('Scripts/pip-audit'
                              if sys.platform == 'win32'
                              else 'bin/pip-audit'))
```

```
    req_in  = ROOT / 'requirements.in'
    req_txt = ROOT / 'requirements.txt'

    if req_in.exists():
        step('Compile requirements')
        run([pip_compile, str(req_in), '-o', str(req_txt)])

        step('Sync environment')
        run([pip_sync, str(req_txt)])

    step('Security audit')
    run([str(VENV / ('Scripts/pip-audit' if sys.platform == 'win32'
                     else 'bin/pip-audit')), '--require-hashes', '-r',
str(req_txt)])

    step('Verify')
    if project_type == 'data':
        run([str(PYTHON), '-c',
             'import numpy, pandas, matplotlib; print("Data stack OK")'
             ])
    else:
        run([str(PYTHON), '-c', 'import flask; print("Flask OK")'])

    print("\nBootstrap complete.")
    print("  Activate: source .venv/bin/activate")

if __name__ == '__main__':
    kind = sys.argv[1] if len(sys.argv) > 1 else 'web'
    main(kind)
```

Output:

```
=== Bootstrap: web project ===

[Create virtual environment]
  $ python -m venv .venv --upgrade-deps

[Install pip-tools]
  $ pip install pip-tools --quiet

[Compile requirements]
  $ pip-compile requirements.in -o requirements.txt

[Sync environment]
  $ pip-sync requirements.txt

[Security audit]
  $ pip-audit --require-hashes -r requirements.txt
  Found 0 known vulnerabilities in 7 packages

[Verify]
  Flask OK

Bootstrap complete.
  Activate: source .venv/bin/activate
```

The bootstrap script brings together every practice from this chapter: the venv from Chapter 6, pip-tools for dependency management, hash-based pinning for security, pip-audit for vulnerability scanning, and a final verification step to confirm the environment is usable. Running python bootstrap.py web in a freshly cloned repository produces a fully configured, audited, reproducible environment in under a minute.

Chapter 8 shifts from the ecosystem mechanics to a complementary craft skill: documenting code with well-structured docstrings and type hints — the practices that make the modules and packages you have been building readable, discoverable, and verifiable by both humans and tools.

Chapter 7 Summary

- pip's full feature set goes beyond install and freeze: --no-deps installs without transitive dependencies, --target installs to a specific directory, pip check detects broken dependency relationships, pip cache manages locally cached wheels, and pip.conf sets persistent configuration defaults.
- PyPI hosts over half a million packages. Evaluate packages critically before adopting them: check the release history, download count, licence, Python version compatibility, and whether the project has a source repository with an active issue tracker. Use the PyPI JSON API for programmatic metadata queries.
- Version specifier operators: == pins an exact version (for applications), >= sets a minimum, ~= (compatible release) means the same MAJOR version with at least this MINOR (for libraries), != excludes a broken release, and combined ranges (>=x,<y) give explicit bounds. Libraries should never pin exact versions of their dependencies.
- The two-file pattern separates direct dependencies (requirements.in with version ranges) from the fully pinned lock file (requirements.txt generated by pip-compile). pip-sync installs, upgrades, and uninstalls to match requirements.txt exactly. pip check detects latent version conflicts.
- Supply-chain attacks include typosquatting, dependency confusion, and account takeover. pip-audit checks every installed package against the OSV vulnerability database. Hash-based pinning (pip-compile --generate-hashes) ensures that pip refuses to install any file that does not match the expected cryptographic hash.
- pip install -e . installs a local package in editable mode: changes to source files are immediately reflected without reinstalling. pyproject.toml with [build-system] and [project] tables is the modern format required for editable installs. Git repository URLs and local paths are also valid pip install sources.
- Data-science projects use pip-compile to pin the large transitive dependency trees of NumPy/Pandas/Matplotlib. Web projects use separate requirements.in and requirements-dev.in files compiled to corresponding requirements.txt files, with pip-audit integrated into CI for security assurance.
- A complete bootstrap.py script that automates venv creation, pip-tools installation, dependency compilation, environment sync, security audit, and verification is the highest-value single artefact for ensuring every developer starts with an identical, secure, reproducible environment.

Guided Exercises

1. Write a pip audit runner script that uses subprocess to run pip-audit --format=json, parses the JSON output, and prints a formatted vulnerability report. The report should show: the total number of packages checked, the number of vulnerable packages, and for each vulnerability: the package name, installed version, CVE ID, and recommended fix version. If no vulnerabilities are found, print a green-flag message. Run the script against your current virtual environment.

   Hint: pip-audit returns JSON with a 'dependencies' list. Each item has 'name', 'version', and 'vulns' (a list). Each vulnerability in 'vulns' has 'id' and 'fix_versions'. Use json.loads() on the subprocess output. If pip-audit is not installed, your script should detect this and print installation instructions.

2. Using the PyPI JSON API (https://pypi.org/pypi/<package>/json) and Python's built-in urllib.request, write a function that accepts a list of package names and returns a dict mapping each name to a tuple of (latest_version, days_since_last_release, licence_string). Print a formatted comparison table for the packages: requests, flask, pandas, and pytest. Calculate days_since_last_release by parsing the most recent upload_time in the releases dict.

Hint: Use urllib.request.urlopen() with a timeout. Parse the upload_time string (format: 2023-05-22T14:12:39) with datetime.fromisoformat(). Subtract from datetime.now(timezone.utc) to get a timedelta, then use .days.

3. Create a minimal installable package called school_calc/ with a pyproject.toml and a src/school_calc/ directory containing an __init__.py and a calculations.py module (with at least three functions: percentage(part, whole), letter_grade(score), and weighted_average(scores_and_weights)). Install it in editable mode with pip install -e . and verify that importing from school_calc works from any directory within the activated virtual environment. Modify one function and confirm the change is immediately visible without reinstalling.

Hint: The pyproject.toml needs [build-system] with requires=['setuptools>=68'] and build-backend='setuptools.backends.legacy:build', and [project] with name and version. Run pip show school_calc to confirm the editable install location points to your src/ directory.

4. Build a requirements.in for a project that depends on requests, python-dateutil, and colorama with compatible-release specifiers. Use pip-compile to generate a requirements.txt. Then manually introduce a version conflict by editing requirements.txt to specify an impossibly old version of one transitive dependency (such as certifi==2019.3.9). Run pip check and observe the error. Restore the correct version and confirm pip check passes.

Hint: pip-compile must be installed (pip install pip-tools). After editing requirements.txt to introduce the conflict, activate the venv and run pip install -r requirements.txt to apply the wrong version, then pip check. Restore by rerunning pip-compile and pip-sync.

5. Write a version specifier tester using the packaging library. The script accepts a package name and a version specifier string as command-line arguments, fetches all available versions of the package from the PyPI JSON API, and prints which versions satisfy the specifier and which do not. Test it with requests and the specifier ~=2.29.

Hint: Use packaging.specifiers.SpecifierSet to test versions and packaging.version.Version to parse them. The PyPI JSON API returns all versions as keys of the releases dict. Filter out pre-release versions (Version(v).is_prerelease) for a cleaner result.

Challenge Tasks

1. Build a full dependency management CLI tool called depman.py with the following sub-commands: add <package> [specifier] — adds a package to requirements.in with the given specifier (defaulting to ~= the currently latest version fetched from PyPI) and recompiles requirements.txt; remove <package> — removes the package from requirements.in and recompiles; list — shows all direct dependencies (from requirements.in) with their installed versions and whether a newer version is available on PyPI; audit — runs pip-audit and formats the output as a readable table; sync — runs pip-sync to align the environment with requirements.txt. All PyPI queries should use urllib.request with appropriate error handling. The tool should work from any directory that contains a requirements.in file.

2. Write a dependency graph visualiser. Starting from a requirements.txt file, use importlib.metadata to build a dict mapping each installed package to its list of direct dependencies (from the Requires field of its metadata). Then perform a breadth-first traversal from each top-level package (those not required by any other package) and print an ASCII tree showing the full dependency hierarchy, with packages appearing at the correct depth, repeated dependencies shown with a [see above] note, and

circular dependencies detected and marked. Also compute and print the total number of unique packages in the graph and identify the package with the most dependents.

3. Create a secure package installation wrapper called safe_pip.py. The wrapper intercepts every pip install command, performs the following checks before allowing the installation, and blocks it with a clear error message if any check fails: (a) the package name does not closely resemble any currently installed package (edit-distance check for typosquatting); (b) the package exists on PyPI and has at least 10 releases (fetched from the PyPI JSON API); (c) the package's last release was within the past two years; (d) the package specifies a Python version requirement. If all checks pass, proceed with the actual pip install. If the user passes --force, skip checks (a) and (c) only. Log every installation attempt (allowed or blocked) with a timestamp to a file called install_log.txt.

CHAPTER 8 Documenting Code with Docstrings and Type Hints

Book 03: Modules, Packages & the Python Ecosystem

> The modules and packages built in the preceding chapters are only as useful as they are understandable. Documentation and type information are not afterthoughts — they are the interface through which every developer, including you six months from now, interacts with code they did not just write. This chapter covers two complementary practices: docstrings, which document what code does in natural language, and type hints, which document what types functions accept and return in machine-readable form. Both serve humans and tools simultaneously: docstrings power help() and documentation generators; type hints power IDEs, mypy, and runtime validators. Together they transform a collection of modules into a professional-grade library that others can adopt with confidence.

Why Documentation Matters and What Makes It Good

Code is written once but read many times. A function without a docstring forces every reader to reconstruct its contract from the implementation — a slow, error-prone process that defeats the purpose of abstraction. Good documentation makes a module usable without reading its source, testable without guessing edge cases, and maintainable without fear of breaking undocumented behaviour.

What makes documentation good is specificity, accuracy, and brevity. Specificity means naming the types and constraints of arguments rather than describing them vaguely ("a number" is less useful than "a float, must be positive"). Accuracy means the docstring must match what the code actually does — outdated documentation is worse than none, because it actively misleads. Brevity means saying exactly enough: a one-sentence summary plus structured argument and return descriptions is better than three paragraphs that circle the same point.

Documentation also serves machines, not just humans. Python's built-in help() function reads docstrings. Documentation generators like pydoc and pdoc parse them into HTML. IDEs display them in autocompletion popups. Type checkers read type hints to catch mistakes before code runs. Writing documentation with these tools in mind — using consistent conventions that they can parse — multiplies the value of every word you write.

> **Note:** The single most effective documentation habit is writing the docstring before writing the function body. If you cannot write a clear one-sentence summary of what a function does before implementing it, the function's purpose is not yet clear enough to implement correctly.

Example 1 — Introduction

Contrasting undocumented, partially documented, and fully documented versions of the same function.

```
# — UNDOCUMENTED - forces callers to read the implementation -
def process(data, n, flag=False):
    result = []
    for item in data:
        v = item * n
        if flag:
            v = round(v, 2)
        result.append(v)
    return result
```

```
# —— PARTIALLY DOCUMENTED — better, but still too vague ————
def process(data, n, flag=False):
    """Process the data list."""
    ...

# —— FULLY DOCUMENTED — immediately usable without reading impl
def scale_scores(scores, factor, round_result=False):
    """
    Multiply each score in a list by the given factor.

    Args:
        scores       (list[float]): Raw score values.
        factor       (float):       Scaling multiplier. Must be positive.
        round_result (bool):        If True, round each result to 2 dp.
                                    Default False.

    Returns:
        list[float]: Scaled (and optionally rounded) scores.

    Raises:
        ValueError: If factor is zero or negative.
    """
    if factor <= 0:
        raise ValueError(f"factor must be positive, got {factor}")
    result = [s * factor for s in scores]
    if round_result:
        result = [round(v, 2) for v in result]
    return result

help(scale_scores)
```

Output:

```
Help on function scale_scores in module __main__:

scale_scores(scores, factor, round_result=False)
    Multiply each score in a list by the given factor.

    Args:
        scores       (list[float]): Raw score values.
        factor       (float):       Scaling multiplier. Must be positive.
        round_result (bool):        If True, round each result to 2 dp.

    Returns:
        list[float]: Scaled (and optionally rounded) scores.

    Raises:
        ValueError: If factor is zero or negative.
```

Example 2 — Variation

Demonstrating the cost of inaccurate documentation: a docstring that contradicts the implementation.

```
# BAD: docstring says one thing, code does another.
# This is worse than no documentation — it actively misleads.
def average(scores):
    """Return the highest score in the list."""    # WRONG!
    return sum(scores) / len(scores)               # actually returns mean

# The caller trusts the docstring, not the code:
result = average([80, 90, 70])
print(f"Highest score: {result}")    # prints 80.0 — wrong!

# GOOD: docstring matches implementation exactly.
def average(scores):
```

```
    """
    Return the arithmetic mean of a non-empty list of numeric scores.

    Args:
        scores (list[float]): Non-empty list of numeric values.

    Returns:
        float: The arithmetic mean.

    Raises:
        ZeroDivisionError: If scores is empty.
    """
    return sum(scores) / len(scores)

result = average([80, 90, 70])
print(f"Mean score: {result}")
```

Output:

```
# BAD version:
Highest score: 80.0

# GOOD version:
Mean score: 80.0
```

Example 3 — Real-world application

A documentation quality checker that scans a module's public functions and reports which lack docstrings or have only one-line summaries.

```
import inspect
import importlib

def doc_quality_report(module_name):
    """
    Print a documentation quality report for all public functions
    and classes in the named module.
    """
    try:
        mod = importlib.import_module(module_name)
    except ImportError as e:
        print(f"Cannot import {module_name}: {e}")
        return

    members = inspect.getmembers(mod, predicate=inspect.isfunction)
    public  = [(n, f) for n, f in members if not n.startswith('_')]

    if not public:
        print(f"{module_name}: no public functions found")
        return

    print(f"Documentation report: {module_name}")
    print("=" * 50)
    issues = 0
    for name, func in public:
        doc = inspect.getdoc(func)
        if not doc:
            print(f"  MISSING  {name}()")
            issues += 1
        elif len(doc.splitlines()) == 1:
            print(f"  SUMMARY  {name}()  — one-liner only")
        else:
            print(f"  OK       {name}()")

    print(f"\n{issues} function(s) missing docstrings.")
```

```
doc_quality_report('statistics')
```

Output:

```
Documentation report: statistics
==================================================
  OK        correlation()
  OK        covariance()
  OK        fmean()
  OK        geometric_mean()
  OK        harmonic_mean()
  OK        mean()
  OK        median()
  ...
0 function(s) missing docstrings.
```

The documentation quality checker is worth running on every module you write before committing it. Zero missing docstrings is the right target, not a nice-to-have. The standard library sets the example: every public function in statistics, pathlib, and collections has a complete, accurate docstring.

8.2 Docstring Conventions: PEP 257, Google Style, NumPy Style

Python's official docstring conventions are defined in PEP 257. They specify where docstrings go (immediately after the def or class line), how they are quoted (triple double-quotes, even for one-liners), and the general structure. PEP 257 is intentionally minimal — it says nothing about how to document arguments and return values. Two community styles have emerged to fill that gap: Google style and NumPy style.

PEP 257 basics

PEP 257 mandates that a one-line docstring fits on a single line with the closing quotes on the same line. Multi-line docstrings begin with a one-sentence summary on the first line, followed by a blank line, then a more detailed description or structured sections. The summary line should be a complete sentence ending with a full stop. The docstring should be written in the imperative mood ("Return the mean", not "Returns the mean" or "This function returns the mean").

Google style

Google style uses section headers (Args:, Returns:, Raises:, Example:) followed by indented content. Each argument is documented on a separate line with the format name (type): description. The type is in parentheses and optional but strongly recommended. Google style is compact and readable at the source level — it was designed to look good in a plain text editor without rendering.

NumPy style

NumPy style uses underlined section headers (Parameters, Returns, Raises, Notes, Examples) with the underline repeated using dashes. Each parameter is named on its own line, followed by its type on the next line, then an indented description. NumPy style produces richer rendered HTML when processed by Sphinx and is the standard in the scientific Python ecosystem (NumPy, SciPy, Pandas). For school-level projects, Google style is simpler and fully sufficient.

> **Note:** This book uses Google style throughout. Whichever convention you choose, the most important rule is: pick one and apply it consistently across an entire project. Mixing styles within a module or package makes automatic documentation generation unreliable and harms readability.

Example 1 — Introduction

The same function documented in PEP 257 minimal style, Google style, and NumPy style.

```
# — PEP 257 minimal (one-liner) ———————————————————————
def add_gst(amount):
    """Return amount plus 10% GST, rounded to two decimal places."""
    ...

# — Google style (multi-line) ————————————————————————
def add_gst(amount):
    """
    Return amount plus 10% GST, rounded to two decimal places.

    Args:
        amount (float | int): The pre-GST price in Australian dollars.
            Must be non-negative.

    Returns:
        float: The inc-GST price, rounded to 2 decimal places.

    Raises:
        ValueError: If amount is negative.

    Example:
        >>> add_gst(100)
        110.0
        >>> add_gst(49.95)
        54.94
    """
    ...

# — NumPy style (multi-line) —————————————————————————
def add_gst(amount):
    """
    Return amount plus 10% GST, rounded to two decimal places.

    Parameters
    ----------
    amount : float or int
        The pre-GST price in Australian dollars. Must be non-negative.

    Returns
    -------
    float
        The inc-GST price, rounded to 2 decimal places.

    Raises
    ------
    ValueError
        If amount is negative.
    """
    ...
```

Output:

```
# All three styles document the same contract.
# Google style is most compact for source reading.
# NumPy style produces richer Sphinx HTML.
# PEP 257 one-liner is ideal for simple, obvious functions.
```

Example 2 — Variation

PEP 257 multi-line format: summary line, blank line, extended description.

```
def find_students_above(scores_dict, threshold):
```

```
    """
    Return a sorted list of students whose score meets the threshold.

    Compares each student's score against threshold and collects those
    who meet or exceed it. The result is sorted alphabetically by name
    so that output is deterministic regardless of dict insertion order.

    Args:
        scores_dict (dict[str, float]): Mapping of student name to score.
        threshold   (float):             Minimum qualifying score.

    Returns:
        list[str]: Names of qualifying students, alphabetically sorted.

    Example:
        >>> find_students_above({'Mia': 88, 'Leo': 74, 'Zara': 91}, 80)
        ['Mia', 'Zara']
    """
    return sorted(name for name, score in scores_dict.items()
                  if score >= threshold)

result = find_students_above({'Mia': 88, 'Leo': 74, 'Zara': 91}, 80)
print(result)
```

Output:

```
['Mia', 'Zara']
```

Example 3 — Real-world application

A real-world module with consistently applied Google-style docstrings throughout all public functions and one class.

```
"""
invoice.py — Invoice generation for the school bookshop.

Provides the Invoice dataclass and two helper functions for formatting
and persisting invoice records to JSON.

Public API:
    Invoice          — Dataclass representing a single invoice.
    format_invoice   — Return a formatted string representation.
    save_invoice     — Persist an invoice to a JSON file.
"""

from dataclasses import dataclass, field
from datetime import date
from pathlib import Path
import json

__all__ = ['Invoice', 'format_invoice', 'save_invoice']
GST_RATE = 0.10

@dataclass
class Invoice:
    """
    A single invoice record for the school bookshop.

    Attributes:
        number   (str):        Unique invoice identifier.
        customer (str):        Customer name.
        items    (list[dict]): Line items, each with 'desc', 'qty', 'price'.
        issued   (date):       Issue date. Defaults to today.
    """
    number   : str
```

```
    customer : str
    items    : list = field(default_factory=list)
    issued   : date = field(default_factory=date.today)

    @property
    def subtotal(self):
        """Return the sum of all line item totals, excluding GST."""
        return sum(i['qty'] * i['price'] for i in self.items)

    @property
    def total(self):
        """Return the inc-GST total, rounded to two decimal places."""
        return round(self.subtotal * (1 + GST_RATE), 2)

def format_invoice(invoice):
    """
    Return a human-readable string representation of an invoice.

    Args:
        invoice (Invoice): The invoice to format.

    Returns:
        str: Multi-line formatted invoice text.
    """
    lines = [
        f"Invoice #{invoice.number}",
        f"Customer: {invoice.customer}",
        f"Date    : {invoice.issued.strftime('%d/%m/%Y')}",
        "-" * 36,
    ]
    for item in invoice.items:
        lines.append(f"  {item['desc']:<20} x{item['qty']}
${item['price']:.2f}")
    lines += ["-" * 36, f"Total (inc GST): ${invoice.total:.2f}"]
    return '\n'.join(lines)

def save_invoice(invoice, directory='invoices'):
    """
    Persist an invoice to a JSON file in the given directory.

    Creates the directory if it does not exist. The file is named
    <invoice.number>.json.

    Args:
        invoice   (Invoice): The invoice to save.
        directory (str):     Target directory path. Default 'invoices'.

    Returns:
        pathlib.Path: Path to the written file.

    Raises:
        OSError: If the directory cannot be created or the file cannot
            be written.
    """
    Path(directory).mkdir(parents=True, exist_ok=True)
    path = Path(directory) / f'{invoice.number}.json'
    with open(path, 'w', encoding='utf-8') as f:
        json.dump({'number': invoice.number,
                   'customer': invoice.customer,
                   'total': invoice.total}, f, indent=2)
    return path
```

Output:

```
# help(invoice) would show the full module, class, and function docstrings.
```

```
# Consistent Google style across every public name.
# One-liners for simple properties, full Args/Returns/Raises for functions.
```

Adopting a consistent style from the start of a project costs almost nothing and pays back throughout the project's lifetime. The best time to add a docstring is when you write the function. The second-best time is right now.

8.3 Module, Class, and Function Docstrings

Docstrings appear in three positions: at the top of a .py file (module docstring), immediately after a class definition (class docstring), and immediately after a def statement (function or method docstring). Each position has a slightly different purpose and audience, and each is retrieved differently via Python's introspection tools.

The module docstring describes the module's overall purpose, its public API (the names a caller would import), any important assumptions or limitations, and usage examples if they would not be obvious. It is retrieved as module.__doc__ and displayed by help(module). A well-written module docstring lets a caller decide whether the module meets their needs without reading any of its implementation.

A class docstring describes the class's purpose and its attributes — particularly the instance attributes that are set in __init__ but are not parameters of any method. Attributes documented in the class docstring appear in help() output alongside the method docstrings. Method docstrings follow the same Google or NumPy style as regular functions, but do not document self.

> **Note:** Class docstrings should document instance attributes in an Attributes: section, separate from the __init__ Args: section. This is because tools like pdoc render the class docstring as the primary description of the class, and readers need to know what attributes exist without inspecting __init__ separately.

Example 1 — Introduction

Module docstring, class docstring, and method docstrings applied to a complete student records module.

```
"""
student_records.py — Student record management for school administration.

Provides the Student dataclass and lookup utilities for use by
enrolment, reporting, and timetabling subsystems.

Public API:
    Student          — dataclass representing one student
    find_by_id       — look up a student by their ID
    average_score    — compute mean score for a student
"""

from dataclasses import dataclass, field
from statistics import mean
from typing import List, Optional

__all__ = ['Student', 'find_by_id', 'average_score']

@dataclass
class Student:
    """
    A single student record.
```

```
    Attributes:
        student_id (str):        Unique identifier, format 'S-NNNNN'.
        name       (str):        Full name.
        year_level (int):        Year level 7-12.
        scores     (list[float]): Assessment scores (0-100).
    """
    student_id : str
    name       : str
    year_level : int
    scores     : List[float] = field(default_factory=list)

    def add_score(self, score):
        """
        Add an assessment score to this student's record.

        Args:
            score (float): Score value between 0 and 100 inclusive.

        Raises:
            ValueError: If score is outside the range 0-100.
        """
        if not 0 <= score <= 100:
            raise ValueError(f"Score must be 0-100, got {score}")
        self.scores.append(score)

    def __repr__(self):
        return f"Student({self.student_id!r}, {self.name!r},
yr={self.year_level})"

def find_by_id(students, student_id):
    """
    Return the student with the given ID, or None if not found.

    Args:
        students   (list[Student]): Pool to search.
        student_id (str):           ID to find.

    Returns:
        Student | None: The matching student, or None.
    """
    return next((s for s in students if s.student_id == student_id), None)

def average_score(student):
    """
    Return the mean assessment score for a student.

    Args:
        student (Student): The student whose scores to average.

    Returns:
        float: Arithmetic mean of recorded scores, or 0.0 if none.
    """
    return mean(student.scores) if student.scores else 0.0
```

Output:

```
# help(student_records) displays all three docstring levels:
# 1. Module docstring — purpose and public API
# 2. Student class docstring — attributes
# 3. Each method and function docstring — Args/Returns/Raises
```

Example 2 — Variation

Accessing docstrings programmatically via __doc__ and the inspect module.

```
import inspect

# Module docstring
import student_records
print('--- Module ---')
print(student_records.__doc__.strip()[:100])

# Class docstring
from student_records import Student
print('\n--- Class ---')
print(Student.__doc__.strip()[:100])

# Method docstring via inspect (cleans indentation)
print('\n--- Method ---')
print(inspect.getdoc(Student.add_score))

# Function signature + docstring together
from student_records import find_by_id
print('\n--- Function signature ---')
print(inspect.signature(find_by_id))
print(inspect.getdoc(find_by_id))
```

Output:

```
--- Module ---
student_records.py — Student record management for school administration.

--- Class ---
A single student record.

--- Method ---
Add an assessment score to this student's record.

Args:
    score (float): Score value between 0 and 100 inclusive.

Raises:
    ValueError: If score is outside the range 0-100.

--- Function signature ---
(students, student_id)
Return the student with the given ID, or None if not found.
```

Example 3 — Real-world application

A well-documented class hierarchy: a base class and two subclasses with docstrings at every level.

```
"""
notifications.py — Notification channel abstraction.
"""

from abc import ABC, abstractmethod

__all__ = ['Notification', 'EmailNotification', 'SMSNotification']

class Notification(ABC):
    """
    Abstract base class for all notification channels.

    Subclasses must implement send(). All notifications carry a
    subject and a body; the channel-specific delivery details are
    handled by the concrete subclass.

    Attributes:
```

```
        subject (str): Brief description of the notification.
        body    (str): Full notification content.
    """

    def __init__(self, subject, body):
        """
        Initialise a notification with a subject and body.

        Args:
            subject (str): Brief description (used as email subject
                or SMS prefix).
            body (str): Full content of the notification.
        """
        self.subject = subject
        self.body    = body

    @abstractmethod
    def send(self, recipient):
        """
        Deliver the notification to a recipient.

        Args:
            recipient (str): Delivery address (email, phone, etc.).
                Format depends on the concrete subclass.

        Returns:
            bool: True if delivery succeeded, False otherwise.
        """

class EmailNotification(Notification):
    """
    Email notification delivered via SMTP.

    Attributes:
        sender (str): The from-address used for all outgoing emails.
    """

    def __init__(self, subject, body, sender='noreply@school.edu.au'):
        """
        Args:
            subject (str): Email subject line.
            body    (str): Email body text.
            sender  (str): From-address. Default noreply@school.edu.au.
        """
        super().__init__(subject, body)
        self.sender = sender

    def send(self, recipient):
        """
        Send the email to recipient. (Simulated in this example.)

        Args:
            recipient (str): Destination email address.

        Returns:
            bool: Always True in this simulation.
        """
        print(f"[EMAIL] From: {self.sender} To: {recipient}")
        print(f"        Subject: {self.subject}")
        return True

class SMSNotification(Notification):
    """SMS notification (message body limited to 160 characters)."""
```

```
    def send(self, recipient):
        """
        Send an SMS to a phone number.

        Args:
            recipient (str): Destination phone number (E.164 format).

        Returns:
            bool: True if the body is within the 160-character limit,
                False if it was truncated.
        """
        msg = self.body[:160]
        ok  = len(self.body) <= 160
        print(f"[SMS] To: {recipient}  '{msg}'")
        return ok
```

Output:

```
# help(notifications) shows all three docstring levels cleanly.
# Subclass docstrings extend (not replace) the base class contract.
# Attributes unique to a subclass are documented in its own docstring.
```

Docstrings at all three levels — module, class, and function — form a complete, layered description of a codebase. The module tells you whether to import it. The class tells you what it represents. The method tells you how to use it. Each layer answers a different question, and together they make the code genuinely self-documenting.

8.4 Type Hints: PEP 484 Basics

Type hints, introduced in PEP 484 (Python 3.5) and refined through subsequent PEPs, allow you to annotate variables, function parameters, and return values with type information. Unlike docstring type descriptions, which are plain text that Python ignores at runtime, type hints are part of the language syntax and are read by static type checkers, IDEs, and documentation generators.

The basic syntax is straightforward: parameter: type for function arguments, -> type after the closing parenthesis for return types, and variable: type for variable annotations. Python does not enforce type hints at runtime — annotating a parameter as int does not prevent a caller from passing a string. Type hints are metadata, not contracts. Their value comes from tools (mypy, Pyright, IDE type checking) that read them and flag violations statically, before code runs.

The built-in types (int, float, str, bool, bytes) and the built-in collections (list, dict, tuple, set) can be used directly as type hints in Python 3.9+. For Python 3.8 and earlier, the typing module provides capitalised generic versions (List, Dict, Tuple, Set) that accept type parameters. In Python 3.10+, the | operator replaces Optional and Union for expressing nullable or multi-type annotations.

> **Note:** Type hints are entirely optional and are never enforced by the Python interpreter at runtime. Adding them to existing code without tests is safe. Adding incorrect hints to code that has no type-checking workflow provides little value — the hints need to be checked by mypy or a similar tool to be useful.

Example 1 — Introduction

Basic type annotations on function parameters and return values.

```
# ── Basic parameter and return annotations ──────────────────
def celsius_to_fahrenheit(c: float) -> float:
    """Convert Celsius to Fahrenheit."""
```

```
    return c * 9 / 5 + 32

def greet(name: str, times: int = 1) -> str:
    """Return a repeated greeting string."""
    return (f'Hello, {name}! ' * times).strip()

def is_passing(score: float, threshold: float = 50.0) -> bool:
    """Return True if score meets or exceeds threshold."""
    return score >= threshold

# — Variable annotations ————————————————————————
max_students: int = 30
school_name: str  = 'Brisbane Heights Secondary'
scores: list[float] = []

# — Collections (Python 3.9+ syntax) ————————————————
def top_students(scores: dict[str, float], n: int) -> list[str]:
    """Return the names of the top n students by score."""
    sorted_names = sorted(scores, key=scores.get, reverse=True)
    return sorted_names[:n]

# — Collections (Python 3.8 compatible typing module syntax) —
from typing import Dict, List

def top_students_38(scores: Dict[str, float], n: int) -> List[str]:
    """Python 3.8-compatible version."""
    return sorted(scores, key=scores.get, reverse=True)[:n]

# Runtime: type hints are stored but not enforced
print(celsius_to_fahrenheit.__annotations__)
```

Output:

```
{'c': <class 'float'>, 'return': <class 'float'>}
```

Example 2 — Variation

Optional types, Union types, and the Python 3.10+ | operator.

```
from typing import Optional, Union

# Optional[X] means the value can be X or None.
# Python 3.10+ equivalent: X | None

# — Optional (pre-3.10 style) ——————————————————
def find_student(students: list, student_id: str) -> Optional[object]:
    """Return the student with the given ID, or None."""
    return next((s for s in students if s.student_id == student_id), None)

# — Optional (Python 3.10+ style) ————————————————
def find_student_modern(students: list, student_id: str) -> object | None:
    """Python 3.10+ syntax: object | None instead of Optional."""
    return next((s for s in students if s.student_id == student_id), None)

# — Union: accept multiple types ——————————————————
def parse_score(raw: Union[str, int, float]) -> float:
    """Convert a raw score value (string, int, or float) to float."""
    return float(raw)

# — Python 3.10+ Union with | ————————————————————
def parse_score_modern(raw: str | int | float) -> float:
    """Python 3.10+ union syntax."""
    return float(raw)
```

```python
# — Annotating None return type ————————————————
def log_score(score: float) -> None:
    """Print a score to stdout. Returns nothing."""
    print(f"Score recorded: {score}")

# — Annotating functions that never return ——————————
from typing import NoReturn

def abort(message: str) -> NoReturn:
    """Raise a RuntimeError unconditionally."""
    raise RuntimeError(message)
```

Output:

```
# Type hints for Optional and Union communicate intent clearly:
# Optional[str] tells the reader this might be None.
# Union[str, int] tells the reader this accepts two types.
# | syntax (3.10+) is more readable and requires no imports.
```

Example 3 — Real-world application

A fully annotated school utilities module using basic type hints throughout.

```python
"""
school_typed.py — Typed school utilities demonstrating PEP 484 annotations.
"""

from dataclasses import dataclass, field
from datetime import date
from typing import Optional

@dataclass
class Student:
    """A student record with full type annotations."""
    student_id : str
    name       : str
    year_level : int
    scores     : list[float] = field(default_factory=list)
    dob        : Optional[date] = None

    @property
    def average(self) -> float:
        """Return mean score, or 0.0 if no scores recorded."""
        return sum(self.scores) / len(self.scores) if self.scores else 0.0

def enrol(name: str, year_level: int, student_id: str) -> Student:
    """
    Create and return a new Student record.

    Args:
        name       (str): Full student name.
        year_level (int): Year level 7-12.
        student_id (str): Unique identifier.

    Returns:
        Student: Newly created record with empty scores list.
    """
    return Student(student_id=student_id, name=name, year_level=year_level)

def honour_roll(students: list[Student], cutoff: float = 80.0) ->
list[Student]:
    """
    Return students whose average meets or exceeds the cutoff.

    Args:
```

```
        students  (list[Student]): Candidates to evaluate.
        cutoff    (float):         Minimum average score. Default 80.0.

    Returns:
        list[Student]: Qualifying students, sorted by average descending.
    """
    eligible = [s for s in students if s.average >= cutoff]
    return sorted(eligible, key=lambda s: s.average, reverse=True)

def add_scores(student: Student, scores: list[float]) -> None:
    """
    Add multiple scores to a student record in place.

    Args:
        student (Student):     The student to update.
        scores  (list[float]): New scores to append.
    """
    student.scores.extend(scores)

if __name__ == '__main__':
    cohort = [
        enrol('Amara Osei',   11, 'S001'),
        enrol('Ben Whitmore', 10, 'S002'),
        enrol('Chloe Nguyen', 11, 'S003'),
    ]
    add_scores(cohort[0], [92.0, 88.0, 95.0])
    add_scores(cohort[1], [74.0, 79.0, 71.0])
    add_scores(cohort[2], [85.0, 90.0, 88.0])
    for s in honour_roll(cohort):
        print(f"{s.name:<20} avg={s.average:.1f}")
```

Output:

```
Amara Osei           avg=91.7
Chloe Nguyen         avg=87.7
```

Type hints on a dataclass are particularly powerful: they serve as both the field declarations and the documentation for what type each field holds. An IDE reading the annotated Student dataclass knows that student_id is a str, and will flag an error if you accidentally pass an int. This feedback appears while you type, not when you run the code.

Type Hints: Generics and the typing Module

The typing module provides advanced type constructs for situations where basic built-in types are insufficient. The most commonly used are TypeVar (for generic functions that work with any type), Callable (for annotating functions that accept other functions as arguments), Sequence and Iterable (for annotating functions that accept any ordered or iterable collection), and TypedDict (for annotating dicts with specific key-value types).

TypeVar allows a function's return type to mirror its argument type — the classic generic pattern. Without TypeVar, a function that accepts any list and returns an element must annotate the return as Any, which disables type checking for the result. With TypeVar T = TypeVar('T'), the annotation def first(items: list[T]) -> T declares that whatever type the list contains, the return type is the same.

Callable[[ArgType1, ArgType2], ReturnType] annotates a parameter that is expected to be a function with a specific signature. This is essential for decorators, strategy patterns, and any higher-order function. Sequence[T] accepts any ordered, indexable collection (list, tuple, str) without committing to a specific one. Protocol, added in Python 3.8, allows structural subtyping — declaring that any object with a specific set of methods satisfies a type, without requiring inheritance.

> **Note:** typing.Any disables type checking for a variable entirely — the checker treats it as compatible with everything. It is the escape hatch for situations where type information is genuinely unavailable (dynamic data from JSON, legacy code). Use Any sparingly: every Any is a hole in your type coverage.

Example 1 — Introduction

TypeVar for generic functions and Callable for higher-order function annotations.

```
from typing import TypeVar, Callable, Sequence

T = TypeVar('T')    # a type variable — represents any type

# Generic function: return type matches input element type
def first(items: Sequence[T]) -> T:
    """Return the first element of any sequence."""
    if not items:
        raise ValueError("Sequence must not be empty")
    return items[0]

# mypy knows that first([1, 2, 3]) returns int,
# and that first(['a', 'b']) returns str.
print(first([10, 20, 30]))    # int
print(first(('x', 'y')))      # str

# Callable[[input_types], return_type]
def apply_to_all(func: Callable[[float], float],
                 values: list[float]) -> list[float]:
    """Apply a float->float function to every element of a list."""
    return [func(v) for v in values]

import math
result = apply_to_all(math.sqrt, [4.0, 9.0, 16.0, 25.0])
print(result)

# The type checker knows func must accept and return float.
# Passing str.upper would be a type error — caught before running.
```

Output:

```
10
x
[2.0, 3.0, 4.0, 5.0]
```

Example 2 — Variation

TypedDict for annotating dictionaries with specific key types, and Protocol for structural subtyping.

```
from typing import TypedDict, Protocol, runtime_checkable

# ── TypedDict ─────────────────────────────────────────
# Declares the expected keys and value types for a dict.
class StudentRecord(TypedDict):
    name       : str
    year_level : int
    average    : float

def format_record(record: StudentRecord) -> str:
    """Format a student record dict for display."""
    return (f"{record['name']:<20} ",
            f"Year {record['year_level']}  ",
            f"avg={record['average']:.1f}")

# The type checker ensures dict has exactly these keys with correct types.
r: StudentRecord = {'name': 'Mia', 'year_level': 10, 'average': 87.5}
```

```
print(''.join(format_record(r)))

# — Protocol: structural subtyping ——————————————————
# Any class with a send(recipient) method satisfies Notifiable,
# even if it does not inherit from anything special.
@runtime_checkable
class Notifiable(Protocol):
    def send(self, recipient: str) -> bool:
        """Send a notification to the recipient."""
        ...

class EmailSender:
    """Satisfies Notifiable by implementing send()."""
    def send(self, recipient: str) -> bool:
        print(f"Email to {recipient}")
        return True

class SMSSender:
    """Also satisfies Notifiable."""
    def send(self, recipient: str) -> bool:
        print(f"SMS to {recipient}")
        return True

def broadcast(notifiers: list[Notifiable], recipient: str) -> None:
    """Send via all provided notifiers."""
    for n in notifiers:
        n.send(recipient)

broadcast([EmailSender(), SMSSender()], 'student@school.edu.au')
print(isinstance(EmailSender(), Notifiable))  # True — runtime check
```

Output:

```
Mia                    Year 10  avg=87.5
Email to student@school.edu.au
SMS to student@school.edu.au
True
```

Example 3 — Real-world application

A generic caching decorator fully annotated with TypeVar, Callable, and ParamSpec.

```
from typing import TypeVar, Callable
from functools import wraps
import time

T = TypeVar('T')

def timed_cache(func: Callable[..., T]) -> Callable[..., T]:
    """
    Decorator: cache results and print timing on first call.

    Args:
        func: The function to wrap. May have any signature.

    Returns:
        Callable: Wrapped function with identical signature,
            caching results by argument tuple.
    """
    cache: dict = {}

    @wraps(func)
    def wrapper(*args):
        if args not in cache:
            start = time.perf_counter()
```

```
            cache[args] = func(*args)
            elapsed = time.perf_counter() - start
            print(f"  [{func.__name__}] computed in {elapsed*1000:.2f}ms")
        return cache[args]
    return wrapper

@timed_cache
def fibonacci(n: int) -> int:
    """Return the nth Fibonacci number."""
    if n <= 1: return n
    return fibonacci(n - 1) + fibonacci(n - 2)

@timed_cache
def year_group(year: int) -> str:
    """Return the school group label for year level."""
    time.sleep(0.01)    # simulated delay
    return {7:'Junior',8:'Junior',9:'Middle',
            10:'Middle',11:'Senior',12:'Senior'}.get(year, 'Unknown')

print(fibonacci(10))
print(fibonacci(10))    # cached — no recompute message
print(year_group(11))
print(year_group(11))    # cached
```

Output:

```
  [fibonacci] computed in 0.05ms
55
55
  [year_group] computed in 10.23ms
Senior
Senior
```

The typing module's constructs become progressively more valuable as a codebase grows. A small script benefits most from basic int, str, float annotations. A library shared across a team benefits from TypeVar, Callable, and Protocol because they document the contracts between components precisely enough that a type checker can catch integration errors before they reach production.

8.6 mypy: Static Type Checking

mypy is the reference static type checker for Python. It reads type annotations and reports type errors — mismatched argument types, functions called with wrong argument counts, None used where a value is expected — without running the code. Installing mypy and running it as part of the development workflow turns type hints from documentation into an enforceable specification.

mypy is installed as a package (pip install mypy) and run from the command line: mypy mymodule.py or mypy src/ to check a whole directory. It produces output in the familiar error format: filename, line number, error category, and a message explaining what is wrong. The strictness of mypy's checking is configurable: running with --strict enables every available check, while the default mode is permissive and suitable as a starting point.

mypy works best when type hints are applied consistently. A function with no type annotations is treated as having all parameters and return values typed as Any, which mypy checks but does not flag as an error by default. The --disallow-untyped-defs flag changes this, requiring all functions to have annotations. For a new project, starting with default mode and gradually increasing strictness is more practical than applying --strict to existing unannotated code.

> **Note:** mypy reads a configuration file called mypy.ini or a [tool.mypy] section in pyproject.toml. Storing mypy configuration in pyproject.toml alongside the rest of the project's tool settings is the modern convention. Options such as ignore_missing_imports, disallow_untyped_defs, and warn_return_any can be set globally or per-module.

Example 1 — Introduction

A module with type errors that mypy catches before the code runs.

```
# typed_errors.py — deliberately contains type errors for mypy to catch

def add_scores(a: float, b: float) -> float:
    """Return the sum of two scores."""
    return a + b

def letter_grade(score: float) -> str:
    """Return the letter grade for a numeric score."""
    if score >= 90: return 'A'
    if score >= 80: return 'B'
    if score >= 70: return 'C'
    return 'D'

# ── Type errors ──────────────────────────────────────────

# Error 1: wrong argument type (str instead of float)
result = add_scores('88', 75.0)

# Error 2: wrong number of arguments
grade = letter_grade(85.0, 'extra')   # extra argument

# Error 3: using None where a float is expected
score: float = None                    # None is not float

# Error 4: returning the wrong type (int instead of str)
def year_label(year: int) -> str:
    return year                        # int, not str

# ── Running mypy ─────────────────────────────────────────
# mypy typed_errors.py
# typed_errors.py:14: error: Argument 1 to 'add_scores' has
#   incompatible type 'str'; expected 'float'  [arg-type]
# typed_errors.py:17: error: Too many arguments for 'letter_grade'
#   [call-arg]
# typed_errors.py:20: error: Incompatible types in assignment
#   (expression has type 'None', variable has type 'float')
#   [assignment]
# typed_errors.py:24: error: Incompatible return value type
#   (got 'int', expected 'str')  [return-value]
# Found 4 errors in 1 file (checked 1 source file)
```

Output:

```
# mypy typed_errors.py
typed_errors.py:14: error: Argument 1 to 'add_scores' has
  incompatible type 'str'; expected 'float'  [arg-type]
typed_errors.py:17: error: Too many arguments for 'letter_grade'
  [call-arg]
typed_errors.py:20: error: Incompatible types in assignment
  (expression has type 'None', variable has type 'float')  [assignment]
typed_errors.py:24: error: Incompatible return value type
  (got 'int', expected 'str')  [return-value]
Found 4 errors in 1 file (checked 1 source file)
```

Example 2 — Variation

Configuring mypy in pyproject.toml and running it with increasing strictness levels.

```
# — pyproject.toml mypy configuration ———————————————
# [tool.mypy]
# python_version          = '3.12'
# warn_return_any         = true
# warn_unused_ignores     = true
# ignore_missing_imports  = true

# Strict mode (uncomment for maximum coverage):
# disallow_untyped_defs    = true
# disallow_any_generics    = true
# check_untyped_defs       = true
# no_implicit_optional     = true

# — Command-line strictness levels ———————————————
# Default (permissive - good starting point):
mypy mymodule.py

# Warn about missing return-type annotations:
mypy mymodule.py --warn-return-any

# Require annotations on all functions:
mypy mymodule.py --disallow-untyped-defs

# Full strict mode:
mypy mymodule.py --strict

# — Suppressing a specific error with a type: ignore comment —
# Use sparingly - each # type: ignore is a gap in type coverage.
legacy_value = get_data_from_old_api()  # type: ignore[no-untyped-call]

# — Checking a whole package or src directory ———————————
mypy src/
mypy src/ --ignore-missing-imports

# — Generating an HTML report (requires lxml) ———————————
mypy src/ --html-report mypy_report/
```

Output:

```
# mypy src/ (clean code)
Success: no issues found in 8 source files

# mypy src/ --strict (with missing annotations)
src/school_typed.py:5: error: Function is missing a return type
  annotation  [no-untyped-def]
src/school_typed.py:12: error: Function is missing a type annotation
  for one or more arguments  [no-untyped-def]
Found 2 errors in 1 file
```

Example 3 — Real-world application

A module that passes mypy --strict: every function fully annotated, no Any, no untyped imports.

```
"""
grade_calculator.py - Grade computation, fully typed for mypy --strict.
"""

from __future__ import annotations
from typing import Final

__all__ = ['compute_grade', 'class_statistics', 'GradeResult']

BOUNDARIES: Final[list[tuple[float, str]]] = [
```

```
    (90.0, 'A'), (80.0, 'B'), (70.0, 'C'), (60.0, 'D'), (0.0, 'E')
]

class GradeResult:
    """Holds a computed grade and its letter."""
    def __init__(self, score: float, letter: str) -> None:
        self.score  = score
        self.letter = letter

    def __repr__(self) -> str:
        return f"GradeResult({self.score}, {self.letter!r})"

def compute_grade(score: float) -> GradeResult:
    """
    Return a GradeResult for the given numeric score.

    Args:
        score (float): Assessment score 0-100.

    Returns:
        GradeResult: Score and letter grade.
    """
    for threshold, letter in BOUNDARIES:
        if score >= threshold:
            return GradeResult(score, letter)
    return GradeResult(score, 'E')

def class_statistics(scores: list[float]) -> dict[str, float]:
    """
    Return mean, min, and max for a list of scores.

    Args:
        scores (list[float]): Non-empty score list.

    Returns:
        dict[str, float]: Keys 'mean', 'min', 'max'.

    Raises:
        ValueError: If scores is empty.
    """
    if not scores:
        raise ValueError("Cannot compute statistics for empty list")
    return {
        'mean': sum(scores) / len(scores),
        'min':  min(scores),
        'max':  max(scores),
    }

if __name__ == '__main__':
    data: list[float] = [88.0, 74.5, 91.0, 63.0, 85.5]
    for s in data:
        r = compute_grade(s)
        print(f"{r.score:>6.1f}  {r.letter}")
    stats = class_statistics(data)
    print(f"Mean: {stats['mean']:.1f}  Min: {stats['min']}  Max:
{stats['max']}")
```

Output:

```
  88.0  B
  74.5  C
  91.0  A
  63.0  D
  85.5  B
Mean: 80.4  Min: 63.0  Max: 91.0
```

```
# mypy grade_calculator.py --strict
Success: no issues found in 1 source file
```

Passing mypy --strict on a module is a meaningful quality signal: it means every input and output is documented in machine-verifiable form, every None is accounted for, and every function is callable with confidence about what it expects and returns. Aim for --strict compliance on all new modules; for legacy code, start with default mode and progressively tighten.

8.7 Generating HTML Documentation with pydoc and pdoc

Python ships with pydoc, a built-in documentation generator that reads module and function docstrings and produces formatted output in the terminal or as HTML. For quick, no-install documentation browsing, pydoc is immediate: python -m pydoc mymodule prints the documentation to the terminal, and python -m pydoc -b starts a local web server with a searchable index of all installed packages.

pdoc is a third-party alternative (pip install pdoc) that produces cleaner, more modern HTML by parsing Google-style and NumPy-style docstrings into structured sections, rendering type hints as clickable links, and including source code navigation. For distributing documentation alongside a Python package, pdoc is the current lightweight recommendation. More complex documentation needs — cross-references, tutorials, versioned docs hosting — are the domain of Sphinx, which is the standard for large open-source projects but has a steeper configuration curve.

Both tools use the same source: the docstrings and type hints already in the code. This is why writing good docstrings from the start is so valuable — the documentation effort is not repeated, and the generated HTML is always in sync with the code. Running pdoc mymodule --output-dir docs/ as a CI step ensures that the documentation is regenerated and published automatically on every merge to the main branch.

> **Note:** pdoc renders type hints as part of the function signature in the generated HTML. If your module has type hints, pdoc will show them. If it does not, only the parameter names appear. This is another reason why type hints and docstrings together are more valuable than either alone.

Example 1 — Introduction

Using Python's built-in pydoc to explore module documentation from the command line and as HTML.

```
# ── Terminal documentation ──────────────────────────────
# Print docs for a module already in the environment
python -m pydoc statistics
python -m pydoc pathlib.Path

# Print docs for a local module
python -m pydoc ./school_typed.py

# ── Start the pydoc web server ──────────────────────────
# Opens a browser with a searchable index of all installed packages
python -m pydoc -b
# Browse to http://localhost:<port> - pydoc prints the port number

# ── Generate a static HTML file ─────────────────────────
python -m pydoc -w school_typed
# Creates school_typed.html in the current directory
```

```
# — Accessing docstrings programmatically ──────────────
import pydoc
import school_typed

# Get the formatted text as a string
text = pydoc.render_doc(school_typed, renderer=pydoc.plaintext)
# Print first 400 characters
print(text[:400])
```

Output:

```
Python Library Documentation: module school_typed

NAME
    school_typed - school_typed.py — Typed school utilities demonstrating
    PEP 484 annotations.

CLASSES
    builtins.object
        Student

    class Student(builtins.object)
     |  Student(student_id: str, name: str, year_level: int, ...)
     |
     |  A student record with full type annotations.
```

Example 2 — Variation

Using pdoc to generate a modern HTML documentation site from a module.

```
# — Install pdoc ──────────────────────────────────
pip install pdoc

# — Preview in browser (starts a live server) ──────────
pdoc school_typed
# Open http://localhost:8080 — updates automatically on file save

# — Generate static HTML files ──────────────────────
pdoc school_typed --output-dir docs/
# Creates docs/school_typed.html

# — Document a package ─────────────────────────────
pdoc src/srs/ --output-dir docs/
# Creates one HTML file per module

# — pdoc reads type hints and renders them in the HTML ─────
# A function annotated as:
#   def enrol(name: str, year_level: int) -> Student:
# renders in HTML as:
#   enrol(name: str, year_level: int) -> Student
# with 'Student' as a clickable link to the Student class docs.

# — CI/CD integration: regenerate on every push ─────────
# In a GitHub Actions workflow (.github/workflows/docs.yml):
# - name: Generate docs
#   run: |
#     pip install pdoc
#     pdoc src/srs/ --output-dir docs/
# - name: Deploy to GitHub Pages
#   uses: peaceiris/actions-gh-pages@v3
#   with:
#     publish_dir: ./docs
```

Output:

```
# pdoc src/srs/ --output-dir docs/
```

```
Generated /home/student/srs_project/docs/srs.html
Generated /home/student/srs_project/docs/srs/models.html
Generated /home/student/srs_project/docs/srs/operations.html
Generated /home/student/srs_project/docs/srs/reports.html

# The HTML pages include:
# - Module docstring as the page introduction
# - Each class with its Attributes: section rendered as a table
# - Each function with Args/Returns/Raises sections
# - Type hints rendered with links between related types
```

Example 3 — Real-world application

A documentation generation script that runs pydoc and pdoc on a package, verifies coverage, and reports undocumented names.

```
"""
gen_docs.py — Generate and audit documentation for a Python package.

Usage: python gen_docs.py <package_path> [--output-dir docs/]
"""

import subprocess
import sys
import inspect
import importlib
from pathlib import Path

def count_undocumented(module_name):
    """Return a list of public names without docstrings."""
    try:
        mod = importlib.import_module(module_name)
    except ImportError:
        return []
    undoc = []
    for name, obj in inspect.getmembers(mod):
        if name.startswith('_'):
            continue
        if inspect.isfunction(obj) or inspect.isclass(obj):
            if not inspect.getdoc(obj):
                undoc.append(name)
    return undoc

def run_pdoc(package_path, output_dir):
    """Generate HTML docs using pdoc."""
    result = subprocess.run(
        ['pdoc', str(package_path), '--output-dir', str(output_dir)],
        capture_output=True, text=True
    )
    if result.returncode != 0:
        print(f"pdoc error: {result.stderr}")
        return False
    for line in result.stdout.splitlines():
        print(f"  {line}")
    return True

def main():
    pkg = sys.argv[1] if len(sys.argv) > 1 else 'statistics'
    out = Path(sys.argv[2]) if len(sys.argv) > 2 else Path('docs')

    print(f"=== Documentation Generation: {pkg} ===")

    # Check for undocumented public names
    undoc = count_undocumented(pkg)
    if undoc:
```

```
        print(f"\nWarning: {len(undoc)} undocumented public name(s):")
        for name in undoc:
            print(f"  - {name}")
    else:
        print("\nAll public names are documented.")

    # Generate HTML documentation
    print(f"\nGenerating HTML docs -> {out}/")
    success = run_pdoc(pkg, out)
    if success:
        print(f"Documentation written to {out}/")
        html_files = list(out.glob('**/*.html'))
        print(f"  {len(html_files)} HTML file(s) generated.")

if __name__ == '__main__':
    main()
```

Output:

```
=== Documentation Generation: statistics ===

All public names are documented.

Generating HTML docs -> docs/
  Generated docs/statistics.html
Documentation written to docs/
  1 HTML file(s) generated.
```

The combination of docstrings, type hints, mypy, and pdoc forms a complete documentation and verification pipeline. Docstrings communicate intent to humans. Type hints communicate types to tools. mypy verifies that calls match the declared types. pdoc publishes everything as browsable HTML. Each layer reinforces the others, and together they raise the quality bar for a Python project from functional to professional.

Chapter 9 builds on the well-documented, properly typed modules developed throughout this book and takes the final step: packaging them for distribution — creating an installable sdist and wheel, writing a pyproject.toml, and publishing to the Python Package Index.

Chapter 8 Summary

- Good documentation is specific, accurate, and brief. Write the docstring before the function body: if you cannot summarise what it does in one sentence, the design needs clarifying first. The single most expensive documentation error is inaccuracy — a docstring that contradicts the code is worse than none.
- PEP 257 defines where docstrings go (immediately after def or class), how they are quoted (triple double-quotes), and their basic structure (one-sentence summary, blank line, detail). Google style and NumPy style extend PEP 257 with Args/Returns/Raises section formats. Pick one convention and apply it consistently.
- Module docstrings describe the module's purpose and public API. Class docstrings document the class's purpose and instance attributes (in an Attributes: section). Method and function docstrings document parameters, return values, and exceptions. All three levels are displayed by help() and rendered by documentation generators.
- Type hints annotate parameters (param: type), return values (-> type), and variables (name: type). They are not enforced at runtime but are read by mypy, IDEs, and pdoc. Python 3.9+ allows list[float], dict[str, int] directly. Python 3.10+ allows X | None instead of Optional[X] and X | Y instead of Union[X, Y].

- The typing module provides advanced constructs: TypeVar for generic functions whose return type mirrors argument type, Callable[[ArgTypes], ReturnType] for higher-order function parameters, TypedDict for annotating dicts with specific key-value types, and Protocol for structural subtyping without inheritance.
- mypy is the reference static type checker. Run mypy mymodule.py to check for type errors without executing code. Configure strictness in pyproject.toml under [tool.mypy]. The --strict flag enables all checks; --disallow-untyped-defs requires annotations on every function. Use # type: ignore[code] sparingly for genuinely unavoidable exceptions.
- pydoc is Python's built-in documentation renderer: python -m pydoc mymodule prints docs to the terminal; python -m pydoc -b starts a searchable web server. pdoc (pip install pdoc) generates modern HTML from docstrings and type hints, with type annotations rendered as clickable links between related types.
- Docstrings, type hints, mypy, and pdoc form a mutually reinforcing pipeline: docstrings communicate intent to humans, type hints communicate types to tools, mypy catches violations before runtime, and pdoc publishes everything as browsable HTML that is always in sync with the source code.

Guided Exercises

1. Take any two modules you wrote in earlier chapters (such as gst_utils.py or school_utils.py from Chapter 3) and add complete Google-style docstrings to every public function, class, and method. Include a module-level docstring listing the public API. Then run python -m pydoc <module> and confirm that the output displays all sections correctly. Identify any places where the existing code behaviour differs from what you wrote in the docstring.

> **Hint:** Use inspect.getdoc() programmatically to retrieve and print each docstring, confirming they are present and clean. Check that Args:, Returns:, and Raises: sections are present on every non-trivial function.

2. Add type hints to the same two modules from Exercise 1. Start with basic annotations (int, float, str, bool, list, dict). Use Optional[X] or X | None for any parameter that can be None. Use list[float] and dict[str, float] for collection types. Run mypy in default mode (mypy mymodule.py) and fix any errors it reports.

> **Hint:** Install mypy with pip install mypy. Common first errors are: missing return type annotations, and Optional types where None was implicitly allowed. Add -> None to functions that do not return a value.

3. Write a new module called converters.py with at least five conversion functions (e.g., km_to_miles, celsius_to_fahrenheit, aud_to_usd, kg_to_lbs, litres_to_gallons). Annotate all parameters and return values with type hints. Add full Google-style docstrings including at least one doctest Example: in each function. Run mypy converters.py --strict and fix all errors until it reports success.

> **Hint:** from __future__ import annotations at the top of the file (Python 3.9 compatibility). For --strict compliance, all functions must have annotations, no Any types, and explicit return types. Add a -> float return type to every conversion function.

4. Use pdoc to generate HTML documentation for the converters.py module from Exercise 3. Install pdoc (pip install pdoc), run pdoc converters.py --output-dir docs/, and open the generated HTML in a browser. Observe how type hints and docstrings are rendered. Then deliberately remove one type hint and one docstring, regenerate, and compare the HTML output before and after.

> **Hint:** pdoc renders type hints in the function signature and formats Args:/Returns:/Raises: sections as structured tables. Without type hints, only parameter names appear. Without the docstring section, that section is missing from the HTML entirely.

5. Write a doc_audit.py script that accepts a module name as a command-line argument and reports: (a) total public functions and classes, (b) names missing docstrings, (c) names with only a one-line summary (no Args/Returns sections), (d) names with both a full docstring and type annotations on all parameters. Run it against the statistics standard library module and then against one of your own modules.

Hint: Use inspect.getmembers with inspect.isfunction and inspect.isclass. Use inspect.getdoc() for the docstring and inspect.signature() to check for annotations. A function has full annotations if all parameters and the return in func.__annotations__ are present.

Challenge Tasks

1. Build a type-safe version of the Student Records System's operations module using the full type-hint toolkit from this chapter. Every function must have complete parameter and return annotations. Use TypedDict for any dict-shaped data, Optional for nullable fields, and list[Student] instead of plain list. Write a dataclass-based GradeReport type that holds a student, a list of GradeResult objects (from the grade_calculator example), a computed average, and a letter summary. Annotate a function generate_report(student: Student) -> GradeReport fully. Run mypy --strict on the entire module and achieve zero errors. Use pdoc to generate HTML documentation for the module.

2. Create a Protocol-based plugin architecture for a report formatter. Define a ReportFormatter Protocol with two required methods: format_row(record: dict[str, str]) -> str and format_header(columns: list[str]) -> str. Write three concrete implementations: TextFormatter (plain text with pipe separators), CSVFormatter (comma-separated), and MarkdownFormatter (Markdown table syntax). Write a generate_report(records: list[dict[str, str]], formatter: ReportFormatter) -> str function that uses any formatter that satisfies the Protocol. Annotate everything completely, run mypy --strict to zero errors, write full Google-style docstrings on every class and function, and generate HTML docs with pdoc.

3. Build a documentation health dashboard. The script accepts a package directory as an argument, imports every module in the package using importlib, and for each public function and class computes: (a) has_docstring (bool), (b) has_summary (bool — first line is non-empty), (c) has_args_section (bool — contains 'Args:' or 'Parameters'), (d) has_return_section (bool), (e) annotation_coverage (float — fraction of parameters and return that are annotated). Output a formatted HTML report (generate it with string formatting, not pdoc) that shows one row per function with colour-coded cells (green=present, red=missing) for each criterion, plus a summary row with overall percentages. Save the report to coverage_report.html.

CHAPTER 9 **Publishing a Simple Package**

Book 03: Modules, Packages & the Python Ecosystem

> The modules, packages, virtual environments, and documentation practices developed across this book are the ingredients of a shareable Python library. This chapter assembles them into a distributable package — something that other developers can install with a single pip install command, just as you have installed packages from PyPI throughout this book. The path from a working local package to a published distribution involves a precise directory structure (the src layout), a configuration file that declares metadata and build instructions (pyproject.toml), a build tool that produces the distributable artefacts, and a publishing workflow that uploads them to the Python Package Index. Understanding this pipeline closes the loop: you are no longer only a consumer of PyPI packages, but a potential contributor to the ecosystem that every Python developer depends on.

9.1 Package Structure for Distribution: src Layout

A package intended for distribution has different structural requirements from one used only within a single project. The most important difference is the src layout: placing all importable source code inside a src/ subdirectory rather than directly at the project root. This single structural choice eliminates an entire category of packaging bugs that are otherwise difficult to diagnose.

The problem the src layout solves is accidental local imports. When a package lives directly at the project root — say, schooltools/__init__.py — running python from that directory puts the root on sys.path. This means import schooltools resolves to the local directory rather than to the installed version. A developer can accidentally pass tests against the local source while having a broken or missing installation, shipping a package that fails to install correctly on any other machine. With the src layout, the source is in src/schooltools/, which is never on sys.path by default, so every import goes through the installed package.

The conventional top-level structure for a distributable package has four elements: pyproject.toml at the root (build configuration and metadata), src/packagename/ (all source code), tests/ (test files, outside src/ so they are not included in the installed package by default), and a README.md and LICENCE file. The src/ directory itself has no __init__.py — it is not a package, just a directory that contains one.

> **Note:** The src layout is not mandatory — pip and setuptools support both flat and src layouts. However, the Python Packaging Authority recommends src layout for all packages intended for distribution, and most modern packaging documentation uses it. Adopting it from the start is the right habit.

Example 1 — Introduction

Flat layout vs src layout — directory structure comparison and the import bug flat layout can cause.

```
# — FLAT LAYOUT (common beginner approach) ————————————————
school_calc/
  school_calc/          # source lives at project root
    __init__.py
    arithmetic.py
  tests/
    test_arithmetic.py
  pyproject.toml
```

```
# Bug: running 'python -m pytest' from school_calc/ adds . to sys.path.
# 'import school_calc' resolves to ./school_calc/ — the local source.
# If school_calc is not installed (or installed at a different version),
# tests pass against local code but the installed package may be broken.

# ── SRC LAYOUT (recommended) ──────────────────────────────────
school_calc/
  src/
    school_calc/          # source inside src/ — never on sys.path by default
      __init__.py
      arithmetic.py
  tests/
    test_arithmetic.py
  pyproject.toml
  README.md
  LICENCE

# With src layout, 'import school_calc' ONLY works if the package
# is installed (editable or otherwise). Tests always run against
# the installed version — no more accidental local imports.
```

Output:

```
# Demonstrating the bug with flat layout:
# $ cd school_calc/          (project root)
# $ python -c 'import school_calc; print(school_calc.__file__)'
# ./school_calc/__init__.py  ← local source, NOT installed package

# With src layout (after pip install -e .):
# $ python -c 'import school_calc; print(school_calc.__file__)'
# .../site-packages/school_calc/__init__.py  ← installed package
```

Example 2 — Variation

The complete src layout directory tree with all conventional files annotated.

```
# Full src layout for a school utility package ready for distribution

school_calc/                  # project root (git repository root)
  src/
    school_calc/              # installable package
      __init__.py             # package version + public API re-exports
      arithmetic.py           # core arithmetic functions
      statistics.py           # statistical utilities
      formatters.py           # output formatting helpers
  tests/                      # test suite (not installed)
    __init__.py               # empty — makes tests a discoverable package
    test_arithmetic.py
    test_statistics.py
    test_formatters.py
  docs/                       # pdoc-generated HTML (not installed)
  dist/                       # build output — in .gitignore
  .venv/                      # virtual environment — in .gitignore
  .gitignore
  pyproject.toml              # build config and package metadata
  README.md                   # shown on PyPI project page
  LICENCE                     # e.g. MIT, Apache 2.0
  requirements-dev.txt        # dev tools: pytest, mypy, black, pdoc

# src/school_calc/__init__.py ──────────────────────────────
"""
school_calc — School mathematics utilities.

Public API:
    add, subtract, multiply, divide   — basic arithmetic
    mean, median, stdev               — descriptive statistics
```

```
    format_score, format_currency      - output formatters
"""
from .arithmetic  import add, subtract, multiply, divide
from .statistics  import mean, median, stdev
from .formatters  import format_score, format_currency

__version__ = "1.0.0"
__all__ = ["add","subtract","multiply","divide",
           "mean","median","stdev",
           "format_score","format_currency"]
```

Output:

```
# Directory listing after pip install -e .
$ pip show school_calc
Name: school-calc
Version: 1.0.0
Location: .../school_calc/src
Editable project location: .../school_calc
```

Example 3 — Real-world application

The src/ source modules for school_calc with type hints and Google-style docstrings.

```
# src/school_calc/arithmetic.py
"""Arithmetic operations for school_calc."""
from __future__ import annotations
__all__ = ['add','subtract','multiply','divide']

def add(a: float, b: float) -> float:
    """Return the sum of a and b."""
    return a + b

def subtract(a: float, b: float) -> float:
    """Return a minus b."""
    return a - b

def multiply(a: float, b: float) -> float:
    """Return the product of a and b."""
    return a * b

def divide(a: float, b: float) -> float:
    """
    Return a divided by b.

    Raises:
        ZeroDivisionError: If b is zero.
    """
    if b == 0:
        raise ZeroDivisionError("Cannot divide by zero")
    return a / b

# src/school_calc/formatters.py
"""Output formatting helpers."""
__all__ = ['format_score','format_currency']

def format_score(name: str, score: float, width: int = 20) -> str:
    """Return a formatted name/score line."""
    return f"{name:<{width}} {score:>6.1f}"

def format_currency(amount: float, symbol: str = '$') -> str:
    """Return amount formatted as currency."""
    return f"{symbol}{amount:,.2f}"
```

Output:

```
# from school_calc import add, format_score
# add(88.5, 11.5)          → 100.0
# format_score('Mia', 88.5)  → 'Mia                    88.5'
```

The src layout enforces a clean separation between the package source and all other project files. Tests, documentation, configuration, and build artefacts each have their own top-level directory, and the boundary between what is installed and what stays on the developer's machine is unambiguous. This structure is the starting point for everything that follows in this chapter.

pyproject.toml: the Modern Build Configuration File

pyproject.toml is the single configuration file that modern Python packaging tools use. It was introduced by PEP 517 and PEP 518 to replace the fragmented combination of setup.py, setup.cfg, and MANIFEST.in that characterised packaging for the previous decade. A single pyproject.toml at the project root describes the build system, the project metadata, and the settings for any tool that supports it (mypy, pytest, black, isort).

The file has two mandatory tables for packaging: [build-system] declares which tool is responsible for building the package and what it needs to do so, and [project] declares the package metadata — name, version, description, and everything that appears on the PyPI project page. The [build-system] table is read by pip before anything else; it tells pip which build backend to install and invoke. setuptools is the default and most widely supported backend; flit and hatchling are modern alternatives that require less configuration for simple packages.

The [project] table is the successor to setup.py's setup() call. Every key in [project] corresponds directly to a field that appears in the package's METADATA file and on its PyPI page. The requires-python field determines which Python versions pip will attempt installation on. The dependencies list is the install_requires from setup.py — the packages needed at runtime. Optional extras (test, dev, docs) let callers install additional packages with pip install school_calc[dev].

> **Note:** pyproject.toml uses TOML syntax, not Python. TOML strings use double quotes, arrays use square brackets, and tables use square-bracket headers. A common mistake is using single quotes (invalid in TOML) or omitting quotes around version specifiers. Validate the file with python -c "import tomllib; tomllib.load(open('pyproject.toml','rb'))" before building.

Example 1 — Introduction

A minimal but complete pyproject.toml using the setuptools backend.

```
# pyproject.toml — minimal complete version for school_calc

[build-system]
requires      = ["setuptools>=68", "wheel"]
build-backend = "setuptools.backends.legacy:build"

[project]
name            = "school-calc"
version         = "1.0.0"
description     = "School mathematics utilities for arithmetic and statistics"
readme          = "README.md"
requires-python = ">=3.10"
license         = {text = "MIT"}

[[project.authors]]
name  = "M. North"
email = "m.north@northwardhouse.com.au"
```

```
[project.urls]
Homepage      = "https://github.com/northward/school-calc"
Documentation = "https://northward.github.io/school-calc"
Issues        = "https://github.com/northward/school-calc/issues"
```

Output:

```
# python -c "import tomllib;
print(tomllib.load(open('pyproject.toml','rb'))['project']['name'])"
school-calc

# pip install -e .   (reads pyproject.toml and installs in editable mode)
Successfully installed school-calc-1.0.0
```

Example 2 — Variation

Comparing setuptools, flit, and hatchling build-backend declarations.

```
# ── setuptools (most widely supported, most configurable) ───
[build-system]
requires      = ["setuptools>=68", "wheel"]
build-backend = "setuptools.backends.legacy:build"

# Optional: tell setuptools where to find packages in src layout
[tool.setuptools.packages.find]
where = ["src"]

# ── flit (minimal config, good for pure-Python packages) ────
[build-system]
requires      = ["flit_core>=3.9"]
build-backend = "flit_core.buildapi"
# flit requires __version__ in the package __init__.py
# and auto-discovers the package without extra config

# ── hatchling (modern, fast, extensible) ──────────────
[build-system]
requires      = ["hatchling"]
build-backend = "hatchling.build"

[tool.hatch.build.targets.wheel]
packages = ["src/school_calc"]

# All three produce identical wheel and sdist artefacts.
# setuptools: most compatible with older tooling.
# flit: simplest setup for pure-Python packages.
# hatchling: best performance and extensibility for large projects.
```

Output:

```
# The choice of build backend does not affect the installed package.
# It only affects what runs when 'python -m build' is invoked.
# All three produce school_calc-1.0.0-py3-none-any.whl
```

Example 3 — Real-world application

A pyproject.toml with tool configuration sections for mypy, pytest, and black alongside the project metadata.

```
# pyproject.toml — production-ready with tool configuration

[build-system]
requires      = ["setuptools>=68","wheel"]
build-backend = "setuptools.backends.legacy:build"

[tool.setuptools.packages.find]
```

```toml
where = ["src"]

[project]
name            = "school-calc"
version         = "1.0.0"
description     = "School mathematics utilities for arithmetic and statistics"
readme          = "README.md"
requires-python = ">=3.10"
license         = {text = "MIT"}
keywords        = ["education","mathematics","school","statistics"]

[[project.authors]]
name  = "M. North"
email = "m.north@northwardhouse.com.au"

[project.classifiers]
# Full list: https://pypi.org/classifiers/
classifiers = [
  "Development Status :: 5 - Production/Stable",
  "Intended Audience :: Education",
  "License :: OSI Approved :: MIT License",
  "Programming Language :: Python :: 3",
  "Programming Language :: Python :: 3.10",
  "Programming Language :: Python :: 3.11",
  "Programming Language :: Python :: 3.12",
  "Topic :: Education",
]

[project.optional-dependencies]
dev  = ["pytest>=8","mypy>=1.9","black>=24","pdoc"]
docs = ["pdoc"]

[tool.mypy]
python_version         = "3.12"
warn_return_any        = true
disallow_untyped_defs  = true
ignore_missing_imports = true

[tool.pytest.ini_options]
testpaths = ["tests"]
addopts   = "-v"

[tool.black]
line-length    = 88
target-version = ["py310","py311","py312"]
```

Output:

```
# pip install -e '.[dev]'  installs the package plus all dev dependencies
# pip install -e '.[docs]' installs the package plus pdoc
# mypy, pytest, and black all read their settings from pyproject.toml
```

Centralising all tool configuration in pyproject.toml means a new developer cloning the repository gets consistent behaviour from every tool without any additional setup. The [project] table alone is sufficient to publish; the [tool.*] tables are optional but strongly recommended for maintaining code quality across a team.

Metadata: name, version, description, dependencies

The metadata in pyproject.toml's [project] table determines how the package appears on PyPI, which Python versions pip will attempt installation on, and what gets installed alongside it. Getting this metadata right is important before publishing — once a version is on PyPI, it cannot be updated or deleted without publishing a new version.

Package names on PyPI are case-insensitive and normalised (hyphens and underscores are equivalent). The name must be unique across all of PyPI. By convention, distribution names use hyphens (school-calc), while import names use underscores (school_calc). The version field must be a valid PEP 440 version string; non-compliant strings cause the build to fail. The description is a one-line summary (shown in search results); the readme points to a file whose contents become the long description shown on the project page.

Classifiers are standardised strings from a controlled vocabulary published at pypi.org/classifiers. They are used by PyPI's search and filtering system and tell users at a glance the maturity, audience, and topic of the package. The Development Status classifier is particularly important: '5 - Production/Stable' signals a package that is safe to rely on, while '2 - Pre-Alpha' warns that the API may change without notice.

> **Note:** The dependencies list in [project] accepts PEP 440 version specifiers (see Chapter 7). Like a library's requirements, these should use ranges (~=, >=,<) rather than pinned versions, so that pip can find a compatible set of packages when the user has other packages installed. Only pin exact versions in an application's requirements.txt, never in a library's pyproject.toml.

Example 1 — Introduction

Reading and validating pyproject.toml metadata programmatically using Python's built-in tomllib.

```
import tomllib
from pathlib import Path

def read_project_metadata(path='pyproject.toml'):
    """Read and return the [project] table from pyproject.toml."""
    with open(path, 'rb') as f:
        data = tomllib.load(f)
    return data.get('project', {})

def validate_metadata(meta):
    """Check that required fields are present and print a report."""
    required = ['name','version','description','requires-python']
    optional = ['readme','license','authors','classifiers','keywords']
    print('Metadata validation report')
    print('=' * 40)
    all_ok = True
    for field in required:
        if field in meta:
            print(f"  OK  [required] {field}: {str(meta[field])[:50]}")
        else:
            print(f"  MISSING [required] {field}")
            all_ok = False
    for field in optional:
        if field in meta:
            print(f"  OK  [optional] {field}")
        else:
            print(f"  --  [optional] {field}: not set")
    print()
    print("All required fields present." if all_ok else "Fix missing fields 
before building.")
    return all_ok

meta = read_project_metadata()
validate_metadata(meta)
```

Output:

```
Metadata validation report
========================================
  OK  [required] name: school-calc
  OK  [required] version: 1.0.0
  OK  [required] description: School mathematics utilities ...
  OK  [required] requires-python: >=3.10
  OK  [optional] readme
  OK  [optional] license
  OK  [optional] authors
  OK  [optional] classifiers
  --  [optional] keywords: not set

All required fields present.
```

Example 2 — Variation

Version string formats: valid and invalid PEP 440 examples, and the normalisation rules for package names.

```
from packaging.version import Version, InvalidVersion
from packaging.utils   import canonicalize_name

# ── Valid PEP 440 version strings ──────────────────────
versions = [
    '1.0.0',         # release
    '1.0.0a1',       # alpha pre-release
    '1.0.0b2',       # beta pre-release
    '1.0.0rc1',      # release candidate
    '1.0.0.post1',   # post-release (e.g. documentation fix)
    '1.0.0.dev1',    # dev release (not for public distribution)
    '2.0',           # two-component release — valid
]

for v in versions:
    try:
        parsed = Version(v)
        print(f"  VALID   {v:<20} normalised: {parsed}")
    except InvalidVersion as e:
        print(f"  INVALID {v:<20} {e}")

# ── Package name normalisation ─────────────────────────
# PyPI normalises names: School_Calc == school-calc == school_calc
names = ['school_calc','School-Calc','SCHOOL.CALC','school calc']
for name in names:
    try:
        norm = canonicalize_name(name)
        print(f"  {name:<20} → {norm}")
    except Exception as e:
        print(f"  {name:<20} INVALID: {e}")
```

Output:

```
  VALID  1.0.0                normalised: 1.0.0
  VALID  1.0.0a1              normalised: 1.0.0a1
  VALID  1.0.0b2              normalised: 1.0.0b2
  VALID  1.0.0rc1             normalised: 1.0.0rc1
  VALID  1.0.0.post1          normalised: 1.0.0.post1
  VALID  1.0.0.dev1           normalised: 1.0.0.dev1
  VALID  2.0                  normalised: 2.0
  school_calc          → school-calc
  School-Calc          → school-calc
  SCHOOL.CALC          → school-calc
  school calc          → school-calc
```

Example 3 — Real-world application

A fully populated [project] table with classifiers, dependencies, optional extras, and project URLs.

```
# pyproject.toml — [project] section with full metadata

[project]
name            = "school-calc"
version         = "1.0.0"
description     = "School mathematics utilities: arithmetic, statistics,
formatting"
readme          = "README.md"
requires-python = ">=3.10"
license         = {text = "MIT"}
keywords        = ["education","maths","school","statistics","australia"]

[[project.authors]]
name  = "M. North"
email = "m.north@northwardhouse.com.au"

[project.classifiers]
# Development status
classifiers = [
  "Development Status :: 5 - Production/Stable",
  # Audience
  "Intended Audience :: Education",
  "Intended Audience :: Developers",
  # Licence
  "License :: OSI Approved :: MIT License",
  # Python versions supported
  "Programming Language :: Python :: 3",
  "Programming Language :: Python :: 3 :: Only",
  "Programming Language :: Python :: 3.10",
  "Programming Language :: Python :: 3.11",
  "Programming Language :: Python :: 3.12",
  # Topic
  "Topic :: Education",
  "Topic :: Scientific/Engineering :: Mathematics",
  # Operating system
  "Operating System :: OS Independent",
]

# Runtime dependencies (use ranges, not pinned versions)
[project.dependencies]
dependencies = ["packaging>=23.0"]

# Optional dependency groups
[project.optional-dependencies]
dev  = ["pytest>=8","mypy>=1.9","black>=24","pip-audit>=2.7","pdoc"]
docs = ["pdoc"]

[project.urls]
Homepage      = "https://github.com/northward/school-calc"
Documentation = "https://northward.github.io/school-calc"
Changelog     = "https://github.com/northward/school-
calc/blob/main/CHANGELOG.md"
Issues        = "https://github.com/northward/school-calc/issues"
```

Output:

```
# pip install school-calc[dev]  installs package + pytest + mypy + black + pdoc
# pip install school-calc[docs] installs package + pdoc
# pip install school-calc       installs package + packaging (runtime dep only)
```

The classifiers table is worth spending time on. PyPI users filter search results by classifier, so a package without Development Status or Topic classifiers is invisible to many potential users. The full controlled vocabulary at pypi.org/classifiers contains hundreds of options; selecting the most accurate half-dozen from it takes five minutes and makes the package significantly more discoverable.

Building a Distribution: python -m build

A distribution is the artefact that pip downloads and installs. There are two distribution formats: a source distribution (sdist) and a wheel (binary distribution). An sdist is a .tar.gz archive of the source code plus metadata; pip builds it into a wheel on the target machine. A wheel is a pre-built archive (a .whl file, which is a renamed zip) that pip installs directly without building. Providing a wheel makes installation faster and avoids requiring a compiler on the target machine.

The build package (pip install build) provides the python -m build command that produces both formats in one step. It creates a clean temporary environment, installs the build backend declared in pyproject.toml, runs the build, and places the results in the dist/ directory. The wheel filename encodes the package name, version, Python version compatibility, ABI tag, and platform: school_calc-1.0.0-py3-none-any.whl means pure Python, any ABI, any platform — the common case for a package with no compiled extensions.

Before uploading to PyPI, the twine check command validates that the distribution metadata is well-formed and that the README renders correctly as reStructuredText or Markdown. A package with malformed metadata will be rejected by PyPI's upload endpoint, so running twine check is an important step in the build workflow. twine is installed with pip install twine.

> **Note:** Never manually edit files inside dist/. If the build output is incorrect, fix the source or pyproject.toml and rebuild. The dist/ directory should be in .gitignore — it contains generated artefacts, not source code.

Example 1 — Introduction

The full build workflow: install build, run python -m build, and inspect the output.

```
# — Step 1: install the build package ————————————————
pip install build

# — Step 2: build from the project root ————————————————
# This creates both sdist (.tar.gz) and wheel (.whl) in dist/
python -m build

# Build sdist only:
python -m build --sdist

# Build wheel only:
python -m build --wheel

# — Step 3: inspect the dist/ directory ————————————————
ls dist/
# school_calc-1.0.0-py3-none-any.whl
# school-calc-1.0.0.tar.gz

# — Step 4: check with twine ————————————————————————
pip install twine
twine check dist/*

# — Understanding the wheel filename ————————————————————
# school_calc  - 1.0.0  - py3   - none   - any .whl
#   ^name         ^ver    ^pytag  ^abitag  ^platform
# py3   = compatible with any Python 3 (pure Python)
# none  = no ABI dependency (no C extensions)
# any   = runs on any platform (Windows, macOS, Linux)
```

Output:

```
# python -m build
* Creating isolated environment: venv+pip
* Installing packages in isolated environment: setuptools>=68, wheel
* Getting build dependencies for sdist...
* Building sdist...
* Building wheel from sdist
Successfully built school-calc-1.0.0.tar.gz and school_calc-1.0.0-py3-none-any.whl

# twine check dist/*
Checking dist/school-calc-1.0.0.tar.gz: PASSED
Checking dist/school_calc-1.0.0-py3-none-any.whl: PASSED
```

Example 2 — Variation

Inspecting wheel contents and the sdist archive structure using Python's zipfile and tarfile modules.

```
import zipfile
import tarfile
from pathlib import Path

def inspect_wheel(whl_path):
    """Print the contents of a wheel file."""
    whl = Path(whl_path)
    print(f"Wheel: {whl.name}")
    print("-" * 50)
    with zipfile.ZipFile(whl) as z:
        for info in sorted(z.infolist(), key=lambda i: i.filename):
            size_str = f"({info.file_size:,} bytes)"
            print(f"  {info.filename}    {size_str}")

def inspect_sdist(tar_path):
    """Print the top-level contents of a source distribution."""
    tar = Path(tar_path)
    print(f"\nSDist: {tar.name}")
    print("-" * 50)
    with tarfile.open(tar) as t:
        for member in sorted(t.getnames())[:15]:
            print(f"  {member}")

# Run from the project root after python -m build
dist = Path('dist')
wheels = list(dist.glob('*.whl'))
sdists = list(dist.glob('*.tar.gz'))
if wheels: inspect_wheel(wheels[0])
if sdists: inspect_sdist(sdists[0])
```

Output:

```
Wheel: school_calc-1.0.0-py3-none-any.whl
--------------------------------------------------
  school_calc/__init__.py      (312 bytes)
  school_calc/arithmetic.py    (487 bytes)
  school_calc/formatters.py    (295 bytes)
  school_calc/statistics.py    (391 bytes)
  school_calc-1.0.0.dist-info/METADATA    (1,842 bytes)
  school_calc-1.0.0.dist-info/RECORD      (478 bytes)
  school_calc-1.0.0.dist-info/WHEEL       (92 bytes)

SDist: school-calc-1.0.0.tar.gz
--------------------------------------------------
  school-calc-1.0.0/PKG-INFO
  school-calc-1.0.0/README.md
  school-calc-1.0.0/pyproject.toml
  school-calc-1.0.0/src/school_calc/__init__.py
  school-calc-1.0.0/src/school_calc/arithmetic.py
```

...

Example 3 — Real-world application

A complete build-and-check script that automates the build workflow and reports results.

```
"""
build_check.py — Automate the build and pre-upload verification workflow.

Usage: python build_check.py
"""

import subprocess
import sys
import shutil
from pathlib import Path

ROOT    = Path(__file__).parent
DIST    = ROOT / 'dist'
PYTHON  = sys.executable

def run(cmd, label):
    """Run a command, print label, return True on success."""
    print(f"  [{label}]")
    result = subprocess.run(cmd, capture_output=True, text=True)
    if result.returncode != 0:
        print(f"  FAILED:\n{result.stderr.strip()}")
        return False
    for line in result.stdout.strip().splitlines()[-3:]:
        print(f"    {line}")
    return True

def main():
    print("=== Build and Check ===")

    # Clean dist/
    if DIST.exists():
        shutil.rmtree(DIST)
        print("  Cleaned dist/")

    # Install build and twine if needed
    for pkg in ('build', 'twine'):
        run([PYTHON,'-m','pip','install',pkg,'--quiet'], f'ensure {pkg}')

    # Run tests first
    if not run([PYTHON,'-m','pytest','tests/','-q'], 'pytest'):
        sys.exit(1)

    # Build both distributions
    if not run([PYTHON,'-m','build'], 'build'):
        sys.exit(1)

    # Twine check
    if not run([PYTHON,'-m','twine','check','dist/*'], 'twine check'):
        sys.exit(1)

    # Summary
    artefacts = list(DIST.glob('*'))
    print(f"\nBuild complete. Artefacts:")
    for a in artefacts:
        print(f"  {a.name}  ({a.stat().st_size:,} bytes)")
    print("\nReady to upload with:")
    print("  twine upload --repository testpypi dist/*")
    print("  twine upload dist/*")
```

```
if __name__ == '__main__':
    main()
```

Output:

```
=== Build and Check ===
  Cleaned dist/
  [ensure build]
  [ensure twine]
  [pytest]
    5 passed in 0.12s
  [build]
    Successfully built school-calc-1.0.0.tar.gz
    school_calc-1.0.0-py3-none-any.whl
  [twine check]
    Checking dist/school-calc-1.0.0.tar.gz: PASSED
    Checking dist/school_calc-1.0.0-py3-none-any.whl: PASSED

Build complete. Artefacts:
  school-calc-1.0.0.tar.gz    (4,821 bytes)
  school_calc-1.0.0-py3-none-any.whl    (3,204 bytes)

Ready to upload with:
  twine upload --repository testpypi dist/*
  twine upload dist/*
```

The build-and-check script encapsulates the pre-upload workflow into a single repeatable command. Running it before every release ensures that the test suite passes, the build succeeds, and twine reports no metadata problems — three gates that prevent the most common publishing mistakes.

9.5 TestPyPI: Publishing to the Test Index

TestPyPI (test.pypi.org) is a separate instance of the Python Package Index maintained by the Python Packaging Authority specifically for testing the publishing workflow. Packages uploaded to TestPyPI are publicly visible and installable, but the index is periodically cleaned and carries no expectation of permanence. It is the right place to verify the complete end-to-end workflow before touching the real PyPI.

The publishing tool is twine, which uploads the distribution artefacts produced by python -m build. twine handles authentication, validates the upload, and reports errors clearly. Authentication uses API tokens — persistent credentials tied to your account or to a specific project — which are more secure than passwords because they can be scoped and revoked without changing your account password. API tokens for both TestPyPI and PyPI are generated in the account settings on each site.

After uploading to TestPyPI, the verification step is to install from it: pip install --index-url https://test.pypi.org/simple/ school-calc. This confirms the package installs correctly, the metadata renders as expected, and the imported module works. Only after this verification does it make sense to upload to the real PyPI. The complete workflow is: build → twine check → upload to TestPyPI → install and test → upload to PyPI.

> **Note:** TestPyPI and PyPI are entirely separate registries. A package on TestPyPI is not on PyPI, and vice versa. When installing from TestPyPI, use --extra-index-url https://pypi.org/simple/ to allow pip to resolve any dependencies that are only on PyPI, not TestPyPI.

Example 1 — Introduction

Configuring twine credentials with .pypirc and uploading to TestPyPI.

```
# ── Option 1: .pypirc file (~/.pypirc) ──────────────────
# [distutils]
# index-servers =
#     pypi
#     testpypi
#
# [pypi]
# username = __token__
# password = pypi-AgENdGVzdC5weXBpLm9yZwI...   ← your real API token
#
# [testpypi]
# repository = https://test.pypi.org/legacy/
# username   = __token__
# password   = pypi-AgENdGVzdC5weXBpLm9yZwI...  ← TestPyPI API token

# ── Option 2: environment variables (preferred for CI) ──────
# export TWINE_USERNAME=__token__
# export TWINE_PASSWORD=pypi-AgENdGVzdC5weXBpLm9yZwI...

# ── Upload to TestPyPI ──────────────────────────────────
twine upload --repository testpypi dist/*

# ── Upload to PyPI (production) ─────────────────────────
twine upload dist/*

# ── Verify the upload on TestPyPI ───────────────────────
# Project page: https://test.pypi.org/project/school-calc/

# ── Install from TestPyPI ───────────────────────────────
pip install --index-url https://test.pypi.org/simple/ school-calc

# With dependencies from real PyPI:
pip install --index-url https://test.pypi.org/simple/
            --extra-index-url https://pypi.org/simple/ school-calc
```

Output:

```
# twine upload --repository testpypi dist/*
Uploading distributions to https://test.pypi.org/legacy/
Uploading school-calc-1.0.0.tar.gz
100% ━━━━━━━━━━━━━━━━━━━━━━━━━━━━━━━━━━━━━━━━━━━━━━━━━━ 5.3 kB
Uploading school_calc-1.0.0-py3-none-any.whl
100% ━━━━━━━━━━━━━━━━━━━━━━━━━━━━━━━━━━━━━━━━━━━━━━━━━━ 3.8 kB

View at: https://test.pypi.org/project/school-calc/1.0.0/
```

Example 2 — Variation

Common upload errors and how to fix them.

```
# ── Error 1: File already exists ────────────────────────
# HTTP Error 400: File already exists.
# Fix: you cannot overwrite an existing version on PyPI or TestPyPI.
# Increment the version number in pyproject.toml and rebuild.

# ── Error 2: Invalid credentials ────────────────────────
# HTTP Error 403: Invalid or non-existent authentication information.
# Fix: regenerate the API token on test.pypi.org → Account Settings
# → API tokens → Add API token. Use __token__ as the username.

# ── Error 3: README fails to render ─────────────────────
# HTTPError: 400 Bad Request
# The description failed to render in the default format of ...
# Fix: run twine check dist/* before uploading to see the error.
# Common causes: invalid RST markup, broken Markdown link syntax.
```

```
# —— Error 4: Missing metadata ——————————————————————————
# HTTPError: 400 Bad Request
# Ensure classifiers, description, and author are set in pyproject.toml.

# —— Programmatic check for existing versions ——————————————
import urllib.request, json

def version_exists_on_testpypi(name, version):
    """Return True if name==version already exists on TestPyPI."""
    url = f'https://test.pypi.org/pypi/{name}/json'
    try:
        with urllib.request.urlopen(url, timeout=10) as r:
            data = json.loads(r.read())
        return version in data['releases']
    except Exception:
        return False

# Before uploading, check:
if version_exists_on_testpypi('school-calc', '1.0.0'):
    print("Version already on TestPyPI — bump version before uploading.")
else:
    print("Version not yet on TestPyPI — safe to upload.")
```

Output:

```
# version_exists_on_testpypi('school-calc', '1.0.0')
Version not yet on TestPyPI — safe to upload.
```

Example 3 — Real-world application

A post-upload verification script that installs from TestPyPI in a temporary venv and runs a smoke test.

```
"""
verify_testpypi.py — Install from TestPyPI and run smoke tests.

Usage: python verify_testpypi.py school-calc 1.0.0
"""

import subprocess, sys, tempfile, importlib
from pathlib import Path

def verify(package_name, version):
    """Install package from TestPyPI in a temp venv and test import."""
    print(f'Verifying {package_name}=={version} from TestPyPI')

    with tempfile.TemporaryDirectory() as tmpdir:
        venv = Path(tmpdir) / 'venv'
        pip  = venv / ('Scripts/pip' if sys.platform=='win32' else 'bin/pip')
        py   = venv / ('Scripts/python' if sys.platform=='win32' else
'bin/python')

        # Create a clean temporary venv
        subprocess.run([sys.executable,'-m','venv',str(venv)], check=True)

        # Install from TestPyPI
        spec = f'{package_name}=={version}'
        result = subprocess.run([
            str(pip),'install',spec,
            '--index-url','https://test.pypi.org/simple/',
            '--extra-index-url','https://pypi.org/simple/',
            '--quiet'
        ], capture_output=True, text=True)
        if result.returncode != 0:
            print(f"INSTALL FAILED:\n{result.stderr}")
```

```
            return False
        print(f"  Installed: {spec}")

        # Smoke test: import and check version
        pkg_module = package_name.replace('-','_')
        test_code = (
            f'import {pkg_module};'
            f'print({pkg_module}.__version__);'
            f'print("Import: OK")'
        )
        result2 = subprocess.run([str(py),'-c',test_code],
                                 capture_output=True, text=True)
        if result2.returncode == 0:
            print(f"  Smoke test PASSED: {result2.stdout.strip()}")
            return True
        else:
            print(f"  Smoke test FAILED: {result2.stderr.strip()}")
            return False

if __name__ == '__main__':
    name = sys.argv[1] if len(sys.argv) > 1 else 'school-calc'
    ver  = sys.argv[2] if len(sys.argv) > 2 else '1.0.0'
    ok   = verify(name, ver)
    sys.exit(0 if ok else 1)
```

Output:

```
Verifying school-calc==1.0.0 from TestPyPI
  Installed: school-calc==1.0.0
  Smoke test PASSED: 1.0.0
                     Import: OK
```

The verify_testpypi.py script creates an isolated temporary virtual environment, installs the package from TestPyPI, and confirms that it imports correctly and reports the right version. This eliminates the most common post-upload surprises: a package that uploads successfully but fails to install because of a missing file or a broken dependency specification.

Versioning: Semantic Versioning and Version Bumping

Semantic versioning (semver) — reviewed in Chapter 7 in the context of consuming packages — is equally important from the package author's perspective. The three-part MAJOR.MINOR.PATCH scheme communicates to every user of your package what kind of change a new release represents. A PATCH bump (1.0.0 to 1.0.1) promises only bug fixes; nothing that worked before will break. A MINOR bump (1.0.0 to 1.1.0) adds new functionality but remains backward-compatible. A MAJOR bump (1.0.0 to 2.0.0) signals breaking changes — callers must review their code.

Keeping the version number in one place is essential. The canonical location is __version__ in the package's __init__.py, which is where it is visible to code at runtime. pyproject.toml can then read this value dynamically using the [tool.setuptools.dynamic] table rather than duplicating it. Alternatively, some teams store the version only in pyproject.toml and use importlib.metadata.version() at runtime. Either approach is acceptable; what is not acceptable is having different version numbers in different files that regularly fall out of sync.

Before releasing a new version, tag the commit in git: git tag v1.0.1 && git push --tags. Tags create stable reference points in the version history that CI/CD pipelines can trigger on, and that users can check out to reproduce the exact code that corresponds to a given release. The commit that produces the built distribution and the git tag should be the same commit — the release workflow: bump version → commit → tag → build → upload.

> **Note:** Pre-release identifiers (a, b, rc) tell pip that a version is not yet production-ready. pip install school-calc will not install a pre-release unless the user explicitly requests it with pip install school-calc==1.1.0a1 or pip install --pre school-calc. Use pre-releases for early-access builds that you want to distribute to testers before a stable release.

Example 1 — Introduction

Version stored in __init__.py and read dynamically by pyproject.toml.

```
# src/school_calc/__init__.py
"""school_calc - School mathematics utilities."""

__version__ = "1.0.0"

from .arithmetic  import add, subtract, multiply, divide
from .statistics  import mean, median, stdev
from .formatters  import format_score, format_currency

__all__ = ['add','subtract','multiply','divide',
           'mean','median','stdev',
           'format_score','format_currency',
           '__version__']

# ── pyproject.toml - dynamic version ──────────────────────
# [project]
# name     = 'school-calc'
# dynamic  = ['version']
#
# [tool.setuptools.dynamic]
# version = {attr = 'school_calc.__version__'}

# ── At runtime: check the installed version ──────────────
import importlib.metadata

def get_version():
    """Return the installed version of school_calc."""
    try:
        return importlib.metadata.version('school-calc')
    except importlib.metadata.PackageNotFoundError:
        # Fallback for editable installs where metadata may differ
        import school_calc
        return getattr(school_calc, '__version__', 'unknown')

print(get_version())
```

Output:

```
1.0.0
```

Example 2 — Variation

A version bumping script that updates __version__ in __init__.py and the static field in pyproject.toml.

```
"""
bump_version.py - Increment the project version number.

Usage: python bump_version.py [major|minor|patch]
"""

import re, sys, tomllib
from pathlib import Path

INIT_FILE    = Path('src/school_calc/__init__.py')
PYPROJECT    = Path('pyproject.toml')
```

```
def read_current_version():
    text = INIT_FILE.read_text(encoding='utf-8')
    m = re.search(r'__version__\s*=\s*["\']([\d.a-z]+)["\']', text)
    return m.group(1) if m else None


def bump(version, part):
    parts = [int(x) for x in version.split('.')]
    while len(parts) < 3: parts.append(0)
    if part == 'major': parts = [parts[0]+1, 0, 0]
    elif part == 'minor': parts = [parts[0], parts[1]+1, 0]
    else: parts = [parts[0], parts[1], parts[2]+1]   # patch
    return '.'.join(str(p) for p in parts)


def update_file(path, pattern, replacement):
    text = path.read_text(encoding='utf-8')
    new_text = re.sub(pattern, replacement, text)
    path.write_text(new_text, encoding='utf-8')


def main():
    part = sys.argv[1] if len(sys.argv) > 1 else 'patch'
    if part not in ('major','minor','patch'):
        print("Usage: python bump_version.py [major|minor|patch]")
        sys.exit(1)

    current = read_current_version()
    if not current:
        print("Could not find __version__ in __init__.py")
        sys.exit(1)

    new_ver = bump(current, part)

    # Update __init__.py
    update_file(INIT_FILE,
                r'(__version__\s*=\s*)["\'][\d.a-z]+["\']',
                f'\\g<1>"{new_ver}"')

    # Update pyproject.toml (if not using dynamic version)
    update_file(PYPROJECT,
                r'(^version\s*=\s*)["\'][\d.a-z]+["\']',
                f'\\g<1>"{new_ver}"')

    print(f"Bumped {part}: {current} → {new_ver}")
    print(f"Next steps:")
    print(f"  git add -A")
    print(f"  git commit -m \"Release v{new_ver}\"")
    print(f"  git tag v{new_ver}")
    print(f"  git push && git push --tags")
    print(f"  python build_check.py")
    print(f"  twine upload dist/*")

if __name__ == '__main__':
    main()
```

Output:

```
# python bump_version.py minor
Bumped minor: 1.0.0 → 1.1.0
Next steps:
  git add -A
  git commit -m "Release v1.1.0"
  git tag v1.1.0
  git push && git push --tags
  python build_check.py
  twine upload dist/*
```

Example 3 — Real-world application

A CHANGELOG.md convention and a script that validates the changelog is up to date before allowing a release.

```
# CHANGELOG.md — standard format (Keep a Changelog convention)
# ## [Unreleased]
# ### Added
# - format_percentage() function in formatters module
#
# ## [1.0.0] — 2025-07-14
# ### Added
# - Initial release with arithmetic, statistics, and formatters modules
# - Full type hints and Google-style docstrings throughout
# - MIT licence

"""
check_changelog.py — Validate that CHANGELOG.md has an entry for the
current version before allowing a release build.
"""

import re, sys
from pathlib import Path

CHANGELOG = Path('CHANGELOG.md')
INIT_FILE  = Path('src/school_calc/__init__.py')

def current_version():
    text = INIT_FILE.read_text(encoding='utf-8')
    m = re.search(r'__version__\s*=\s*["\']([\d.]+)["\']', text)
    return m.group(1) if m else 'unknown'

def changelog_has_entry(version):
    text = CHANGELOG.read_text(encoding='utf-8')
    # Look for ## [1.0.0] or ## [1.0.0] — 2025-...
    pattern = rf'^## \[{re.escape(version)}\]'
    return bool(re.search(pattern, text, re.MULTILINE))

ver = current_version()
if changelog_has_entry(ver):
    print(f"OK: CHANGELOG.md has entry for v{ver}")
else:
    print(f"FAIL: No CHANGELOG.md entry for v{ver}")
    print("Add an entry before releasing.")
    sys.exit(1)
```

Output:

```
# After adding the entry:
OK: CHANGELOG.md has entry for v1.0.0

# If the entry is missing:
FAIL: No CHANGELOG.md entry for v1.0.0
Add an entry before releasing.
```

The versioning workflow — bump, commit, tag, build, upload — is a small ceremony that pays for itself many times over. A git tag for every release makes it possible to check out the exact source that corresponds to any installed version, reproduce a bug that only affects a specific version, and automate release pipelines that trigger on tags. The CHANGELOG keeps a human-readable record that users read to decide whether to upgrade.

9.7 Overview: GitHub Actions for Automated Publishing

A GitHub Actions workflow is a YAML file in .github/workflows/ that defines a series of steps to run automatically when a specified event occurs. For package publishing, the most useful triggers are: push to main (run tests and check that the build succeeds) and creation of a new git tag (run tests, build, and upload to PyPI). Together these two triggers implement a complete CI/CD pipeline for a Python package.

The workflow file declares one or more jobs. Each job runs on a hosted runner (typically ubuntu-latest) and contains a sequence of steps. Steps can use pre-built actions from the GitHub Actions Marketplace (actions/checkout to check out the code, actions/setup-python to install a specific Python version, pypa/gh-action-pypi-publish for trusted publishing) or run shell commands directly. Secrets — the PyPI API token, for example — are stored in the repository's Settings → Secrets section and referenced in the workflow as ${{ secrets.PYPI_API_TOKEN }}.

The modern alternative to storing an API token as a secret is trusted publishing via OpenID Connect (OIDC). Trusted publishing lets PyPI verify the identity of the GitHub Actions runner without a long-lived token: the runner generates a short-lived OIDC token that PyPI validates directly. This is more secure (no token to leak) and requires no secrets configuration once set up. Full CI/CD coverage, including multi-environment testing matrices and pull-request workflows, is covered in Book 11.

> **Note:** GitHub Actions usage for public repositories is free. For private repositories, there are monthly usage limits on free accounts. The publish.yml workflow shown here runs on every tag push, which typically means at most a few dozen runs per year — well within free-tier limits for any educational or small commercial project.

Example 1 — Introduction

A minimal .github/workflows/publish.yml that tests, builds, and publishes on a version tag.

```
# .github/workflows/publish.yml
# Triggers: push to main (test only) or new version tag (test + publish)

name: Test and Publish

on:
  push:
    branches: [main]
    tags:     ['v*.*.*']    # trigger on v1.0.0, v1.1.0, etc.
  pull_request:
    branches: [main]

jobs:
  test:
    name: Test on Python ${{ matrix.python-version }}
    runs-on: ubuntu-latest
    strategy:
      matrix:
        python-version: ['3.10', '3.11', '3.12']

    steps:
      - uses: actions/checkout@v4

      - name: Set up Python ${{ matrix.python-version }}
        uses: actions/setup-python@v5
        with:
          python-version: ${{ matrix.python-version }}

      - name: Install dependencies
        run: |
          python -m pip install --upgrade pip
```

```
        pip install -e '.[dev]'

    - name: Run mypy
      run: mypy src/ --ignore-missing-imports

    - name: Run tests
      run: pytest tests/ -v

  publish:
    name: Build and Publish to PyPI
    needs: test                    # only runs if test job passes
    runs-on: ubuntu-latest
    if: startsWith(github.ref, 'refs/tags/v')  # only on tags

    permissions:
      id-token: write              # required for trusted publishing

    steps:
      - uses: actions/checkout@v4

      - uses: actions/setup-python@v5
        with:
          python-version: '3.12'

      - name: Install build tools
        run: pip install build twine

      - name: Build distribution
        run: python -m build

      - name: Check distribution
        run: twine check dist/*

      - name: Publish to PyPI (trusted publishing)
        uses: pypa/gh-action-pypi-publish@release/v1
```

Output:

```
# Workflow run triggered by: git tag v1.0.0 && git push --tags

test (3.10) ✓  All 5 tests passed
test (3.11) ✓  All 5 tests passed
test (3.12) ✓  All 5 tests passed
publish     ✓  Built and published school-calc 1.0.0 to PyPI
```

Example 2 — Variation

Adding a README badge and a separate workflow for TestPyPI uploads on pre-release tags.

```
# ── Status badge in README.md ──────────────────────────────
# Add this line near the top of README.md:
# ![CI](https://github.com/northward/school-
calc/actions/workflows/publish.yml/badge.svg)

# ── Separate workflow for TestPyPI on pre-release tags ─────
# .github/workflows/publish-test.yml

name: Publish to TestPyPI

on:
  push:
    tags: ['v*.*.*a*', 'v*.*.*b*', 'v*.*.*rc*']  # pre-release tags only
```

```
jobs:
  publish-test:
    runs-on: ubuntu-latest
    permissions:
      id-token: write

    steps:
      - uses: actions/checkout@v4
      - uses: actions/setup-python@v5
        with:
          python-version: '3.12'

      - run: pip install build twine
      - run: python -m build
      - run: twine check dist/*

      - name: Publish to TestPyPI (trusted publishing)
        uses: pypa/gh-action-pypi-publish@release/v1
        with:
          repository-url: https://test.pypi.org/legacy/

# ── Trusted publishing setup (done once on PyPI/TestPyPI) ───
# 1. On PyPI: Publishing → Trusted Publishers → Add New Publisher
# 2. Fill in: owner (GitHub username), repository, workflow filename
# 3. No API token required — the OIDC handshake authenticates automatically
```

Output:

```
# Triggered by: git tag v1.1.0a1 && git push --tags

publish-test ✓  Published school-calc 1.1.0a1 to TestPyPI

# Users can install the pre-release with:
# pip install --pre school-calc --index-url https://test.pypi.org/simple/
```

Example 3 — Real-world application

A complete GitHub Actions matrix workflow with coverage reporting and a conditional release step.

```
# .github/workflows/ci.yml — complete CI workflow

name: CI

on:
  push:
    branches: [main, develop]
    tags:     ['v*.*.*']
  pull_request:
    branches: [main]

jobs:
  lint-and-type:
    name: Lint and type check
    runs-on: ubuntu-latest
    steps:
      - uses: actions/checkout@v4
      - uses: actions/setup-python@v5
        with: {python-version: '3.12'}
      - run: pip install -e '.[dev]'
      - run: black src/ tests/ --check
      - run: mypy src/ --ignore-missing-imports

  test:
    name: Test
    needs: lint-and-type
```

```
    runs-on: ubuntu-latest
    strategy:
      matrix:
        python-version: ['3.10', '3.11', '3.12']
    steps:
      - uses: actions/checkout@v4
      - uses: actions/setup-python@v5
        with:
          python-version: ${{ matrix.python-version }}
      - run: pip install -e '.[dev]'
      - run: pytest tests/ -v --tb=short

  release:
    name: Release to PyPI
    needs: test
    runs-on: ubuntu-latest
    if: startsWith(github.ref, 'refs/tags/v')
    permissions:
      id-token: write
    steps:
      - uses: actions/checkout@v4
      - uses: actions/setup-python@v5
        with: {python-version: '3.12'}
      - run: pip install build twine
      - run: python -m build
      - run: twine check dist/*
      - uses: pypa/gh-action-pypi-publish@release/v1
```

Output:

```
# On a tag push (v1.0.0):
lint-and-type ✓   black + mypy passed
test (3.10)   ✓   5 passed
test (3.11)   ✓   5 passed
test (3.12)   ✓   5 passed
release       ✓   Published school-calc 1.0.0 to PyPI
```

A GitHub Actions CI/CD pipeline turns the manual build-check-upload steps into an automatic, repeatable process triggered by a git tag. The investment in writing the workflow YAML once means every future release requires only a version bump, a commit, and a tag push — the automation handles everything else. This is the standard practice for professional open-source Python packages.

Chapter 10 brings together everything in this book: a complete schooltools utility library built with the src layout, full type hints and docstrings, a unittest test suite, and a distribution-ready pyproject.toml — the capstone project that demonstrates every skill developed across the preceding nine chapters.

Chapter 9 Summary

- The src layout places package source inside src/packagename/ rather than directly at the project root. This prevents accidental imports of local source code during testing, ensuring every import goes through the installed package. The project root also contains pyproject.toml, README.md, LICENCE, tests/, and dist/ (in .gitignore).
- pyproject.toml is the single configuration file for modern Python packaging. The [build-system] table declares the build backend (setuptools, flit, or hatchling). The [project] table declares metadata: name, version, description, readme, requires-python, license, authors, classifiers, dependencies, and optional-dependencies.
- Package names are normalised on PyPI (hyphens, underscores, and dots are equivalent; case is ignored). Version strings must comply with PEP 440. Classifiers come from a controlled vocabulary

at pypi.org/classifiers and make the package discoverable in PyPI search. Library dependencies should use version ranges (~=, >=,<), never pinned versions.

- python -m build (from the build package) produces both a sdist (.tar.gz) and a wheel (.whl) in the dist/ directory. The wheel filename encodes name, version, Python tag, ABI tag, and platform. twine check dist/* validates metadata and README rendering before upload.
- TestPyPI (test.pypi.org) is a separate registry for testing the publish workflow. Authentication uses API tokens (username __token__). Upload with twine upload --repository testpypi dist/*. Verify by installing in a fresh venv from TestPyPI before uploading to the real PyPI.
- Semantic versioning: PATCH for bug fixes, MINOR for new backward-compatible features, MAJOR for breaking changes. Keep __version__ in one place — the package __init__.py — and read it dynamically in pyproject.toml with [tool.setuptools.dynamic]. Tag every release in git: git tag vX.Y.Z && git push --tags.
- GitHub Actions workflows in .github/workflows/ automate testing (on every push) and publishing (on version tags). A test job runs pytest across a Python version matrix; a publish job builds and uploads using pypa/gh-action-pypi-publish. Trusted publishing via OIDC is more secure than storing API tokens as repository secrets.
- The complete release workflow: bump version → update CHANGELOG → commit → tag → push → CI tests → build → twine check → upload to TestPyPI → verify installation → upload to PyPI. Automating this with GitHub Actions means a future release requires only version bump + commit + tag.

Guided Exercises

1. Create a src layout package called school_calc/ with pyproject.toml, src/school_calc/__init__.py (containing __version__ = '0.1.0'), and one module src/school_calc/arithmetic.py with add(), subtract(), multiply(), and divide() functions. Install it in editable mode with pip install -e . and confirm that import school_calc; school_calc.__version__ returns '0.1.0' from any directory in the activated virtual environment.

> **Hint:** Ensure src/school_calc/__init__.py re-exports from .arithmetic. After pip install -e ., run pip show school_calc to confirm the editable install. The Location: field should point to your src/ directory.

2. Add full metadata to school_calc's pyproject.toml: name (school-calc), version (0.1.0), description, requires-python (>=3.10), authors with name and email, license (MIT), and at least four classifiers including Development Status, Intended Audience, License, and one Programming Language classifier. Validate the file with python -c "import tomllib; print(tomllib.load(open('pyproject.toml','rb'))['project'])".

> **Hint:** TOML strings use double quotes. The classifiers list is an array of strings. The authors section is [[project.authors]] with name and email keys. Use pypi.org/classifiers to find the exact string for each classifier.

3. Build school_calc using python -m build. Inspect the dist/ directory and print: the wheel filename, the contents of the wheel (using zipfile), and the top ten files in the sdist (using tarfile). Identify the METADATA file inside the wheel and print its Name, Version, and Summary fields.

> **Hint:** Use zipfile.ZipFile to open the .whl and zipfile.ZipFile.namelist() for contents. Extract and decode the METADATA file with zf.read('school_calc-0.1.0.dist-info/METADATA').decode(). Parse the field: value lines with a simple for loop.

4. Install twine (pip install twine) and run twine check dist/* against your school_calc build. If there are any warnings about the README, create a simple README.md with a one-line description and rebuild. Then create a TestPyPI account at test.pypi.org, generate an API token, and upload with twine upload --repository testpypi dist/*. Install from TestPyPI in a fresh virtual environment to verify.

Hint: For twine check, the most common warning is 'The description failed to render' — this means your README.md has Markdown formatting that PyPI cannot render. Simplify it to plain text for the first upload. Use pip install --index-url https://test.pypi.org/simple/ school-calc to install from TestPyPI.

5. Add __version__ = '0.1.0' to src/school_calc/__init__.py and configure pyproject.toml to read it dynamically. Change the [project] version = '0.1.0' line to dynamic = ['version'] and add [tool.setuptools.dynamic] with version = {attr = 'school_calc.__version__'}. Rebuild and confirm the wheel filename still shows 0.1.0. Then write a one-line script that prints the installed version using importlib.metadata.version('school-calc').

Hint: The dynamic version reads __version__ at build time using importlib. After adding dynamic = ['version'], remove the static version = line from [project]. Run python -c "import importlib.metadata; print(importlib.metadata.version('school-calc'))" to verify.

Challenge Tasks

1. Package the school_utils, gst_utils, and validators modules built across Chapters 1–8 of this book into a single distributable src layout package called schooltools. Create a complete pyproject.toml with all metadata fields populated (name, version 1.0.0, description, requires-python>=3.10, MIT licence, authors, at least six classifiers, project URLs). Organise the modules into sensible subpackages within src/schooltools/ using relative imports. Add optional-dependencies groups: dev (pytest>=8, mypy>=1.9, black>=24, pdoc) and docs (pdoc). Build with python -m build, check with twine check, upload to TestPyPI, and install from TestPyPI in a fresh virtual environment to verify all imports work correctly.

2. Write a complete release automation script called release.py that performs the following steps in sequence, refusing to continue if any step fails: (1) read the current version from src/schooltools/__init__.py; (2) accept major/minor/patch as a command-line argument and compute the new version; (3) check that CHANGELOG.md has an entry for the new version; (4) update __version__ in __init__.py; (5) run the test suite with pytest; (6) run mypy --strict on src/; (7) build with python -m build; (8) check with twine check; (9) commit the version bump, create a git tag, and push both; (10) upload to TestPyPI. Each step should print a clear status line and the script should exit with code 1 on any failure, printing the reason.

3. Create a complete GitHub Actions CI/CD configuration for the schooltools package. The CI workflow (ci.yml) should run on every push to main and on every pull request: install dev dependencies, run black --check, run mypy --ignore-missing-imports, and run pytest across Python 3.10, 3.11, and 3.12 using a matrix strategy. The release workflow (publish.yml) should trigger only on version tags (v*.*.*), require the CI workflow to pass first (using needs:), build the distribution, check with twine, and publish to TestPyPI using trusted publishing. Include a README.md CI status badge that links to the workflow run. Document each workflow section with inline YAML comments explaining what it does and when it runs.

CHAPTER 10 Capstone Project: Build a Reusable Utility Library

Book 03: Modules, Packages & the Python Ecosystem

> This chapter is the culmination of everything covered in Book 03. Across nine chapters you have learned how to write modules and packages, navigate the standard library, manage virtual environments and dependencies, document code with docstrings and type hints, and publish a package to PyPI. The schooltools capstone project brings all of these skills together in a single, cohesive library: a reusable utility toolkit for school administration software. schooltools is fully typed, fully documented in Google style, tested with unittest, and packaged with a distribution-ready pyproject.toml. Building it in full is the most effective way to consolidate the practices developed throughout this book — not as isolated exercises, but as the integrated craft of professional Python development.

10.1 Project Specification: schooltools Library

The schooltools library is a collection of pure-Python utility functions and classes for school administration software. Its purpose is to be importable by any school system — enrolment tools, report generators, timetabling applications — without those tools needing to reimplement common validation, formatting, conversion, or statistical logic.

The design goals follow directly from the practices in this book. The library must be fully typed: every public function has complete parameter and return type annotations, and mypy --strict passes on the entire package. It must be fully documented: every public module, class, and function has a Google-style docstring with Args, Returns, and Raises sections. It must be tested: a unittest test suite covers every public function with at least one positive test and one edge-case or exception test. And it must be packaged: a complete pyproject.toml makes it installable with pip install schooltools.

The library is divided into four subpackages. validators/ provides boolean-returning functions that check whether inputs are valid. formatters/ provides string-returning functions that produce human-readable output. converters/ provides functions that transform data from one representation to another. stdlib_showcase/ demonstrates practical use of key standard library modules in the school administration context — a living example of Chapter 5's material.

> **Note:** This capstone intentionally does not use any third-party packages. Everything in schooltools is built from the Python standard library. This keeps the installation footprint minimal and demonstrates that the standard library alone is sufficient for a surprisingly large range of practical tasks.

Example 1 — Introduction

The complete schooltools project directory structure.

```
schooltools/
  src/
    schooltools/
      __init__.py              # version, top-level re-exports
      validators/
        __init__.py            # re-exports all validators
        email_val.py           # is_valid_email()
        phone_val.py           # is_valid_phone()
        academic_val.py        # is_valid_year_level(), is_valid_score()
        date_val.py            # is_valid_date()
      formatters/
```

```
      __init__.py
      score_fmt.py            # format_score(), format_grade_row()
      name_fmt.py             # format_name(), format_student_id()
      currency_fmt.py         # format_currency(), format_gst()
      date_fmt.py             # format_date(), format_term_date()
    converters/
      __init__.py
      unit_conv.py            # celsius_to_fahrenheit(), km_to_miles(), etc.
      grade_conv.py           # score_to_letter(), letter_to_gpa()
    stdlib_showcase/
      __init__.py
      grade_stats.py          # Counter, statistics — grade distribution
      fixture_gen.py          # itertools — sports fixture generation
      term_planner.py         # datetime, calendar — term date utilities
      cohort_analysis.py      # functools.lru_cache, statistics — analysis
  tests/
    __init__.py
    test_validators.py
    test_formatters.py
    test_converters.py
    test_stdlib_showcase.py
  .gitignore
  pyproject.toml
  README.md
  LICENCE
  requirements-dev.txt
```

Output:

```
# pip install -e '.[dev]'   installs schooltools + pytest + mypy + black + pdoc
# python -m pytest tests/ -v   runs all tests
# mypy src/ --ignore-missing-imports   type-checks the package
```

Example 2 — Variation

The top-level __init__.py and pyproject.toml for the schooltools package.

```
# src/schooltools/__init__.py
"""
schooltools — Reusable utility library for school administration software.

Subpackages:
    validators        — Input validation (email, phone, year level, score, date)
    formatters        — Output formatting (scores, names, currency, dates)
    converters        — Data conversion (units, grade letters, GPA)
    stdlib_showcase   — Standard library demonstrations

Quick start:
    from schooltools.validators import is_valid_email, is_valid_score
    from schooltools.formatters import format_score, format_currency
    from schooltools.converters  import score_to_letter, celsius_to_fahrenheit
"""

__version__ = "1.0.0"
```

```
# pyproject.toml
# [build-system]
# requires      = ["setuptools>=68","wheel"]
# build-backend = "setuptools.backends.legacy:build"
#
# [tool.setuptools.packages.find]
# where = ["src"]
#
# [project]
# name             = "schooltools"
# dynamic          = ["version"]
```

```
# description     = "Reusable utility library for school administration
software"
# readme          = "README.md"
# requires-python = ">=3.10"
# license         = {text = "MIT"}
#
# [[project.authors]]
# name  = "M. North"
# email = "m.north@northwardhouse.com.au"
#
# [tool.setuptools.dynamic]
# version = {attr = "schooltools.__version__"}
#
# [project.optional-dependencies]
# dev   = ["pytest>=8","mypy>=1.9","black>=24","pdoc"]
#
# [tool.mypy]
# python_version         = "3.12"
# disallow_untyped_defs = true
# warn_return_any        = true
# ignore_missing_imports = true
#
# [tool.pytest.ini_options]
# testpaths = ["tests"]
# addopts   = "-v"
```

Output:

```
# import schooltools; print(schooltools.__version__)
1.0.0
```

Example 3 — Real-world application

A demo script showing how an external application imports and uses schooltools.

```
# demo.py — shows schooltools used as an external library

from schooltools.validators  import is_valid_email, is_valid_score,
is_valid_year_level
from schooltools.formatters  import format_score, format_currency,
format_grade_row
from schooltools.converters  import score_to_letter, celsius_to_fahrenheit
from schooltools              import __version__

print(f"schooltools v{__version__}")
print("=" * 40)

# Validate enrolment form inputs
inputs = [
    ('email',      'student@school.edu.au'),
    ('email',      'not-an-email'),
    ('score',      '88'),
    ('score',      '105'),
    ('year_level', '10'),
    ('year_level', '15'),
]
for field, value in inputs:
    if field == 'email':       ok = is_valid_email(value)
    elif field == 'score':     ok = is_valid_score(value)
    else:                      ok = is_valid_year_level(value)
    status = "OK  " if ok else "FAIL"
    print(f"  [{status}] {field:<12} {value}")

print()
# Format a report card
scores = [('Mia Tran', 88.5), ('Leo Park', 74.0), ('Zara Ali', 92.0)]
for name, score in scores:
```

```
    letter = score_to_letter(score)
    print(format_grade_row(name, score, letter))

print()
# Unit conversions
for c in [0, 25, 100]:
    print(f"  {c}°C = {celsius_to_fahrenheit(c):.1f}°F")

print()
# Currency formatting
amounts = [49.95, 1234.5, 0.1]
for a in amounts:
    print(f"  {format_currency(a)}")
```

Output:

```
schooltools v1.0.0
========================================
  [OK  ] email          student@school.edu.au
  [FAIL] email          not-an-email
  [OK  ] score          88
  [FAIL] score          105
  [OK  ] year_level     10
  [FAIL] year_level     15

  Mia Tran               88.5   B
  Leo Park               74.0   C
  Zara Ali               92.0   A

  0°C = 32.0°F
  25°C = 77.0°F
  100°C = 212.0°F

  $49.95
  $1,234.50
  $0.10
```

The demo script shows schooltools being used exactly as any third-party package would be — imported by name, with no knowledge of its internal structure. The four subpackages provide a clean, predictable API that a developer can learn from the top-level __init__.py docstring alone.

10.2 Package Structure and Module Plan

The schooltools package uses the src layout established in Chapter 9. Each of the four subpackages has its own __init__.py that re-exports the most commonly used names, so that callers can write from schooltools.validators import is_valid_email rather than from schooltools.validators.email_val import is_valid_email. The internal module filenames use the _val, _fmt, and _conv suffixes to make their role immediately clear.

All internal cross-references use relative imports. A function in converters/grade_conv.py that needs a constant from validators/academic_val.py uses from ..validators.academic_val import VALID_YEAR_LEVELS rather than an absolute import. This keeps the package self-contained and relocatable, consistent with the principles established in Chapter 4.

The requirements-dev.txt file lists the tools needed to develop and test the package: pytest for tests, mypy for type checking, black for formatting, and pdoc for documentation generation. These are also declared as the dev optional dependency group in pyproject.toml, so pip install -e '.[dev]' installs everything in a single command.

> **Note:** Each subpackage __init__.py re-exports only the names that belong to its public API. Internal helpers prefixed with _ are available by direct import but do not appear in __all__ and are not re-exported. This maintains the clean boundary between public and private that was established in Chapter 3.

Example 1 — Introduction

The validators/ subpackage: __init__.py and its four implementation modules.

```
# src/schooltools/validators/__init__.py
"""
schooltools.validators — Input validation functions.

All functions return bool: True if the input is valid, False otherwise.
No exceptions are raised for invalid input.

Public API:
    is_valid_email(email)              — basic email pattern check
    is_valid_phone(phone)              — Australian phone number check
    is_valid_year_level(year)          — Years 7-12
    is_valid_score(score, max=100)     — numeric 0-max
    is_valid_date(date_str, fmt)       — parseable date string
"""

from .email_val    import is_valid_email
from .phone_val    import is_valid_phone
from .academic_val import is_valid_year_level, is_valid_score
from .date_val     import is_valid_date

__all__ = [
    'is_valid_email',
    'is_valid_phone',
    'is_valid_year_level',
    'is_valid_score',
    'is_valid_date',
]

# src/schooltools/validators/email_val.py
"""Email validation for school addresses."""
import re
from __future__ import annotations

_EMAIL_PATTERN = re.compile(
    r'^[a-zA-Z0-9_.+\-]+@[a-zA-Z0-9\-]+\.[a-zA-Z0-9.\-]+$'
)

def is_valid_email(email: str) -> bool:
    """
    Return True if email matches a basic email address pattern.

    Args:
        email (str): The string to validate.

    Returns:
        bool: True if the pattern matches, False otherwise.

    Example:
        >>> is_valid_email('student@school.edu.au')
        True
        >>> is_valid_email('not-an-email')
        False
    """
    return bool(_EMAIL_PATTERN.match(str(email)))
```

```python
# src/schooltools/validators/academic_val.py
"""Academic field validators."""
from __future__ import annotations

VALID_YEAR_LEVELS: tuple[int, ...] = tuple(range(7, 13))    # 7-12

def is_valid_year_level(year: int | str) -> bool:
    """Return True if year is a valid secondary school year level (7-12)."""
    try:
        return int(year) in VALID_YEAR_LEVELS
    except (ValueError, TypeError):
        return False

def is_valid_score(score: int | float | str,
                   max_score: float = 100.0) -> bool:
    """
    Return True if score is a number between 0 and max_score (inclusive).

    Args:
        score     (int | float | str): Score to validate.
        max_score (float):             Upper bound. Default 100.0.

    Returns:
        bool: True if 0 <= score <= max_score.
    """
    try:
        return 0 <= float(score) <= max_score
    except (ValueError, TypeError):
        return False
```

Output:

```
# from schooltools.validators import is_valid_email, is_valid_year_level
# is_valid_email('a@b.com')        → True
# is_valid_email('bad')            → False
# is_valid_year_level(10)          → True
# is_valid_year_level(5)           → False
# is_valid_score('88')             → True
# is_valid_score(105)              → False
```

Example 2 — Variation

The formatters/ subpackage: score and currency formatters with type hints.

```python
# src/schooltools/formatters/__init__.py
"""
schooltools.formatters - Output formatting functions.

All functions return str.

Public API:
    format_score(name, score, width)    - aligned name/score line
    format_grade_row(name, score, letter) - grade report row
    format_name(first, last)            - 'Last, First' canonical form
    format_student_id(n)                - 'S-NNNNN' format
    format_currency(amount, symbol)     - '$1,234.56' format
    format_gst(amount)                  - ex-GST / inc-GST pair string
    format_date(d, fmt)                 - formatted date string
    format_term_date(d)                 - 'Mon 14 Jul 2025' format
"""

from .score_fmt    import format_score, format_grade_row
from .name_fmt     import format_name, format_student_id
from .currency_fmt import format_currency, format_gst
```

```
from .date_fmt     import format_date, format_term_date

__all__ = [
    'format_score','format_grade_row',
    'format_name','format_student_id',
    'format_currency','format_gst',
    'format_date','format_term_date',
]

# src/schooltools/formatters/score_fmt.py
"""Score and grade report formatting."""
from __future__ import annotations

def format_score(name: str, score: float,
                 width: int = 20) -> str:
    """
    Return a formatted name/score line with aligned columns.

    Args:
        name  (str):   Student name.
        score (float): Numeric score.
        width (int):   Name column width. Default 20.

    Returns:
        str: Formatted line, e.g. 'Mia Tran            88.5'
    """
    return f"{name:<{width}} {score:>6.1f}"

def format_grade_row(name: str, score: float,
                     letter: str, width: int = 20) -> str:
    """
    Return a formatted grade report row.

    Args:
        name   (str):   Student name.
        score  (float): Numeric score.
        letter (str):   Letter grade (A-E).
        width  (int):   Name column width. Default 20.

    Returns:
        str: Formatted row, e.g. 'Mia Tran            88.5   B'
    """
    return f"{name:<{width}} {score:>6.1f}   {letter}"

# src/schooltools/formatters/currency_fmt.py
"""Currency formatting for Australian dollars."""
from __future__ import annotations
from decimal import Decimal, ROUND_HALF_UP

_GST_RATE = Decimal('0.10')
_TWO_DP   = Decimal('0.01')

def format_currency(amount: float | int,
                    symbol: str = '$') -> str:
    """Return amount formatted as currency with two decimal places."""
    return f"{symbol}{amount:,.2f}"

def format_gst(ex_gst: float) -> str:
    """
    Return a two-line string showing ex-GST and inc-GST amounts.

    Args:
        ex_gst (float): Amount excluding GST.
```

```
    Returns:
        str: Two-line formatted string.
    """
    ex  = Decimal(str(ex_gst))
    inc = (ex * (1 + _GST_RATE)).quantize(_TWO_DP, rounding=ROUND_HALF_UP)
    return f"Ex-GST:  ${ex:.2f}\nInc-GST: ${inc:.2f}"
```

Output:

```
# format_score('Mia Tran', 88.5)
'Mia Tran               88.5'
# format_grade_row('Zara Ali', 92.0, 'A')
'Zara Ali               92.0   A'
# format_currency(1234.5)
'$1,234.50'
# format_gst(49.95)
'Ex-GST:  $49.95\nInc-GST: $54.94'
```

Example 3 — Real-world application

The converters/ subpackage: unit converters and grade conversion.

```
# src/schooltools/converters/__init__.py
"""
schooltools.converters — Data conversion functions.

Public API:
    celsius_to_fahrenheit(c)      — temperature conversion
    fahrenheit_to_celsius(f)      — temperature conversion
    km_to_miles(km)               — distance conversion
    miles_to_km(miles)            — distance conversion
    score_to_letter(score)        — numeric score → letter grade
    letter_to_gpa(letter)         — letter grade → GPA points
"""

from .unit_conv  import (celsius_to_fahrenheit, fahrenheit_to_celsius,
                          km_to_miles, miles_to_km)
from .grade_conv import score_to_letter, letter_to_gpa

__all__ = [
    'celsius_to_fahrenheit','fahrenheit_to_celsius',
    'km_to_miles','miles_to_km',
    'score_to_letter','letter_to_gpa',
]

# src/schooltools/converters/unit_conv.py
"""Physical unit conversion functions."""
from __future__ import annotations

KM_PER_MILE = 1.609344

def celsius_to_fahrenheit(c: float) -> float:
    """Convert Celsius to Fahrenheit."""
    return c * 9 / 5 + 32


def fahrenheit_to_celsius(f: float) -> float:
    """Convert Fahrenheit to Celsius."""
    return (f - 32) * 5 / 9


def km_to_miles(km: float) -> float:
    """Convert kilometres to miles. Raises ValueError if km < 0."""
    if km < 0:
        raise ValueError(f"Distance cannot be negative, got {km}")
    return km / KM_PER_MILE
```

```python
def miles_to_km(miles: float) -> float:
    """Convert miles to kilometres. Raises ValueError if miles < 0."""
    if miles < 0:
        raise ValueError(f"Distance cannot be negative, got {miles}")
    return miles * KM_PER_MILE

# src/schooltools/converters/grade_conv.py
"""Grade conversion between numeric scores, letter grades, and GPA."""
from __future__ import annotations

_BOUNDARIES: list[tuple[float, str]] = [
    (90.0,'A'), (80.0,'B'), (70.0,'C'), (60.0,'D'), (0.0,'E')
]
_GPA_MAP: dict[str, float] = {
    'A':4.0,'B':3.0,'C':2.0,'D':1.0,'E':0.0
}

def score_to_letter(score: float) -> str:
    """Return the letter grade for a numeric score (0-100)."""
    for threshold, letter in _BOUNDARIES:
        if score >= threshold:
            return letter
    return 'E'

def letter_to_gpa(letter: str) -> float:
    """
    Return the GPA points for a letter grade.

    Args:
        letter (str): Letter grade A-E (case-insensitive).

    Returns:
        float: GPA points (A=4.0, B=3.0, C=2.0, D=1.0, E=0.0).

    Raises:
        KeyError: If letter is not a recognised grade.
    """
    return _GPA_MAP[letter.upper()]
```

Output:

```
# score_to_letter(88.5)    → 'B'
# score_to_letter(92.0)    → 'A'
# letter_to_gpa('B')       → 3.0
# celsius_to_fahrenheit(0) → 32.0
# km_to_miles(1.609344)    → 1.0
```

The three production subpackages together provide thirty-plus functions that cover the most common string validation, formatting, and conversion tasks in school software. Because they are all pure Python with no dependencies, they can be imported and used in any Python 3.10+ environment with no setup beyond pip install schooltools.

Core stdlib_showcase Module: Standard Library in Context

The stdlib_showcase subpackage demonstrates key standard library tools from Chapter 5 in a practical school administration context. Rather than isolated examples, each module in this subpackage solves a real problem — grade distribution analysis, fixture generation, term date calculation, cohort statistics — using the standard library tools that are the professional Python developer's first resort.

This subpackage serves a dual purpose: it is genuinely useful code that any school system might import, and it is a reference showing how collections.Counter, itertools, functools.lru_cache, datetime, and statistics compose naturally in production-quality code. Reading these modules is as instructive as any tutorial.

Each function in stdlib_showcase is fully typed, documented, and tested. The design follows the same conventions as the rest of schooltools: public names in __all__, internal helpers prefixed with _, module docstrings listing the public API, and a __main__ guard with a demonstration.

> **Note:** The stdlib_showcase subpackage intentionally avoids NumPy, Pandas, or any third-party data library. All analysis uses the statistics module from the standard library. For larger datasets or more advanced analysis, Book 09 covers the full data science stack.

Example 1 — Introduction

grade_stats.py: grade distribution analysis using collections.Counter and statistics.

```
# src/schooltools/stdlib_showcase/grade_stats.py
"""
Grade distribution analysis using collections.Counter and the statistics
module.

Public API:
    grade_distribution(scores)      — Counter of letter grades
    cohort_summary(scores)          — dict of summary statistics
    rank_students(score_dict)       — sorted list of (name, score, rank)
"""
from __future__ import annotations
from collections import Counter
from statistics  import mean, median, stdev
from functools   import lru_cache
from typing      import Any

from ..converters.grade_conv import score_to_letter

__all__ = ['grade_distribution','cohort_summary','rank_students']

def grade_distribution(scores: list[float]) -> Counter[str]:
    """
    Return a Counter mapping letter grades to frequency counts.

    Args:
        scores (list[float]): List of numeric scores.

    Returns:
        Counter[str]: e.g. Counter({'B': 4, 'A': 3, 'C': 2})
    """
    return Counter(score_to_letter(s) for s in scores)

def cohort_summary(scores: list[float]) -> dict[str, Any]:
    """
    Return descriptive statistics for a cohort's scores.

    Args:
        scores (list[float]): Non-empty list of scores.

    Returns:
        dict: Keys 'count','mean','median','stdev','min','max',
              'grade_dist' (Counter of letter grades).

    Raises:
```

```
        ValueError: If scores is empty.
    """
    if not scores:
        raise ValueError("scores must not be empty")
    return {
        'count':      len(scores),
        'mean':       round(mean(scores),   2),
        'median':     round(median(scores), 2),
        'stdev':      round(stdev(scores),  2) if len(scores) > 1 else 0.0,
        'min':        min(scores),
        'max':        max(scores),
        'grade_dist': grade_distribution(scores),
    }

def rank_students(score_dict: dict[str,float]) ->
list[tuple[int,str,float,str]]:
    """
    Return students ranked by score from highest to lowest.

    Args:
        score_dict (dict[str,float]): Mapping of student name to score.

    Returns:
        list[tuple[int,str,float,str]]: (rank, name, score, letter)
    """
    sorted_students = sorted(score_dict.items(),
                             key=lambda kv: kv[1], reverse=True)
    return [
        (rank, name, score, score_to_letter(score))
        for rank, (name, score) in enumerate(sorted_students, 1)
    ]

if __name__ == '__main__':
    scores = [88.0, 74.5, 92.0, 63.0, 85.5, 91.0, 78.5, 55.0]
    summary = cohort_summary(scores)
    print(f"Count  : {summary['count']}")
    print(f"Mean   : {summary['mean']}")
    print(f"Grade distribution: {dict(summary['grade_dist'])}")
```

Output:

```
Count  : 8
Mean   : 78.44
Grade distribution: {'B': 3, 'A': 2, 'C': 2, 'D': 1}
```

Example 2 — Variation

fixture_gen.py: sports fixture generation using itertools.permutations and grouping logic.

```
# src/schooltools/stdlib_showcase/fixture_gen.py
"""
Sports fixture generation using itertools.

Public API:
    round_robin(teams)           - all ordered match pairs
    fixtures_by_round(teams, n)  - pairs grouped into rounds of n matches
"""
from __future__ import annotations
import itertools

__all__ = ['round_robin','fixtures_by_round']

def round_robin(teams: list[str]) -> list[tuple[str,str]]:
    """
    Return all ordered (home, away) pairs for a round-robin competition.
```

```
    Args:
        teams (list[str]): Team names (at least 2).

    Returns:
        list[tuple[str,str]]: All ordered pairs. Length = n*(n-1).

    Raises:
        ValueError: If fewer than 2 teams are provided.
    """
    if len(teams) < 2:
        raise ValueError("At least 2 teams required")
    return list(itertools.permutations(teams, 2))

def fixtures_by_round(teams: list[str],
                      matches_per_round: int | None = None
                      ) -> list[list[tuple[str,str]]]:
    """
    Group all round-robin fixtures into rounds.

    Args:
        teams             (list[str]): Team names.
        matches_per_round (int|None):  Matches per round.
            Defaults to len(teams) // 2.

    Returns:
        list[list[tuple[str,str]]]: Each inner list is one round.
    """
    all_matches = round_robin(teams)
    n = matches_per_round or (len(teams) // 2)
    rounds = []
    it = iter(all_matches)
    while chunk := list(itertools.islice(it, n)):
        rounds.append(chunk)
    return rounds

if __name__ == '__main__':
    teams = ['Brisbane', 'Sydney', 'Melbourne', 'Perth']
    for i, rnd in enumerate(fixtures_by_round(teams), 1):
        print(f"Round {i}:")
        for home, away in rnd:
            print(f"  {home} vs {away}")
```

Output:

```
Round 1:
  Brisbane vs Sydney
  Brisbane vs Melbourne
Round 2:
  Brisbane vs Perth
  Sydney vs Brisbane
Round 3:
  Sydney vs Melbourne
  Sydney vs Perth
...
```

Example 3 — Real-world application

term_planner.py and cohort_analysis.py completing the stdlib_showcase subpackage.

```
# src/schooltools/stdlib_showcase/term_planner.py
"""Term date utilities using datetime and calendar."""
from __future__ import annotations
from datetime import date, timedelta
import calendar

__all__ = ['school_days_in_range','weeks_in_term']
```

```python
def school_days_in_range(start: date, end: date,
                         holidays: frozenset[date] | None = None
                         ) -> list[date]:
    """
    Return all school days (Mon-Fri, excluding holidays) in [start, end].

    Args:
        start     (date):                First day of the range.
        end       (date):                Last day of the range.
        holidays  (frozenset[date]):      Public holidays to exclude.
            Defaults to empty set.

    Returns:
        list[date]: Sorted list of school days.
    """
    hols = holidays or frozenset()
    days = []
    d = start
    while d <= end:
        if d.weekday() < 5 and d not in hols:
            days.append(d)
        d += timedelta(days=1)
    return days

def weeks_in_term(start: date, end: date) -> list[list[date]]:
    """Group school days into weeks (Mon-Fri groupings)."""
    days = school_days_in_range(start, end)
    weeks: list[list[date]] = []
    week: list[date] = []
    for d in days:
        if week and d.weekday() == 0:   # new Monday
            weeks.append(week)
            week = []
        week.append(d)
    if week:
        weeks.append(week)
    return weeks

# src/schooltools/stdlib_showcase/cohort_analysis.py
"""Memoised cohort statistics using functools.lru_cache."""
from __future__ import annotations
from functools import lru_cache
from statistics import mean, stdev, correlation

__all__ = ['yearly_means','year_correlation']

@lru_cache(maxsize=256)
def _cached_mean(scores: tuple[float,...]) -> float:
    """Memoised mean for an immutable scores tuple."""
    return mean(scores)


def yearly_means(cohort: dict[int,list[float]]) -> dict[int,float]:
    """
    Return the mean score for each year level.

    Args:
        cohort (dict[int,list[float]]): year_level → scores.

    Returns:
        dict[int,float]: year_level → mean score.
    """
    return {yr: _cached_mean(tuple(scores))
            for yr, scores in cohort.items()}
```

```python
def year_correlation(cohort: dict[int,list[float]]) -> float:
    """Return the correlation between year level and mean score."""
    means = yearly_means(cohort)
    years = list(means.keys())
    avgs  = [means[y] for y in years]
    if len(years) < 2:
        return 0.0
    return round(correlation(years, avgs), 3)
```

Output:

```
# from schooltools.stdlib_showcase import grade_stats, term_planner
# grade_stats.grade_distribution([88, 74, 92, 63]) →
Counter({'B':1,'A':1,'C':1,'D':1})
# term_planner.school_days_in_range(date(2025,7,14), date(2025,7,18))  → 5 days
```

The stdlib_showcase subpackage demonstrates a core principle: the standard library, used well, is sufficient for most data manipulation and analysis tasks that arise in school administration software. Counter for frequency analysis, itertools for combinatorial generation, datetime for calendar arithmetic, lru_cache for performance — these are not advanced techniques, they are the standard tools of professional Python.

10.4 Type Hints and Docstrings Throughout

Every public name in schooltools is fully annotated with type hints and documented with a Google-style docstring. This section demonstrates how the completed library looks when checked with mypy --strict and how it renders with pdoc.

The key annotation decisions in schooltools are: functions that accept both numeric strings and actual numbers use int | float | str unions (validated with try/except float()); functions that return None are annotated -> None explicitly; Optional is used sparingly — only where None is a meaningful sentinel, not as a shortcut to avoid annotating properly; and all public collection parameters use the specific collection type (list[float] not Sequence) to make the expected mutability clear.

Running mypy src/schooltools/ --ignore-missing-imports --disallow-untyped-defs on the completed package reports zero errors. The --ignore-missing-imports flag is needed only because mypy may not have stubs for all standard library generics on all Python versions; in a properly configured environment with mypy's bundled stubs it is not required.

> **Note:** The from __future__ import annotations line at the top of each module enables the postponed evaluation of annotations (PEP 563), which allows forward references and union types to work correctly on Python 3.10 without runtime overhead. It is best practice to include it in every module that uses type hints.

Example 1 — Introduction

Demonstrating mypy --strict compliance on the validators subpackage.

```
# Run mypy --strict on the validators subpackage
# mypy src/schooltools/validators/ --strict --ignore-missing-imports

# Expected output for a fully annotated module:
# Success: no issues found in 4 source files

# Common mypy strict errors and how they were resolved in schooltools:
```

```
# 1. Function is missing a return type annotation
#    Fix: every function has -> bool, -> str, -> float, or -> None

# 2. Function is missing a type annotation for one or more arguments
#    Fix: every parameter annotated, including **kwargs if used

# 3. Incompatible return value type
#    Fix: ensure all branches return the declared type

# 4. Item 'None' has no attribute
#    Fix: explicitly check for None before attribute access

# Accessing type hints programmatically (after pip install -e .)
import inspect
from schooltools.validators import is_valid_email, is_valid_score

for func in [is_valid_email, is_valid_score]:
    hints = {k: v.__name__ if hasattr(v,"__name__") else str(v)
             for k, v in func.__annotations__.items()}
    print(f"{func.__name__}: {hints}")
```

Output:

```
is_valid_email: {'email': 'str', 'return': 'bool'}
is_valid_score: {'score': 'str', 'max_score': 'float', 'return': 'bool'}
```

Example 2 — Variation

Generating HTML documentation with pdoc showing how type hints and docstrings render together.

```
# Generate HTML documentation for all four subpackages
# pdoc src/schooltools/ --output-dir docs/

# ── What pdoc generates ──────────────────────────────────────
# docs/
#   schooltools.html              — top-level module page
#   schooltools/
#     validators.html             — validators subpackage
#     formatters.html             — formatters subpackage
#     converters.html             — converters subpackage
#     stdlib_showcase.html        — stdlib_showcase subpackage
#   (plus one HTML per implementation module)

# ── How type hints render in pdoc ────────────────────────────
# Function signature in HTML:
# is_valid_score(score: int | float | str, max_score: float = 100.0) -> bool
# score_to_letter(score: float) -> str

# ── Checking docs coverage programmatically ──────────────────
import inspect, importlib

def doc_coverage(package_name):
    """Count documented vs total public functions in a package."""
    mod = importlib.import_module(package_name)
    total = 0
    documented = 0
    for name, obj in inspect.getmembers(mod, inspect.isfunction):
        if name.startswith('_'):
            continue
        total += 1
        if inspect.getdoc(obj):
            documented += 1
    pct = documented/total*100 if total else 0
    print(f"{package_name}: {documented}/{total} documented ({pct:.0f}%)")
```

```
for pkg in ['schooltools.validators','schooltools.formatters',
            'schooltools.converters']:
    doc_coverage(pkg)
```

Output:

```
schooltools.validators: 5/5 documented (100%)
schooltools.formatters: 8/8 documented (100%)
schooltools.converters: 6/6 documented (100%)
```

Example 3 — Real-world application

The complete __init__.py for each subpackage showing the final public API.

```
# src/schooltools/converters/__init__.py — full public API
"""
schooltools.converters — Data conversion functions.

Converts between measurement systems and academic grade representations.
All functions raise ValueError for out-of-range inputs.

Unit conversions:
    celsius_to_fahrenheit(c)     — temperature
    fahrenheit_to_celsius(f)     — temperature
    km_to_miles(km)              — distance (raises ValueError if negative)
    miles_to_km(miles)           — distance (raises ValueError if negative)

Grade conversions:
    score_to_letter(score)       — 0-100 numeric → A/B/C/D/E
    letter_to_gpa(letter)        — A→4.0, B→3.0, C→2.0, D→1.0, E→0.0
                                   Raises KeyError for unrecognised letter.
"""
from .unit_conv  import (celsius_to_fahrenheit, fahrenheit_to_celsius,
                         km_to_miles, miles_to_km)
from .grade_conv import score_to_letter, letter_to_gpa

__all__ = [
    'celsius_to_fahrenheit', 'fahrenheit_to_celsius',
    'km_to_miles',           'miles_to_km',
    'score_to_letter',       'letter_to_gpa',
]

# Accessing the API from outside the package:
# from schooltools.converters import score_to_letter
# from schooltools.converters import celsius_to_fahrenheit, km_to_miles
# from schooltools            import converters   # then
converters.score_to_letter(88)
```

Output:

```
# pdoc renders this docstring as the subpackage introduction page,
# with each function listed with its full type-annotated signature.
# 100% annotation coverage + 100% docstring coverage = professional-grade
library.
```

The documentation coverage report showing 100% across all three subpackages is the standard schooltools should aspire to and maintain. A CI step that runs doc_coverage and fails the build if coverage drops below 100% is a simple but effective quality gate that prevents the gradual decay of documentation that afflicts many codebases over time.

10.5 Tests Using unittest

The schooltools test suite uses Python's built-in unittest framework (Book 11 covers pytest and coverage in depth). Each subpackage has a dedicated test file. Tests are organised into TestCase subclasses, with setUp() used where common fixtures are needed. Every public function has at least one positive test and one edge-case or exception test.

Running python -m unittest discover -s tests/ from the project root discovers and runs all test files matching the test*.py pattern. The -v flag produces verbose output showing each test method name. Running individual test files with python -m unittest tests/test_validators works during development of a specific module.

The test suite demonstrates three patterns that are worth adopting: assertRaises() as a context manager for testing that exceptions are raised correctly, assertEqual() for comparing return values, and subTest() for running the same assertion against multiple inputs without writing a test method per input. The subTest() pattern is particularly valuable for validation functions that should accept a range of valid inputs and reject a range of invalid ones.

> **Note:** Keep test files outside src/ so they are not included in the installed package. The tests/ directory at the project root is the correct location. Adding tests/__init__.py (empty) makes the test directory a proper package, which helps pytest and some IDEs discover tests correctly.

Example 1 — Introduction

test_validators.py: testing all five validator functions with positive and negative cases.

```
# tests/test_validators.py
import unittest
from schooltools.validators import (
    is_valid_email, is_valid_phone,
    is_valid_year_level, is_valid_score, is_valid_date
)

class TestEmailValidator(unittest.TestCase):

    def test_valid_emails(self):
        valid = [
            'student@school.edu.au',
            'a.b+c@example.com',
            'user123@domain.org',
        ]
        for email in valid:
            with self.subTest(email=email):
                self.assertTrue(is_valid_email(email))

    def test_invalid_emails(self):
        invalid = ['not-an-email', '@nodomain', 'missing@', '', '   ']
        for email in invalid:
            with self.subTest(email=email):
                self.assertFalse(is_valid_email(email))

class TestYearLevelValidator(unittest.TestCase):

    def test_valid_year_levels(self):
        for yr in range(7, 13):    # 7 through 12 inclusive
            with self.subTest(year=yr):
                self.assertTrue(is_valid_year_level(yr))

    def test_invalid_year_levels(self):
        for yr in [6, 13, 0, -1, 'abc', None]:
            with self.subTest(year=yr):
                self.assertFalse(is_valid_year_level(yr))
```

```python
class TestScoreValidator(unittest.TestCase):

    def test_valid_scores(self):
        for s in [0, 50, 100, '88', 75.5]:
            with self.subTest(score=s):
                self.assertTrue(is_valid_score(s))

    def test_invalid_scores(self):
        for s in [-1, 101, 'abc', None]:
            with self.subTest(score=s):
                self.assertFalse(is_valid_score(s))

    def test_custom_max(self):
        self.assertTrue(is_valid_score(50, max_score=50.0))
        self.assertFalse(is_valid_score(51, max_score=50.0))

if __name__ == '__main__':
    unittest.main()
```

Output:

```
# python -m unittest tests/test_validators.py -v
test_invalid_emails (TestEmailValidator) ... ok
test_valid_emails (TestEmailValidator) ... ok
test_invalid_year_levels (TestYearLevelValidator) ... ok
test_valid_year_levels (TestYearLevelValidator) ... ok
test_custom_max (TestScoreValidator) ... ok
test_invalid_scores (TestScoreValidator) ... ok
test_valid_scores (TestScoreValidator) ... ok
----------------------------------------------------------------------
Ran 7 tests in 0.003s
OK
```

Example 2 — Variation

test_converters.py: testing grade and unit converters including exception cases.

```python
# tests/test_converters.py
import unittest
from schooltools.converters import (
    celsius_to_fahrenheit, fahrenheit_to_celsius,
    km_to_miles, miles_to_km,
    score_to_letter, letter_to_gpa
)

class TestTemperatureConverters(unittest.TestCase):

    def test_celsius_to_fahrenheit_known_values(self):
        cases = [(0, 32.0), (100, 212.0), (-40, -40.0)]
        for c, expected in cases:
            with self.subTest(celsius=c):
                self.assertAlmostEqual(celsius_to_fahrenheit(c), expected)

    def test_round_trip(self):
        for c in [0, 25, 100, -10]:
            with self.subTest(celsius=c):
                self.assertAlmostEqual(
                    fahrenheit_to_celsius(celsius_to_fahrenheit(c)), c,
places=6
                )

class TestDistanceConverters(unittest.TestCase):

    def test_km_to_miles(self):
```

```
        self.assertAlmostEqual(km_to_miles(1.609344), 1.0, places=5)

    def test_negative_distance_raises(self):
        with self.assertRaises(ValueError):
            km_to_miles(-1.0)
        with self.assertRaises(ValueError):
            miles_to_km(-0.5)

class TestGradeConverters(unittest.TestCase):

    def test_score_to_letter_boundaries(self):
        cases =
[(90,'A'),(89,'B'),(80,'B'),(79,'C'),(70,'C'),(69,'D'),(60,'D'),(59,'E')]
        for score, expected in cases:
            with self.subTest(score=score):
                self.assertEqual(score_to_letter(score), expected)

    def test_letter_to_gpa(self):
        self.assertEqual(letter_to_gpa('A'), 4.0)
        self.assertEqual(letter_to_gpa('e'), 0.0)  # case-insensitive

    def test_invalid_letter_raises(self):
        with self.assertRaises(KeyError):
            letter_to_gpa('Z')

if __name__ == '__main__':
    unittest.main()
```

Output:

```
# python -m unittest tests/test_converters.py -v
test_celsius_to_fahrenheit_known_values ... ok
test_round_trip ... ok
test_km_to_miles ... ok
test_negative_distance_raises ... ok
test_score_to_letter_boundaries ... ok
test_letter_to_gpa ... ok
test_invalid_letter_raises ... ok
----------------------------------------------------------------------
Ran 7 tests in 0.002s
OK
```

Example 3 — Real-world application

Running the complete test suite and interpreting the results.

```
# Run all tests from the project root
python -m unittest discover -s tests/ -v

# ── Expected output ──────────────────────────────────────────
# test_invalid_emails (test_validators.TestEmailValidator) ... ok
# test_valid_emails (test_validators.TestEmailValidator) ... ok
# test_invalid_year_levels (test_validators.TestYearLevelValidator) ... ok
# test_valid_year_levels (test_validators.TestYearLevelValidator) ... ok
# test_custom_max (test_validators.TestScoreValidator) ... ok
# test_invalid_scores (test_validators.TestScoreValidator) ... ok
# test_valid_scores (test_validators.TestScoreValidator) ... ok
# test_celsius_to_fahrenheit_known_values ... ok
# test_round_trip ... ok
# test_km_to_miles ... ok
# test_negative_distance_raises ... ok
# test_score_to_letter_boundaries ... ok
# test_letter_to_gpa ... ok
# test_invalid_letter_raises ... ok
# test_format_score_alignment (test_formatters.TestScoreFormatters) ... ok
```

```
# test_format_currency_thousands (test_formatters.TestCurrencyFormatters) ...
ok
# test_grade_distribution (test_stdlib.TestGradeStats) ... ok
# test_cohort_summary_empty_raises (test_stdlib.TestGradeStats) ... ok
# ...
# Ran 22 tests in 0.008s
# OK

# ── Programmatic test runner with result summary ──────────────
import unittest
loader = unittest.TestLoader()
suite  = loader.discover('tests/')
runner = unittest.TextTestRunner(verbosity=0)
result = runner.run(suite)
print(f"\nTests run     : {result.testsRun}")
print(f"Failures      : {len(result.failures)}")
print(f"Errors        : {len(result.errors)}")
print(f"Status        : {"PASS" if result.wasSuccessful() else "FAIL"}")
```

Output:

```
......................
----------------------------------------------------------------------
Ran 22 tests in 0.008s
OK

Tests run     : 22
Failures      : 0
Errors        : 0
Status        : PASS
```

Twenty-two tests covering all four subpackages in under ten milliseconds — that is the profile of a well-designed pure-Python library. Fast tests run on every save, providing immediate feedback that a change has not broken anything. The combination of subTest() for parameterised cases and assertRaises() for exception verification covers the two test patterns that apply to nearly every function in schooltools.

10.6 Packaging and Distribution with pyproject.toml

The schooltools package is ready for distribution. The pyproject.toml has all required metadata, the src layout prevents accidental local imports, the test suite passes, mypy reports zero errors, and pdoc generates clean HTML documentation. The final step is to build and distribute.

The schooltools package represents the complete arc of Book 03: it began as separate module concepts in Chapter 1, grew into a package in Chapter 4, gained standard library tools in Chapter 5, acquired proper documentation in Chapter 8, and now, in this chapter, becomes something that any Python developer can install with pip install schooltools and use immediately without reading the source.

This closing section presents the complete build, check, and publish workflow as a unified script, and reflects on what the schooltools library demonstrates about professional Python development: that quality comes not from any single practice, but from the consistent application of many small habits — naming, structure, types, docstrings, tests, and packaging — applied together across every file in the project.

> **Note:** A package published to PyPI is a public commitment. Once version 1.0.0 is on PyPI, users will depend on it. Before publishing, ensure: all tests pass, mypy reports no errors, the README is accurate,

the CHANGELOG is complete, and the licence is appropriate for the intended audience. Retiring a published version is difficult; publishing a correct one is straightforward.

Example 1 — Introduction

The complete pyproject.toml for schooltools version 1.0.0 ready for distribution.

```
# pyproject.toml - schooltools v1.0.0 complete distribution configuration

[build-system]
requires      = ["setuptools>=68","wheel"]
build-backend = "setuptools.backends.legacy:build"

[tool.setuptools.packages.find]
where = ["src"]

[project]
name            = "schooltools"
dynamic         = ["version"]
description     = "Reusable utility library for school administration software"
readme          = "README.md"
requires-python = ">=3.10"
license         = {text = "MIT"}
keywords        = ["education","school","utilities","validation","formatting"]

[[project.authors]]
name  = "M. North"
email = "m.north@northwardhouse.com.au"

[project.classifiers]
classifiers = [
  "Development Status :: 5 - Production/Stable",
  "Intended Audience :: Education",
  "Intended Audience :: Developers",
  "License :: OSI Approved :: MIT License",
  "Programming Language :: Python :: 3",
  "Programming Language :: Python :: 3 :: Only",
  "Programming Language :: Python :: 3.10",
  "Programming Language :: Python :: 3.11",
  "Programming Language :: Python :: 3.12",
  "Topic :: Education",
  "Topic :: Software Development :: Libraries :: Python Modules",
  "Operating System :: OS Independent",
]

[project.optional-dependencies]
dev  = ["pytest>=8","mypy>=1.9","black>=24","pdoc","pip-audit>=2.7"]
docs = ["pdoc"]

[project.urls]
Homepage      = "https://github.com/northward/schooltools"
Documentation = "https://northward.github.io/schooltools"
Issues        = "https://github.com/northward/schooltools/issues"

[tool.setuptools.dynamic]
version = {attr = "schooltools.__version__"}

[tool.mypy]
python_version         = "3.12"
disallow_untyped_defs  = true
warn_return_any        = true
ignore_missing_imports = true
```

```
[tool.pytest.ini_options]
testpaths = ["tests"]
addopts   = "-v"

[tool.black]
line-length     = 88
target-version = ["py310","py311","py312"]
```

Output:

```
# python -m build
* Creating isolated environment: venv+pip
* Building sdist...
* Building wheel from sdist
Successfully built schooltools-1.0.0.tar.gz
  and schooltools-1.0.0-py3-none-any.whl

# twine check dist/*
Checking dist/schooltools-1.0.0.tar.gz: PASSED
Checking dist/schooltools-1.0.0-py3-none-any.whl: PASSED
```

Example 2 — Variation

A final integration test that installs schooltools in a clean venv and exercises the complete public API.

```
"""
integration_test.py — Final verification that schooltools installs and
works correctly from the wheel.

Usage: python integration_test.py
"""
import subprocess, sys, tempfile
from pathlib import Path

def run_integration_test(wheel_path):
    """Install wheel in a temp venv and verify the full public API."""
    with tempfile.TemporaryDirectory() as tmp:
        venv = Path(tmp) / 'venv'
        pip  = venv / ('Scripts/pip' if sys.platform=='win32' else 'bin/pip')
        py   = venv / ('Scripts/python' if sys.platform=='win32' else
'bin/python')
        subprocess.run([sys.executable,'-m','venv',str(venv)], check=True)
        subprocess.run([str(pip),'install',wheel_path,'--quiet'], check=True)

        test_code = '''
import schooltools
from schooltools.validators import is_valid_email, is_valid_score
from schooltools.formatters import format_score, format_currency
from schooltools.converters import score_to_letter, celsius_to_fahrenheit
from schooltools.stdlib_showcase.grade_stats import cohort_summary

assert schooltools.__version__ == '1.0.0'
assert is_valid_email('student@school.edu.au') is True
assert is_valid_email('bad') is False
assert is_valid_score(88) is True
assert is_valid_score(105) is False
assert format_score('Mia', 88.5).startswith('Mia')
assert format_currency(49.95) == '$49.95'
assert score_to_letter(92.0) == 'A'
assert celsius_to_fahrenheit(0) == 32.0
summary = cohort_summary([88.0, 74.0, 92.0, 63.0])
assert summary['count'] == 4
print("Integration test: ALL ASSERTIONS PASSED")
print(f'schooltools {schooltools.__version__} installed and working.')
'''
        result = subprocess.run([str(py),'-c',test_code],
```

```
                                capture_output=True, text=True)
        if result.returncode == 0:
            print(result.stdout.strip())
        else:
            print(f"FAILED:\n{result.stderr}")
        return result.returncode == 0

# Find the wheel in dist/
wheels = list(Path('dist').glob('schooltools*.whl'))
if wheels:
    ok = run_integration_test(str(wheels[0]))
    sys.exit(0 if ok else 1)
else:
    print("No wheel found. Run: python -m build")
    sys.exit(1)
```

Output:

```
Integration test: ALL ASSERTIONS PASSED
schooltools 1.0.0 installed and working.
```

Example 3 — Real-world application

A reflection on what schooltools demonstrates about professional Python development.

```
# schooltools by the numbers — what this library demonstrates

# ── Chapters applied ─────────────────────────────────────────
# Ch 1: module design principles (cohesion, __all__, module docstrings)
# Ch 2: import forms, relative imports, __init__.py re-exports
# Ch 3: module structure, constants, __main__ guards, doctest examples
# Ch 4: package hierarchy, subpackages, lean __init__.py, public API curation
# Ch 5: collections.Counter, itertools, functools.lru_cache, datetime,
statistics
# Ch 6: venv, requirements-dev.txt, .gitignore
# Ch 7: pyproject.toml dependencies, optional extras, editable install
# Ch 8: Google-style docstrings, type hints, mypy --strict, pdoc HTML
# Ch 9: src layout, pyproject.toml metadata, python -m build, TestPyPI

# ── Quality metrics ──────────────────────────────────────────
QUALITY_METRICS = {
    'Public functions'          : 25,
    'Docstring coverage'        : '100%',
    'Type annotation coverage'  : '100%',
    'mypy --strict'             : 'PASS',
    'Unittest tests'            : 22,
    'Test pass rate'            : '100%',
    'Third-party dependencies'  : 0,
    'Python versions tested'    : '3.10, 3.11, 3.12',
    'Licence'                   : 'MIT',
}

for metric, value in QUALITY_METRICS.items():
    print(f"  {metric:<32} {value}")
```

Output:

```
  Public functions                 25
  Docstring coverage               100%
  Type annotation coverage         100%
  mypy --strict                    PASS
  Unittest tests                   22
  Test pass rate                   100%
  Third-party dependencies         0
  Python versions tested           3.10, 3.11, 3.12
  Licence                          MIT
```

The quality metrics table is not a goal in itself — it is the natural outcome of applying each chapter's practices consistently. No single metric makes schooltools good; the combination of all of them does. A library with 100% docstring coverage but no tests is fragile. A library with 22 passing tests but no type hints requires more mental effort to use correctly. Professional quality is not any single practice applied once; it is many small practices applied everywhere, every time.

With schooltools complete, Book 03 is complete. You have covered the full Python ecosystem — from a single .py file through packages, virtual environments, third-party libraries, documentation, and distribution — and assembled these skills into a library that is genuinely useful, professionally structured, and ready to be installed by anyone with pip. The practices in this book apply equally to every Python project you will write from here forward.

10.7 What We Built: Book 03 in Review

The schooltools capstone brings together every concept in Book 03 and closes the loop from a single module to a distributed package. Looking back across the ten chapters, the progression is both technical and conceptual: from understanding what a module is to publishing one; from managing a single file to managing a full package hierarchy; from installing packages to creating ones that others can install.

The technical skills are specific and immediately applicable: writing cohesive modules with clean public interfaces, organising them into packages with relative imports, managing virtual environments and dependencies with pip and pyproject.toml, annotating code with type hints that mypy can verify, documenting with docstrings that pdoc can render, and publishing distributions to PyPI. Each of these skills addresses a real problem that arises in professional Python projects.

The conceptual shift is perhaps more important: from writing code that works to writing code that can be shared, maintained, and built upon by others. The src layout, __all__ declarations, Google-style docstrings, and semantic versioning are not bureaucratic overhead — they are the means by which code becomes useful to people who were not present when it was written. That is the difference between a script and a library, and between a programmer and a developer.

Chapter 10 Summary

- schooltools is a pure-Python utility library for school administration software, organised into four subpackages: validators/ (boolean validators), formatters/ (string formatters), converters/ (data transformers), and stdlib_showcase/ (standard library demonstrations). It uses the src layout from Chapter 9 and installs with pip install schooltools.
- Every module uses relative imports for intra-package references and exports a curated public API through its __init__.py with an explicit __all__ list. This keeps the library self-contained and relocatable, and ensures that from schooltools.validators import is_valid_email works without knowledge of internal module names.
- All 25 public functions have complete type hints (mypy --strict passes on the entire package) and Google-style docstrings with Args, Returns, and where applicable Raises sections. pdoc generates HTML documentation from these annotations automatically with pdoc src/schooltools/ --output-dir docs/.
- The stdlib_showcase subpackage demonstrates collections.Counter for grade distribution, itertools.permutations and islice for fixture generation, datetime and calendar for term date

planning, and functools.lru_cache for memoised cohort statistics — practical applications of the standard library tools from Chapter 5.

- The 22-test unittest suite uses subTest() for parameterised validation cases and assertRaises() for exception testing. All tests are in the tests/ directory outside src/, so they are not included in the installed package. Running python -m unittest discover -s tests/ -v executes the complete suite.
- The pyproject.toml includes all required metadata (name, version 1.0.0, description, requires-python>=3.10, MIT licence, authors, twelve classifiers, project URLs), optional dependency groups for dev and docs, and tool configuration for mypy, pytest, and black. The version is read dynamically from __version__ in __init__.py.
- Building with python -m build produces schooltools-1.0.0.tar.gz and schooltools-1.0.0-py3-none-any.whl in dist/. twine check dist/* validates both artefacts. The integration_test.py script installs from the wheel in a clean venv and verifies every public import works correctly.
- Book 03 has progressed from a single .py file (Chapter 1) through packages and virtual environments (Chapters 4–6), third-party library management (Chapter 7), professional documentation (Chapter 8), and distribution (Chapter 9) to a complete, tested, typed, documented, published utility library. The practices applied throughout are the standard of professional Python development.

Guided Exercises

1. Build the validators/ subpackage in full. Create src/schooltools/validators/ with __init__.py and the four implementation modules (email_val.py, phone_val.py, academic_val.py, date_val.py). Each function must have type hints and a Google-style docstring. Install the package in editable mode with pip install -e . and verify from schooltools.validators import is_valid_email works. Run mypy src/schooltools/validators/ and fix any errors reported.

Hint: Start with academic_val.py (the simplest validators — no regex needed). Add email_val.py second (one compiled regex constant). The __init__.py re-exports all four public functions with from .module import name. Confirm pip show schooltools shows the editable install location.

2. Add the formatters/ subpackage. Implement format_score, format_grade_row, format_name, format_student_id, format_currency, format_gst, format_date, and format_term_date. All must accept and return str. Write a test_formatters.py with at least two test methods per function. Run the test suite with python -m unittest tests/test_formatters.py -v and ensure all tests pass.

Hint: format_gst uses Python's Decimal type for precision — import from the decimal module, not float arithmetic. format_name should produce 'Last, First' canonical form. subTest() is useful for format_score tests with multiple widths.

3. Implement the converters/ subpackage. The unit converters (celsius_to_fahrenheit, fahrenheit_to_celsius, km_to_miles, miles_to_km) must raise ValueError for invalid inputs. The grade converters (score_to_letter, letter_to_gpa) must be case-insensitive and raise KeyError for unrecognised letters. Add a test_converters.py with tests for known values, round-trip conversions, and all exception cases.

Hint: Use assertAlmostEqual for floating-point comparisons (never assertEqual on floats). Test round-trips with assertAlmostEqual(fahrenheit_to_celsius(celsius_to_fahrenheit(c)), c, places=6). Use assertRaises as a context manager for exception tests.

4. Implement grade_stats.py in the stdlib_showcase subpackage. The three public functions (grade_distribution, cohort_summary, rank_students) must use collections.Counter, the statistics module, and the converters.grade_conv.score_to_letter function via a relative import. Add docstring examples and run python -m doctest src/schooltools/stdlib_showcase/grade_stats.py -v to verify them.

Hint: The relative import for score_to_letter from grade_stats.py is from ..converters.grade_conv import score_to_letter. doctest examples must match the repr() of the returned value exactly — for Counter, this means the example must show Counter({'B':3,'A':2}) with correct ordering.

5. Build the complete schooltools package and run the full integration test. Run python -m build from the project root, then twine check dist/*. Create a minimal integration_test.py that installs the wheel in a temporary venv (using subprocess and tempfile.TemporaryDirectory) and imports at least one name from each of the four subpackages. Confirm mypy src/schooltools/ --ignore-missing-imports --disallow-untyped-defs reports zero errors.

Hint: The integration test's test code string should import from all four subpackages and assert at least one value for each. Pass the wheel path as a subprocess argument to pip install inside the temp venv. Check result.returncode == 0 and print result.stdout to see the pass confirmation.

Challenge Tasks

1. Build the complete schooltools library as specified in this chapter: all four subpackages (validators/, formatters/, converters/, stdlib_showcase/), a top-level __init__.py with the version and re-exports, a complete pyproject.toml, a README.md that could serve as a real project landing page (overview, installation instructions, quick-start example, API summary table), and a LICENCE file. Every public function must have complete type hints and a Google-style docstring. Run mypy src/schooltools/ --strict --ignore-missing-imports and achieve zero errors. Run the full 22-test suite and achieve 100% pass rate. Build the wheel with python -m build, check with twine check, and upload to TestPyPI. Install from TestPyPI in a fresh virtual environment and run the integration test.

2. Extend schooltools with a fifth subpackage: schooltools/reports/. The subpackage should contain three modules: text_report.py (generates a plain-text report from a list of StudentRecord TypedDicts), csv_report.py (generates a CSV string using the csv module from the standard library), and html_report.py (generates an HTML table string using Python's built-in string formatting and html.escape). All three modules must expose a generate(records, title) -> str function. The reports/__init__.py must re-export all three and declare their __all__. Add full type hints, Google docstrings, and a test_reports.py test file. Update the version to 1.1.0, rebuild, and upload the new version to TestPyPI.

3. Write a complete development workflow automation script called dev.py that implements the following sub-commands as a simple command-line interface: test (runs python -m unittest discover), typecheck (runs mypy --ignore-missing-imports --disallow-untyped-defs on src/), format-check (runs black src/ tests/ --check), doc-coverage (uses inspect and importlib to report docstring coverage for all public functions in all four subpackages, failing if coverage drops below 100%), build (runs python -m build after all checks pass), and release (runs test + typecheck + format-check + doc-coverage + build + twine check + bump_version.py + git commit + tag + push in sequence, refusing to proceed if any step fails). The script must exit with code 0 only if every requested step completes successfully.

Made in United States
North Haven, CT
05 November 2026

21766803R00137